University of St. Francis

P9-ARR-108

3 0301 00117705 0

1992

PAINFUL
PASSAGES

PAINFUL PASSAGES

Working with Children with Learning Disabilities

Elizabeth Dane

LIBRARY
College of St. Francis
JOLIET, ILLINOIS

NASW PRESS

National Association of Social Workers, Inc.
Silver Spring, MD 20910

Richard L. Edwards, ACSW, *President*
Mark G. Battle, ACSW, *Executive Director*

© 1990 by the NASW Press

All rights reserved. No part of this book may be reproduced or transmitted in any form or by any means, electronic or mechanical, including photocopying, recording, or by any information storage and retrieval system, without permission in writing from the publisher.

Library of Congress Cataloging-in-Publication Data

Dane, Elizabeth.
    Painful passages: working with children with learning
disabilities / Elizabeth Dane.
       p. cm.
    Includes bibliographical references and index.
    ISBN 0-87101-175-1
    1. Learning disabled children—Education—United States.
2. Learning disabilities—United States.   I. Title.
LC4705.D36   1990
371.9—dc20
                                                  90-6463
                                                      CIP

Printed in the United States of America

Cover and interior design by Michael David Brown, Inc.

Contents

371.9
D179

142, 5-33

Contents

Foreword

Learning is a form of growing. Growing is an exhilarating process and, intermittently, a painful one. Just as there are growing pains, there are most certainly learning pains. These pains are experienced by all learners as they strive to expand their sensitivities and acquire the skills to uncover knowledge and fortify feelings of personal efficacy. The pathways that culminate in learning make up the passages that enable us to explore modes of intellectual fulfillment as we mature.

For many children, the passages are far too narrow and exceedingly painful—painful because these children harbor elusive handicapping attributes of the nervous system that make learning and academic productivity exasperating for them. These children have specific learning disabilities and constitute a rather paradoxical and puzzling group. Yet, in recent years, we have come to understand so much about the nature of their plight and the urgency of their needs. In this book, *Painful Passages: Working with Children with Learning Disabilities,* the subject of learning disabilities is examined closely and practically, so that its implications for all of us are clearly depicted.

Painful Passages is timely and necessary because our current knowledge of learning disabilities requires us to act swiftly and judiciously to prevent the tragic complications of needless failure in early life. Our keen awareness of learning disabilities should provide the impetus for collaboration among educators, clinicians (from multiple disciplines), parents, siblings, and peer groups. The need for collaboration is all too evident when we consider how much is at stake as a child struggles to be and to feel adequate. It is therefore highly appropriate that there be a book about learning disabilities presented from the unique and broad perspective of the field of social work. As any discipline seeks to determine its role or level of commitment, it is important to consider carefully exactly what is at stake. In the case of learning disabilities, there are devastating risks as well as extraordinary opportunities for redemption along the painful passages. To understand these high stakes, it will be helpful to describe 10 critical realizations about learning disabilities, the individuals who harbor them, and the effects they commonly generate.

Critical Realization One: *Children with learning disabilities are an extremely heterogeneous group.*

There are many children who manifest unusual patterns of "central nervous system function." Their profiles of strengths and weaknesses are such that they are destined to have difficulties acquiring certain academic skills and achieving proficiency in school. Although this group of students shares the fact that they are underachieving because of maladaptive neurological development, there is enormous heterogeneity among them, particularly regarding the precise nature of their disabilities.

There are some children who experience serious fatigue when they try to concentrate or attend to relevant information. Other children contend with memory deficiencies. Still others are unable to keep pace with the language demands of the school curriculum. Problems with processing visual information, forming concepts, deploying workable problem-solving skills, organizing materials and time, retaining information in the correct order, and moving one's fingers precisely enough to allow writing to keep pace with thinking are among the multitude of possible dysfunctions that commonly impede learning-disabled children.

Children with learning disabilities most often have more than one disability. They have clusters or combinations of weaknesses. One child may have a deficiency of memory and difficulties with attention. Another child may have fine motor weaknesses, a language dysfunction, and organizational problems. The precise manifestations of a child's learning disabilities are likely to vary dramatically depending on that child's cluster of dysfunctions, his or her strengths, personality factors, and a wide range of environmental and educational variables. Thus, it is not at all surprising that no two children with learning disabilities are alike. In a sense, therefore, we do an injustice to these students if we categorize them all under the rigid diagnostic label "LD kids," implying that if you've seen one, you've seen them all. In fact, there are many more ways to be different than there are to be the same!

Critical Realization Two: *Learning disabilities affect more than just learning.*

Children with learning disabilities are vulnerable to a diversity of associated and complicated problems. Some of these youngsters have social cognitive weaknesses, which means that the processing deficiencies that affect learning are also interfering with their social lives. There are also those who have trouble picking up social feedback clues, predicting social consequences, or understanding how they are affecting other people. Still others have language problems that make it exceedingly hard for them to praise, to influence, and to express their feelings verbally. Such children are often misunderstood by their peers; many of them experience outright rejection or ridicule. Learning difficulties can also be closely associated with behavior problems. Sometimes disturbed (and disturbing) actions are actually a part of the learning disability. For example, many children with attention deficits act impulsively. They respond to stress, provocation, or boredom without thinking or predicting outcomes. Consequently, they commit acts of aggression or disruption that masquerade as willful (premeditated) transgressions. Other children develop behavior problems as defense mechanisms. A child who is embarrassed about not learning may become a class clown or exhibit overly controlling behaviors toward others to divert attention from his or her daily displays of inadequacy. In some cases, a learning disability may be closely associated with depression or excessive anxiety and low self-esteem. Furthermore, psychosomatic symptoms, such as headaches or abdominal pains, are not an unusual concomitant of academic success deprivation.

Critical Realization Three: *Learning disabilities change over time.*
It is possible to have the onset of a learning disability at any age. As expectations evolve, new disabilities may surface. For example, as children proceed through school, there are heavier demands placed on memory. Those children who are born with tendencies toward memory dysfunction may not develop serious school problems until they reach junior or senior high school. Similarly, it is possible to evolve into one's strengths. A student may have much more difficulty learning at one stage of his or her education than at another. As the expectations evolve, it is possible that one's strengths will become tapped increasingly.

It is essential to recognize that a disability is only a disability when it is elicited at a time and place where a particular vulnerable function is demanded. Thus, learning disabilities depend very much on the context in which they occur. Some children with learning disabilities are destined to become highly competent adults, especially when they are permitted to practice their specialties, to pursue their personal strengths, and to sidestep those contexts that somehow amplify their shortcomings. In childhood, one is expected to be good at just about everything! Such an expectation may well exaggerate the effects of learning disabilities during the school years.

Critical Realization Four: *Learning disabilities affect families and are affected by families.*
There is no question that learning disabilities have a powerful reciprocal relationship with families. Many children inherit their disabilities from one or both parents. In addition, parents become powerful role models. Their patterns of learning, their intellectual inclinations (or disinclinations), their attitudes toward education, and their parenting practices exert powerful impacts on their child's learning style. Conversely, a child's success or failure at learning reverberates throughout a family. Children who are experiencing inordinate failure are likely to incite recurring family crises. Parents are apt to become confused, disappointed, embarrassed, and even angry at a child who is not learning or exhibiting sufficient academic productivity. It is common for parents to experience guilt over a child's learning difficulty or to believe that somehow they caused the problem. Parents

may blame their marital difficulties, economic struggles, personal career strivings, or genes for a child's disabilities. Siblings are critical. A brother or sister may become jealous of the attention diverted to a child with learning disabilities. Siblings may also feel ashamed of a brother or sister whom they may perceive as a negative indicator of their family worth.

Critical Realization Five: *There are some advantages to having learning disabilities.*

Learning disabilities are not all bad. Children with learning disabilities *universally* possess some extraordinary strengths. Many children with language disabilities develop excellent nonverbal reasoning and conceptual abilities. Many children with attention deficits possess scintillating imaginations and a high level of entrepreneurialism. Frequently students who have had to struggle academically develop some extraordinary tactics for coping with stress. When thinking about a child with learning disabilities, it is essential that we identify that youngster's notable assets and that we not simply seek to devise ways of overcoming weaknesses but also ways of fortifying preexisting strengths.

Critical Realization Six: *Children with learning disabilities pose some important ethical dilemmas.*

There are many moral questions that arise as we strive to study, understand, and support children with learning disabilities. First, we have to question the value and the potential effects of the label "learning disability." Are there self-fulfilling prophecies inherent in such labels? Does the "LD label" preclude other factors (such as emotional disturbance)? Does it make us overlook a child's strengths? Does it stigmatize a youngster in the minds of his or her parents, peers, and teachers? Does the label of learning disability somehow make a child feel less accountable, more crippled, or more out of control? Ethical issues also arise when we try to evaluate these children. How can we guarantee a child a well-balanced, high-quality assessment, one that is free of conflicts of interest or strong disciplinary biases? Finally, there is the issue of how much of a right we have to change a child. If a girl or boy is born with a certain pattern of "central nervous system wiring," should we help that child to realize the full potential of that pattern? Or should we try to modify the wiring itself? These are issues that should never be ignored as we consider the needs and rights of children with learning disabilities.

Critical Realization Seven: *Learning-disabled children require informed advocacy and faithful case management.*

In part because of the ethical dilemmas enumerated above, there is a compelling need for staunch advocacy and continuing vigilance as children with learning disabilities navigate the painful passages. They must have their rights represented so that they will not be lost or damaged within the community (especially school) or sacrificed to the needs of groups of children rather than individuals. These children and their parents crave applicable advice. There is a need for help in day-to-day decision making and for developmentally oriented practical suggestions. Parents seek assistance in finding and evaluating services for their learning-disabled children. Case management becomes vital. Not only must such management be constructive, optimistic, and practical, but it must also represent a longitudinal commitment. Families of learning disabled children need a long-term alliance with a clinician who is willing and able to assist in the intricate process of decision making along the painful passages.

Critical Realization Eight: *Children with learning disabilities are susceptible to the damaging effects of misunderstanding.*

The long-term impacts of learning disabilities are probably not nearly as malignant as the long-term impacts of the misunderstandings that learning disabilities commonly engender. A child's mental health can be seriously impaired if he or she grows up hearing the refrain, "You can do better," when those who are voicing such admonitions are utterly wrong. Children should never be punished or publicly humiliated for their disabilities. To retain a child in sixth grade because he or she has a language disability and the school has no language therapist is cruel and unusual punishment. To assume a child is lazy when he or she has fine motor problems that make writing too difficult can inflict potentially irreversible damage on that child's self-esteem.

Parents are often victims of misunderstandings. Consequently, they are prone to many questionable interventions that offer a quick fix for learning disabilities. Radical diets, pills, exercises, or other narrowly defined and incompletely validated panaceas may be accepted by confused parents who do not have a grasp on their child's learning disability.

Affected children themselves have a desperate need for "demystification," as many of them come to fantasize that they are retarded or pervasively inept because they do not grasp the discrete nature of their disabilities. In almost all cases, their fantasies are far worse than their disabilities.

Critical Realization Nine: *Learning disabilities are amenable to good evaluation and good management.*

We are now able to offer excellent assessments and treatment programs for children with learning disabilities. It is critical that such processes be multidisciplinary or multimodal. Any testing of a child needs to include various kinds of examinations administered by professionals from different disciplines. There needs to be a search for recurring themes or issues that emerge repeatedly in a child's academic work, in various kinds of testing, in a carefully elicited history, in observations made by teachers, and in what the child reports. Similarly, management must be eclectic or multimodal.

At times children with learning disabilities warrant independent evaluations. Although students are entitled to evaluations within their schools, it is not unusual for a parent to seek an outside opinion, an assessment that is free from any possible conflicts of interest that may prevail when a school evaluates one of its own students.

Critical Realization Ten: Learning disabilities provide important insights into the development and learning abilities of all children.

Children with learning disabilities amplify certain aspects of the learning process that represent struggles for *all* children. By studying and getting to know students with learning disabilities, we learn a great deal about learning in general. Such knowledge has potent implications for teaching. The study of learning disabilities also exemplifies the nature-nurture balance. We appreciate that all individuals are born with certain predispositions to success or failure, to particular pathways toward gratification, and to intrinsic behaviors and temperamental arrays that are uniquely their own. These endogenous contributions interact and transact with a wide range of environmental influences emanating from the culture, the family, social transactions, and critical life experiences of a child either to minimize or aggravate the effects of any inborn disability. Therefore, in a sense, the study of learning disabilities is the study of success and failure, of human resiliency, and of ongoing interactions between heredity and environment.

In scanning these 10 critical realizations, it should indeed be evident that learning disabilities are not just another item on a list of common childhood afflictions. Indeed, learning disabilities do not fit neatly into a traditional model of disease. It is virtually impossible to separate an understanding of learning disabilities from an understanding of human development. Because so much is at stake as individuals grow and develop, it is clear that by reckoning with learning disabilities, we come to grapple with a series of very basic life struggles. This book, *Painful Passages,* will go a long way toward empowering and informing professionals as they become more sensitized to the complex, exciting, and potentially life-enhancing implications of learning disabilities. Indeed, the book merits reading with care and reflection.

MELVIN D. LEVINE, M.D.
Professor of Pediatrics
University of North Carolina
School of Medicine
Chapel Hill

Acknowledgments

During the past four years I have received support from many colleagues: Florence Wexler Vigilante, who identified the importance of social work involvement with children with learning disabilities and their families; Judith Rosenberger, who shared her works in progress for inclusion in this book; Carmen Ortiz Hendricks and Martha Fraad Haffey, who read early versions of several chapters; and Harold Lewis, who persistently expanded my understanding of the critical issues. Expert editorial assistance, and much encouragement, came from Martha F. Browne. There also were many readers in the community—parents, social workers in practice, and social work administrators—who generously contributed their experiences and observations. This book was undertaken with the support of the Foundation for Children with Learning Disabilities, now the National Center for Learning Disabilities, Inc. The foundation staff members were consistently encouraging in their support of this endeavor. Finally I wish to thank my family—Patrick, Samuel Lee, and Krystyna Elizabeth—for their patience.

Acknowledgments

Introduction

C hildren with learning disabilities present many puzzling images to people around them. These children may excel in reading but fail in math. Their attention in school may be unfocused, but they might have intense hobbies outside the classroom. Their physical awkwardness or lack of organizational skills may constrain their abilities on the playing field or in the classroom, but they may swim and sail with consummate skill. They may have vivid imaginations and great creativity but lack the skills to communicate their ideas. They may have a wide circle of acquaintances but be unable to sustain individual friendships.

Although some children with learning disabilities ultimately compensate for and overcome the effects of their disabilities, other children are overcome by their failures and have few outlets that meet their needs for success and mastery. Low self-esteem, chronic self-doubt, anxiety, depression, anger, and frustration haunt the inner lives of these children well into adulthood. These children's families, burdened by guilt, unclear choices, and competing priorities, struggle to maintain a balanced perspective. Their siblings often are confused and angered by the concern and attention that seems to be directed unfairly to a brother or sister without visible differences or handicaps.

Because of their unpredictable learning and behavior patterns and their consequential difficulties in academic and social encounters, children with learning disabilities come into contact with a wide spectrum of educational, health, and mental health specialists. Researchers in many fields have worked toward identification of possible biological or physical developmental influences. Cognitive and psychological indicators of deviation from age-related norms have been developed. Significant gains in these areas have produced numerous hypotheses about the complex phenomena of learning disabilities. Extensive curricula and teaching models in academic and social skills for use in the classroom have been created.

The interdependent nature of a child's cognitive, social, and emotional development and his or her family, school, and community environment during the growing years now is recognized widely. Nevertheless, the varied professional interventions that focus on changing the nature of the fit between the child and his or her many environments have received little attention. Too often, specialists emphasize the need for individual change and adjustment, following a diagnosis based on a medical model (Rosenberger, 1988), and neglect the need for changes in the family, professional, and institutional environments in which the child functions.

Historically, social workers have lagged in providing services for children with learning disabilities and their families. Despite the exponential growth in numbers of children with learning disabilities in special education classes, the increasing awareness of the role that learning disabilities may play in truancy and "dropping out," the destructive influence on family cohesion, the number of adjudicated youths with learning disabilities, and the long-term residues of school and social failure on employment status and adult adjustment, there has not been a corresponding growth of interest in the social work profession.

Nevertheless, social workers in educational, recreational, health, mental health, family, child welfare, and protective settings encounter many children with learning disabilities. Social workers have a biopsychosocial perspective that could help them play a unique role among the many diverse professional groups working with these children and their families. Social workers could offer a continuum of critical services, including individual and family counseling, group intervention, institutional advocacy, program design, organization of community support, and lobbying for legislative change.

A recent national study of social work involvement with children with learning disabilities in child welfare and family agencies revealed that most social workers learned about this complex condition in a piecemeal fashion—for example, through individual field experiences in graduate school, the rare graduate course, or work with children in agencies employing psychologists or special education specialists (Dane, 1984). Informal discussions with members of other disciplines drew from knowledge bases and practice perspectives that did not necessarily encompass social work involvement. The social workers participating in the study recognized that the comprehensive needs of these children and their families often were neither identified nor addressed. Many social services agencies provided little in the way of direct support for social workers to expand their knowledge or skills to work with this client population. Frequently, social agency executives cited other priorities as taking precedence in the competition for scarce agency resources. The social workers taking part in the study consistently stressed their frustration with the limited literature and models of practice emanating from their profession.

This book was created to give social workers ready access to the wealth of information available from the research and experience of diverse disciplines, as a basis for increased practice knowledge and for new approaches for the social work profession. Specific social work contributions to the literature are highlighted, as is the work of related professionals who offer perspectives that support a biopsychosocial understanding of human functioning. The book is designed to meet a need expressed by social work practitioners, supervisors, and administrators for greater knowledge about learning disabilities as these professionals seek to respond effectively to children and their families. A deeper understanding of the issues that face both the child and the family should lead to more targeted social work interventions at the individual, group, institutional, and community levels. It is hoped that by highlighting new directions for social work involvement, this book will provide a stimulus for new models of social work practice.

Students at both undergraduate and graduate levels should find this book to be a resource that will further their understanding of specific characteristics of learning disabilities; of the professional, organizational, and political issues in the field that guide the interpretation of needs; and of the design of services and the patterns of access for children with learning disabilities. Ultimately, this understanding should help the student or new practitioner ensure that clients gain the optimum resources to meet their needs.

PERSPECTIVE ON LEARNING DISABILITIES

The literature on learning disabilities has grown rapidly during the past 15 years. Research from the biological, behavioral, and social sciences has contributed to a broader understanding of possible etiologies and neurodevelopmental processes that are relevant to prevention and remediative strategies. In part, the current controversies in the field regarding definitional inadequacies are the result of the lack of a comprehensive knowledge base, which has led to little uniformity of assessment processes and inconsistent identification of the population.

The term *learning disabilities* is used in this book because of its familiarity and is based on the legislative definition in the Education for All Handicapped Children Act of 1975. Other terms are discussed and their relative merits also are presented. Readers are invited to select their own nomenclature and to be cognizant of the many ways all of the current labels—or even nonlabels—can be misinterpreted to the detriment or advantage of children, at different times and in different places.

The discussion of learning disabilities in this book is based on the assumption that central nervous system dysfunction underlies the vulnerability to disability. Levine's (1982) perspective that a developmental vulnerability to disability may be influenced significantly by the aggravating or mediatory roles of family, school, culture, and environment is adopted, and the importance of multicausality is stressed. It follows then that multiple approaches toward assessment and intervention require interdisciplinary collaboration. The complex interdependency of innate biological tendencies and the opportunities available in the environment offer a background for a broader consideration of the role and function of social work with children with learning disabilities.

Social work is a unique profession because it encompasses both the individual and his or her environment. Social workers can intervene in existing situations and also can assist in early identification and prevention of learning disabilities. The diversity of settings in which social workers practice maximizes the potential for early intervention and continuity through a child's different life stages. The principle of social work practice that ensures that the individual is seen in the context of the environment and family situation also ensures a broad conceptualization of need and strategy that does not focus exclusively on the child's dysfunction as the sole source of the problems. Social workers can separate underlying problems from their impact on the social functioning of a child and reach out to parents, teachers, and others in the child's immediate environment (Vigilante, 1983). The social worker's recognition of the need to link available community resources and ability to design new resources place the social worker in a pivotal role in program development.

The emphasis on professional knowledge and intervention in this book does not diminish the important, multifaceted roles that parents play as nurturers, educators, service coordinators, mediators, advocates, and organizers. In fact, a key social work objective in work with families is to support, teach, and empower families to become more skilled in these capacities. Throughout the child's life, the family must be continuing advocates and champions for effective services (Dane, 1985).

This overview of current knowledge about the multiple phenomena of learning disabilities and the variety of approaches used in different settings should be useful to social workers. Additionally, access to a discussion of the current issues in the field, interdisciplinary literature, and an extensive bibliography may stimulate social workers to develop a deepened perspective on their work and to expand the unique contribution of the social work profession to the literature. The profession has the potential for a far wider involvement with, and on behalf of, children with learning disabilities and their families. This book is designed to prepare social workers to assume these multiple roles.

Chapter 1 presents the evolution of the term *learning disability* and its impact on the conceptualization and understanding of the complex multiple phenomena now grouped within this category. Lay, professional, and legislative contributions and limits to definitional clarity are explored. New proposals for eliminating the label of "learning disability" and the resulting politicization of the process of defining the multiple special needs of, and obtaining services for, children with learning disabilities are explored in terms of social work roles and functions. Finally, some of the health and environmental variables influencing the demography of learning disabilities are reviewed, and implications for early social work intervention are explored.

Chapter 2 presents a discussion of learning-related developmental differences, organized according to the specific functional areas most relevant to children. A classification system drawing heavily on work by Levine (1987) serves as the basis for discussion. Levine's perspective provides a general framework for the observation and initial identification of variations in children's functioning that may require more in-depth analysis of specific needs for social work intervention. Factors of time; individualization; heightened sensitivity to the interrelationship of cognitive, emotional, and social development; and strategic environmental changes to minimize frustration and failure emerge as important arenas for social work attention.

Current issues and controversies are highlighted in Chapter 3, which examines how learning disabilities are assessed. The potential impact of the evaluation process on children and families is discussed, and several of the most frequently used evaluation instruments and approaches in key areas are reviewed. The importance of multidisciplinary involvement and the resulting need for effective coordination and establishment of priorities are explored. Opportunities for social work participation in different institutional settings are considered.

Chapter 4 focuses on the impact of learning disabilities on psychosocial development. Recent works that examine ego functioning, the use of defenses, and implications for personality are presented. Rosenberger's (1988) adaptation of principles of self-psychology to work with children with learning disabilities offers viable approaches for understanding the impact of daily events on the developing child and on the creation of appropriate interventions. Specific issues in individual and group strategies are explored.

The effects of the developmental stages of children with learning disabilities on family life are examined in Chapter 5. Specific family issues of mourning, unmet expectations, and sibling reactions are explored. Areas for early intervention and differential analysis of family needs are examined, adapting an existing model of family types. Issues of parental empowerment, mutual aid group development, and collaboration for institutional change and community action also are discussed.

Chapter 6 summarizes key elements of the Education for All Handicapped Children Act (1975) and the more recent early intervention program included in later amendments to this act. The needs of especially vulnerable subgroups in the larger categories of eligible children are described. Particular emphasis is given to the legislative mandate and sanction for social work intervention. Critical questions are raised to encourage the expansion of social work conceptualization of service parameters to children and their families. Other relevant legislative mandates providing services and opportunity to persons with disabilities are presented.

Finally, Chapter 7 offers some suggestions for a broader view of social work intervention with, and on behalf of, children with learning disabilities and their families. A review of recent social work contributions to the integration of theory and practice with children with learning disabilities and their families leads to the development of principles of practice. The role of social work educators in supporting social work movement in the field of learning disabilities is discussed. The profession is challenged to move into closer collaboration with other disciplines and to work toward greater definition of its distinctive function.

REFERENCES

Dane, E. (1984). [The child welfare and family service systems: A national survey of social work involvement with learning disabled children.] Unpublished raw data.

Dane, E. (1985). Professional and lay advocacy in the education of handicapped children. *Social Work, 30,* 505–510.

Education for All Handicapped Children Act, Pub. L. No. 94–142, §5, 6, 89 Stat. 773–796 (1975).

Levine, M. D. (1982). The high prevalence–low severity developmental disorders of school children. In L. Barness (Ed.), *Advances in pediatrics* (pp. 529–554). Chicago: Medical Yearbook Publishers.

Levine, M. D. (1987). *Developmental variation and learning disorders.* Cambridge, MA: Educators Publishing Service.

Rosenberger, J. (1988). Self-psychology as a theoretical base for understanding the impact of learning disabilities. *Child and Adolescent Social Work, 5,* 269–280.

Vigilante, F. W. (1983). Working with families of learning disabled children. *Child Welfare, 62,* 429–436.

Chapter 1

Definitions and Demography of Learning Disabilities

Historically, the problem of defining what learning disabilities are has made their diagnosis, treatment, and integration into a single theoretical category very difficult. Although many of the diverse group of subtle neurological impairments now referred to collectively as *learning disabilities* have been recognized and documented since the early 1800s, most research done until the 1920s examined the impact of trauma on the communication skills of previously "normal" adult subjects. It was not until the 1930s that a developmental perspective emerged linking specific disorders in speech, writing, and perception to certain difficulties in learning observed in children (Chalfant, 1987). The inadequacy of such alternative diagnoses as mental retardation or visual impairment was evidenced by the failure of the treatment modalities they entailed. These failures left a residue of problem cases that previous theories of learning—whether psychologically, medically, educationally, or socially based—could not handle.

Defining these cases as resulting from "learning disabilities" required much more than the introduction of a new term; it required a reworking of existing paradigms. The research on trauma-caused communication deficits offered guideposts for further work on the role of brain structure in language competence. The research also created a taxonomy of specific behavioral manifestations of learning disabilities. The elevation of the former "problem cases" into the new category of "learning disabilities," however, involved the acceptance of those new manifestations as arising—at least in some cases—from an organic condition, rather than from an environmental disadvantage or a traumatic event.

Emerging interest in learning disorders of children was stimulated by educational reforms addressing the needs of children with mental retardation or hearing deficits. This interest led to the establishment of a variety of professional and lay groups dedicated to furthering understanding of the causes, prevention, and treatment of what now was perceived to be a widespread problem. The Council for Exceptional Children, formed in 1922, is now the largest professional organization in the world focused on research, service, and policy issues to support the education of both handicapped and gifted children. Its 13 special interest groups respond to the specific needs of targeted handicapped groups and of the professional groups represented in the council's membership. Another early organization dedicated to specific written language disabilities was the Orton

Dyslexia Society (ODS), founded in 1949 in recognition of the earlier pioneering work of Samuel T. Orton, a neurologist who studied the role of the structure of the brain in the development of severe reading disabilities in children. Today the ODS focus is on specific reading and written language disabilities and on support of biological, cognitive, and educational research, with a continuing emphasis on brain research.

During the 1950s, many scholarly and professional groups, parents' organizations, and other interested individuals continued to work on differentiating the various handicapping conditions that contribute to the development of learning problems. Despite many differences of perspective, there was growing agreement on the existence of a significant group of children, exhibiting diverse behavioral symptoms but linked by specific patterns of learning difficulties, who could not be included in the well-established categories of the severely brain-injured, deaf, blind, or mentally retarded.

By the early 1960s, efforts to integrate the different perspectives were under way. The growth in acceptance of the umbrella term "learning disabilities" promoted the identification of, and the first steps toward understanding, the problems of a group of children who had fallen through the cracks of existing service programs. Children who today would be identified as having learning disabilities frequently were misidentified as mentally retarded or emotionally disturbed (Levine, 1982; Mercer, 1973). Placed in classes or groups with children with different behavioral characteristics, these children failed to learn, and often adopted behavior that seemed to confirm the faulty diagnosis. Other children whose problems were less severe were seen as slow, and graduated from school only to emerge as functionally illiterate. Other children dropped out or left school as soon as they were legally able to make that choice. In their demands for increased funding for the treatment of learning disabilities, the new advocacy groups also stressed the need for specially trained professionals to work with these children and the importance of research that would yield greater understanding of their learning needs. The major focus of both professional and lay attention continues to be the development of methods to promote academic achievement.

The 1960s also brought the consolidation and redirection of a number of the earlier advocacy organizations. The 1963 Chicago meeting of parents' groups at which the term "learning disabilities" was introduced (by Samuel Kirk) provided the impetus for the establishment of the Association for Children with Learning Disabilities (ACLD) in 1964. This organization, now the Learning Disabilities Association of America, consists of parents, professionals, adults with learning disabilities, and others concerned with children and adults who have "perceptual, conceptual or coordinative problems" (ACLD, 1963, p. 1). The Division for Children with Learning Disabilities, founded in 1968 by a group of educators in the Council for Exceptional Children, split in the early 1980s to become a separate organization for professionals oriented toward the delivery of educational services for children with specific learning disabilities. Reflecting its incorporation of adult concerns in recognition of the lingering impacts of learning disabilities on adults, the division subsequently changed its name to the Council for Learning Disabilities. Each of these organizations holds a national conference and offers newsletters, periodicals, and occasional publications to local and national members. Although the groups do not agree on the definitions and parameters of learning disabilities, each group has played a major role in the growth in—and recognition of the need for—national and local legislative support, educational resources, and many other services for children, adults, and their families.

The historical focus on educational remediation and the accompanying lack of emphasis on the psychosocial needs of children and their families have contributed to the poor integration of the social work profession into the area of learning disabilities and to a sparse representation of social workers in these organizations. Until recently, learning-disabled children's social and emotional problems and needs have been presented most forcefully by psychologists and psychiatrists.

The emphasis on diagnostic tests and personality inventories in schools has integrated the educational psychologist into the educational service setting, and orientation toward psychopathology and psychoanalytic perspectives has involved the psychiatric profession. The biopsychosocial perspective offered by the social work profession brings a much-needed broader view. Assessment and intervention that focus on changes in the child, as well as changes in family, school, and community systems, will emphasize meeting the child's normal growth and developmental needs. Specific social and emotional needs of both the child and his or her family must be identified.

Social work practitioners and planners must create opportunities to share their perspectives with other professionals. To build the important bridges to other disciplines, social workers need to be more active in interdisciplinary activities held by leading advocacy organizations for learning-disabled persons.

LEGISLATIVE CONTRIBUTIONS TO DEFINITIONAL CLARITY

From the mid-1960s through the mid-1970s, state and federal legislation began to address the rights of all persons with disabilities to education. Work on the major piece of enabling legislation that revolutionized federal involvement in education for children with disabilities was begun in 1974. The Education for All Handicapped Children Act of 1975 (P.L. 94–142) (EHA) established a general definition of *learning disabilities:*

> Specific learning disability means a disorder in one or more of the basic psychological processes involved in understanding and using language, spoken or written, which may manifest itself in an imperfect ability to listen, think, speak, read, write, spell, or to do mathematical calculations. The term includes such conditions as perceptual handicaps, brain injury, minimal brain dysfunction, dyslexia and developmental aphasia. The term does not

include children who have learning problems which are primarily the result of visual, hearing or motor handicaps, or mental retardation or of environmental, cultural or economic disadvantage. (EHA, 1975)

In fact, this definition had been developed in 1967 by the National Advisory Committee on Handicapped Children (Lynn, 1979). The category of *learning disabilities* is defined to include deficits in visual, spatial, auditory, and motor functioning that create a discrepancy between general ability and documented achievement. Note, however, that despite the existence of a variety of instruments to assess ability and achievement, there is no consensus regarding what approach should be used to quantify the gap between the two (McLaughlin & Lewis, 1986). Also, although different handicapping conditions may present similar behavioral manifestations, the legislation is an attempt to restrict the category to more severe underlying dysfunctions that are the primary causes of the learning problems.

The EHA definition continues to confound professionals, who are attempting to develop research, assessment, and intervention strategies in response to its vague parameters. Chalfant (1987) noted that "the behavioral symptoms of specific learning disabilities might also arise from visual or hearing impairments, mental retardation, emotional disturbance, social maladjustment, health problems, cultural differences, family problems or poor instruction" (p. 924). For example, a 5-year-old adopted child from another culture showed signs of functional problems in a number of areas in kindergarten. Because of the difference in cultural background and the child's limited facility in English, it was difficult for teachers to determine the extent to which his difficulties reflected cultural dislocation, social adjustment, or a specific learning disability. For 3 years, teachers saw cultural dislocation and difficulties in social adjustment as the primary problems affecting the child's learning. Only when he reached second grade was a specific learning disability identified by an educational evaluation. The ambiguities in the diagnosis of learning disabilities have led to both overdiagnosis and underdiagnosis, wasting valuable time for children whose learning disabilities, whatever their source, have placed them at high risk for educational failure.

EHA included both the first federally sponsored definition of learning disabilities and a mandate for its use within schools across the country. Dislocation and upset were inevitable. Change within systems—especially such massive institutions as the educational and service organizations affected by the legislation—is never tranquil, and this change provoked many levels of controversy. Boundaries between existing categories of handicapping conditions were redefined, and new groups of children suddenly were identified as having handicapping conditions. Disciplinary and professional turfs and areas of expertise underwent parallel changes in response to the new pupil categories.

The vague parameters for learning disabilities established in the legislation and the operational difficulties that emerged elicited a flood of criticism. Both in practice and in policy-making areas, deficiencies in the definition became apparent almost immediately. In particular, the wording of the definition implied that learning disability reflected a homogeneous condition. However, the fact that no single salient feature, no single syndrome of dysfunction or behavior characteristic, unites all learning-disabled children has led to continued questioning of the EHA definition in professional and lay circles. The seemingly endless discussion of the definition encompasses pragmatic, fiscal, and service issues, as well as the more theoretical concerns expressed by researchers.

On the theoretical front, some of the most recent and vocal questioning of the federal definition has come from Gerald Coles (1988), a clinical psychologist. Addressing the problems associated with the use of the term "learning disabilities" through an analysis of relevant research, Coles concluded that the emergence of learning disabilities as a field is not the result of a "scientific breakthrough" (p. 189). According to Coles, among children formally designated as having learning disabilities there are very few children with minimal neurological dysfunction, and there are significantly more for whom other risk factors are more salient. Concerned professionals and lay persons, he argued, should put more energy toward "addressing, challenging and trying to change the systemic conditions that are the wellsprings of learning failure" (p. 212).

Coles (1988) described learning disabilities as a fabrication of middle-class families meant to focus attention on special learning needs of their children without having to label them mentally retarded or emotionally disturbed. He asserted that the growth in popularity of the term has served political, discriminatory, professional, and institutional ends, without particularly benefiting the children in question. Coles mustered ample expert documentation of the difficulties of implementing the legislation's provisions to assist children with learning disabilities. For example, testing and evaluation procedures do not correspond closely to the conceptual definitions of learning disabilities (Ysseldyke, 1983), the technical adequacy of the tests used in decision making is faulty (Ysseldyke et al., 1982), and the classification judgments have proven to be highly variable from school to school and district to district (Epps, Ysseldyke, & Algozzine, 1982; Thurlow, Ysseldyke, & Casey, 1984).

Others have criticized the definition of learning disability as focusing on what it is not, without offering any clarity about what it is. They cite the vagueness of referrals to disorders in psychological processes involved in understanding and using language and the questionable exclusion of children who have learning problems primarily due to other handicaps or environmental, cultural, or economic disadvantage.

Levine questioned the presumption of defining a true learning disability as having a purity of diagnosis (Levine, Brooks, & Shonkoff, 1980, p. 2). Levine (1987) considered the uniqueness and endless variation of children's learning styles, and provided a continuum along which to assess the unique developmental patterns of the individual. He offered the following progression: "a variation in development need not be a dysfunction; a dysfunction need not create disability; and a disability may never become a handicap" (p. 3). Levine's (1987) sequence makes it clear that the extent to which social structures and the child's immediate environment facilitate specific overcoming or bypassing strategies is a major determinant in the progression from variation to disability to handicap. (Social structures also play a strong role in defining the tasks constituting developmental milestones or progress, of course; different cultures value different achievements.) Levine (1987) explicitly disavowed umbrella categories and labels, such as "learning disabilities."

Levine probably would agree with Coles (1988) that a narrow and exclusive focus on a biologically based description of learning problems under the label of learning disabilities impedes the exploration of a wider source of influential factors. As a result, society narrows the acceptable strategies for intervention, places artificial limits on service design, and fails to examine the quality of opportunities available, permitting an inevitably inequitable distribution of resources.

Despite significant difficulties with its application, the EHA definition has not been modified significantly. The definition still is used by each state government to determine the types of services to be provided to different categories of students. Parents, educators, evaluators, researchers, social workers, and administrators must continue to use the definition, while struggling with the implications of opposing views. Still, the imposition of a single, federal definition of learning disabilities has had some positive outcomes. The EHA definition does reflect current political and economic realities of attention, funding, and the allocation of professional resources. It serves as a focus for advocacy by providing specific identification parameters for a previously ill-defined population, as well as enhanced visibility for a wide set of problems. Greater visibility and the resulting heightened perceptions of need lead, in turn, to greater public attention to the diversity of learning problems and disorders, and also provide both motivation and guidelines for professional involvement. Definitional clarity—even an illusory clarity—is particularly crucial to the struggle for financial support, providing a rallying point in the competition with well-established categories of need for funding at federal, state, and local levels.

Although the current federally imposed definition has had some positive effects for the various groups concerned with learning disabilities, it is essential to remember that these groups have purposes and goals that are inherently—and appropriately—divergent. The search for a single definition that would meet the needs of researchers, theorists, practitioners, and evaluations may be futile. According to Keogh (1987), the confusion in the field of learning disabilities that has led some critics to refer to learning disabilities as a nonexistent phenomenon arises from the failure to distinguish a conceptual definition from an operational definition. She proposed that professional and lay groups alike adopt and use more narrowly worded definitions, based on their specific purposes and tasks. As an example, Keogh noted that school systems have one kind of operational definition to conform to their bureaucratic, economic, political, altruistic, and self-serving needs. Researchers, however, should have a distinct operational definition that is tailored to criteria such as validity, reliability, and transferability of outcomes.

Unfortunately, improved definitional clarity at the level of the individual discipline or group has the paradoxical result of greater confusion in the broader area of policy-making. Research, assessment, intervention, and outcomes are studied under distinct operational definitions. In contrast, policy decisions must be based on generalizations. Difficulties are inevitable when integrating fundamentally incompatible data. Even the preliminary step of identifying the target group for a study of learning disabilities is fraught with danger. Some studies have used children identified by the local school evaluation team, and others have performed their own selection process. Tests used may be interpreted in different ways, depending on the goals and skills of the researcher. Variables seen as important and screened in by one researcher will be eliminated by another. The development of a sound knowledge base has been, and continues to be, exceedingly difficult under these circumstances.

In 1981, the National Joint Council for Learning Disabilities (NJCLD) responded to the criticism of earlier definitions by providing a new one:

> Learning disabilities is a generic term that refers to a *heterogeneous* group of disorders manifested by significant difficulties in the acquisition and use of listening, speaking, reading, writing, reasoning or mathematical abilities. These disorders are *intrinsic to the individual and presumed to be due to central nervous system dysfunction.* Even though a learning disability may occur concomitantly with other handicapping conditions (e.g., sensory impairment, mental retardation, social and emotional disturbance) or environmental influences (e.g., cultural differences, insufficient/inappropriate instruction, psychogenic factors), it is not the direct result of those conditions or influences. [Italics added] (Hammill, Leigh, McNutt, & Larsen, 1981, p. 331)

The italicized portions of the definition highlight the additional stress placed on the heterogeneity of conditions, the flat assertion that they are intrinsic (based in the individual), and the acknowledged presumption that there is a neurological base for the conditions listed in the definition.

The federal Interagency Committee on Learning Disabilities (ICLD) (1987) was mandated by Section 9 of the Health Research Extension Act of 1985 (P.L. 99–158) to review and assess federal research priorities, activities, and findings regarding learning disabilities (including central nervous system dysfunction in children). In 1987, ICLD proposed three significant additions to the NJCLD definition: (1) social skills were newly identified as subject to specific learning disability, (2) a noncausal relationship between hyperactivity/attention deficit disorder and learning disability was posited, and (3) the presumed relationship of other handicapping conditions to learning disabilities was specified in greater detail. The ICLD goal was to establish a definition that could be used with equal effectiveness as a basis for research, diagnosis, administration, and legislation, obviating the need for separate, competing definitions. The following definition was proposed:

> Learning disabilities is a generic term that refers to a heterogeneous group of disorders manifested by significant difficulties in the acquisition and use of listening, speaking, reading, writing, reasoning, or mathematical abilities *or of social skills.* These disorders are intrinsic to the individual and presumed to be due to central nervous system dysfunction. Even though a learning disability may occur concomitantly with other handicapping conditions (e.g., sensory impairment, mental retardation, social and emotional disturbance), *with socio*environmental influences (e.g., cultural differences, insufficient or inappropriate instruction, psychogenic factors), *and especially with attention deficit disorder, all of which may cause learning problems, a learning disability* is not the direct result of those conditions or influences. [Italics added] (Kavanagh & Truss, 1988, pp. 550–551)

All ICLD members, except the U.S. Department of Education (DOE), accepted the 1987 modifications. DOE officials rejected the new definition for two reasons (ICLD, 1987). First, the inclusion of social skills in the definition would involve a change in EHA, possibly increasing the number of learning-disabled children legally entitled to special education services. At the time, DOE was involved in a "regular education initiative" aimed at returning children to the regular education classroom whenever possible. Second, the new language left unclear to what degree a learning disability might be the *indirect* result of other handicapping conditions or socioenvironmental influences. DOE attorneys raised the possibility of conflict with the explicit point that learning disability was intrinsic to the individual (Silver, 1988). This recent effort on a national level illustrates the ongoing search for understanding and a common conceptual base among professional groups working in the area. The struggle for definitional clarity continues to reflect both the unknowns in the field and the realities of fiscal and political constraints.

PROFESSIONAL CONTRIBUTIONS TO DEFINITIONAL CLARITY

Despite the legally mandated and widespread use of the federal definition of learning disabilities, several other terms still are in common use: minimal brain dysfunction syndrome (MBD) or central nervous system dysfunction (CNS), neurological impairment (NI), and dyslexia. Each term has different connotations for professionals and parents. A professional group's choice of nomenclature typically guides its identification of problems, its selection of intervention strategies, and its range of referrals for collateral or supportive services. Frequently, a professional group's terminology reflects beliefs about the location of the dysfunction or problem, such as minimal *brain* dysfunction or *central nervous system* dysfunction. Other professions may use terminology emphasizing specific impairments, such as *visual perception* or *expressive language* deficit, which imply a specific direction for intervention. A brief review of some of the most frequently used terms will provide a background for assessing points of disagreement and will facilitate social workers' discussions with families and other professionals about the selection and sequencing of appropriate steps in evaluation and treatment.

Implicit in the terms MBD, CNS, and NI is an emphasis on the functioning of the central nervous system as the locus of a broad range of disorders. These terms highlighting brain and central nervous system involvement should be used with great care. Not all persons with neurological impairments are learning disabled, whereas many (but not all) professionals in the field believe that nearly every individual with a specific learning disability has some neurological impairment resulting in a central nervous system dysfunction (Myers & Hammill, 1982). In the past, members of the medical professions often have been most comfortable with this nomenclature—a terminology that, with its implications of irremediable brain injury or damage, has left a legacy of fear, stigma, and confusion among parents. Many parents have assumed that such terms were just other ways of saying that their child was mentally retarded and faced definite limits to potential achievement. Tragically, parents' lowered expectations and professionals' selection of less demanding remediative strategies often have resulted in self-fulfilling prophecies about the child. *Dyslexia,* one of the first descriptive labels, refers to the manifestation of a primary reading disorder based on central nervous system dysfunction. Much of the research on learning disabilities has focused on the specific problem of reading disability (ICLD, 1987), with recent research emphasizing visual information processing and verbal processing of language. As the complexities of dyslexia become better understood, the term is being applied to a broad range of writing, reading, and speaking disorders, which may be influenced themselves by widely differing auditory, visual, or sequencing dysfunctions. Many other terms pinpointing specific difficulties with word recognition, word memory, spelling, calculating, and so forth, have begun to be used by educators as testing methodologies have been developed to isolate different areas of academic weakness. These terms generally lead to specific therapeutic interventions that might be prescribed: for example, *receptive language problems* suggests need for a language therapist; *visual perceptual problems,* developmental optometry; *motor skill deficits,* sensory motor integration therapy (Lynn, 1979).

However, the lay community still associates dyslexia with letter and word reversals, even though this is only one possible manifestation of the problem. To the general public, dyslexia connotes a contained and remediable problem, without the accompanying emotional, behavioral, or social components that recently have been associated with the term "learning disabilities." Parents often prefer the term "dyslexia" because the word "disability" is absent. The widely publicized identification of such well-known figures as Winston Churchill and Nelson Rockefeller as dyslexic has popularized the term and has even fostered an association between dyslexia and creative accomplishment in adult life. The term occasionally has carried socioeconomic overtones, as some of the earlier expensive private special schools were established for "dyslexic" children.

Although the term "learning disabilities" avoids the stigma of explicit reference to brain damage, operationally it may have other stigmatizing effects. The legal definition is used in a variety of ways in public school systems. Some of the children to whom it is applied have genuine specific learning dysfunctions that constitute disabilities; others may not, but may be seen as too divergent from the classroom norm in terms of emotionally volatile behavior or pace of learning. Such divergences may be related to cultural, racial, class, or experiential background and have nothing to do with specific learning disabilities. Labels also may be inappropriately affixed to reduce class size, to lessen the need for individualized instruction in the regular classroom, or, by excluding less advanced readers from the statistical pool, to promote higher class reading scores. All children so labeled—whether correctly or not—represent an increasingly large population in the public school system, a population that is both very diverse and poorly served.

In return for the presumed advantages of smaller classes and remedial attention, children identified as having specific learning disabilities must accept the status—and the stigma—inherent in the "special education" classification. The trade is not necessarily a fair one. As has been shown repeatedly, the adoption of the classification of learning disability does not automatically bring improvements to a child's learning situation. Despite legislative mandates, many children fall farther and farther behind, receiving both poor instruction and limited monitoring of their progress. Relatively few children gain the skills they need to move back into regular education (Gartner & Lipsky, 1987).

The implications of labeling in the educational system have led to a series of position statements from professional groups, lay organizations, and governmental agencies. Concerned by the ever-increasing number of children receiving special education outside regular classrooms, Madeleine Will (1986), assistant secretary of the DOE Office of Special Education and Rehabilitative Services, discussed the concept of "shared responsibility." She stated that "building level administrators must be empowered to assemble appropriate professional and other resources for delivering effective, coordinated, comprehensive services for all students, based on individual educational needs rather than eligibility for special programs" (p. 413). Will's (1986) statement stressed the governmental commitment to the rights of children with learning disabilities to education established under P.L. 94–142, but underlined the goal of educating learning-disabled children in the regular education classroom. This "regular education initiative" has drawn equal numbers of supporters and detractors. The National Association of Social Workers, together with the National Association of School Psychologists and the Coalition of Advocates for Students, has adopted a "rights without labels" position statement supporting a student's right to obtain services in school without being labeled or removed from the regular education programs. The focus is on prereferral screening and intervention in the regular classroom by both regular and special education staff.

The concept underlying rights without labels is appealing on many levels, because the stigmatization involved in labeling the student is avoided without the concomitant loss of specially trained staff. The effect of the ongoing debate over the quality of *regular* education on education for children with special needs cannot be ignored, however. Professional groups have noted a possible erosion of legislative protection and special services for students with mild to severe learning disabilities (Lerner, 1987). Parents, regular educators, or advocacy groups have not been vocal in support of these protections and services. The abandonment of compensatory strategies to correct for past discrimination, changes in fiscal support structures, the lack of specially trained teachers, and the blurring of the rights of children with handicaps are just a few of the fears being voiced by opponents of the proposed change (McKinney & Hocutt, 1988).

Social workers outside the school system who work with children with learning disabilities and their families usually are responding to a family's concerns about the behavior or emotional state of their child. Rather than using a special education label, these social workers are likely to use a labeling system for mental disorders established by the American Psychiatric Association (1987) *Diagnostic and Statistical Manual of Mental Disorders* (DSM-III-R). Since the first edition (1952), DSM authors have sought continually to refine and clarify diagnostic categories amid continuing controversy (Kutchins & Kirk, 1988). Developmental disorders and learning disabilities were not included in DSM until 1980, which spurred debate on whether children diagnosed with these problems would be stigmatized as having a mental disorder (Rutter & Shaffer, 1980). This DSM-III edition (APA, 1980) presented core symptoms and subsets of additional symptoms, and identified a range of other factors to be considered (such as duration of the problems, age of onset, course, predisposing factors, and requirements for a differential diagnosis). Other 1980 innovations reflected a move away from a psychoanalytic perspective toward a theoretical approach that focused on identification of symptoms rather than causes. A revised DSM-III (DSM-III-R) (APA, 1987) was published amid increasing controversy, and questions about reliability studies and the basis for the changes it embodied have been raised (Kutchins & Kirk, 1988). Categorizations again are more specific, based on the primary symptoms manifested by children. There is a basic division between physical versus sensory impairments (such as visual or hearing limitations), and behavioral or emotional pathology (such as conduct or cognitive disorders). DSM-III-R categories focus on the psychological characteristics and impacts of the specific disorders or adaptive behaviors associated with them, without stressing their educational implications (Unruh, 1987).

The experience of having a learning disability has been found to play a major—and lifelong—role in an individual's organization of experience and overall development. With its focus on single dimensions, the classification system approach of DSM may not be helpful to a holistic conceptualization of the issues facing children and their families. Finally, there is the still-unresolved question of whether the DSM classification carries with it the automatic implication of mental disorder and accompanying stigma.

The most recent contribution to the terminological debate is the suggestion that the term "learning disabilities" be abandoned in favor of the phrase "learning differences," to avoid the connotation of disability, while stressing institutional responses that focus on individualized intervention strategies. The key disagreement over use of the term concerns whether or not "differences" lessens the idea of need and will lead to a reduction in the resources necessary to deal with special problems. There is fear that protective legislation may be abandoned, and that rights and entitlements associated with "disability" will be lost (Brown, 1989).

IMPLICATIONS FOR FAMILIES AND CHILDREN

Each term precipitates a reaction from professionals and parents. The social worker cannot function effectively without an awareness of how learning disorders have been identified for parents and their children, and of the different connotations these terms may carry. Clues to such latent meanings (which may vary by region, class, cultural and ethnic background, and past history of the use of the term for members of a particular sociocultural group) should emerge from discussion with families regarding what terms they have heard, what their extended family and friends have said, and how the child's problems are referred to and defined colloquially. This discussion also will help to clarify the level of support and the expectations and attitudes in the child's home and community environment. Finally, it is essential to determine the family's level of knowledge about the disabling condition, familial biases and stereotypes, family definitions of the role of academic success in negotiating the adult world, and the reality of service availability with and without potentially stigmatizing labeling. This clarification of values helps the family and the social worker to develop a cooperative relationship, to ensure that the psychosocial and educational needs of the child will be addressed.

Social workers should cover the following six areas in exploring labels and terminology with children with learning disabilities and their families:

1. Help parents clarify their understanding of the labels that have been applied to their child. Misconceptions and fears often overwhelm reasoned thinking and selection of appropriate next steps. For example, parents' fears that a child may be mentally retarded may have been reinforced by daily experiences in which the child is labeled as stupid. Clear definitions must be developed.

2. Correct children's misperceptions of themselves, and help them develop their own definition of their learning disability.

3. Analyze the extent to which the label(s) used by parents reflect appropriate understanding of the issues confronting them and their children. For example, a term may reveal denial, overreadiness to assume the worst prognosis, or confusion with mental retardation.

4. Educate parents about the different definitions of learning disabilities and the controversies surrounding them. This begins the demystification process and introduces the different professional perspectives, while acknowledging the current gaps in knowledge about this complex set of conditions.

5. Help parents perceive the specific description of their child's strengths and weaknesses as not only legitimate but preferable to nondescriptive labels and categories. Any legal or service definition applied to their child always must include the individualized description.

6. Help parents understand current, relevant legislative issues, so that they can become affiliated with appropriate groups. Changes in legal definitions may have direct repercussions—good or bad—on services and resources for children in their schools and communities. Empowering parents to see their roles as multidimensional, linking the struggle for appropriate services for their own child with ways to support the needs of others, is part of the social worker's task.

The definition of learning disabilities encompasses many configurations of dysfunctional developmental variations. The politicization of the process of defining learning disabilities will continue to affect both the children who live with these disabilities and their families. Simultaneously, lay and professional groups are struggling with revised definitions of the problem and its parameters, which will have significant implications for service access and continuity. Social workers must recognize that, at the many junctures where professional, political, economic, and parental perspectives may clash, the needs of the child must take precedence. Those needs must be kept clearly in view in all deliberations aimed at improving a given group's access to available resources.

DEMOGRAPHY OF LEARNING DISABILITIES

Not surprisingly, given the absence of definitional unanimity, the basic issue of determining the extent of learning disabilities among children on a national basis has plagued professionals and confounded planning for resources at all levels of public and private services. According to the literature, the prevalence of learning disabilities (based on the number of people with the condition relative to the general population at a specified point in time) has varied from 2 percent to more than 20 percent of the total population (Broman, Bien, & Shaughnessy, 1985). In 1987, between 5 and 10 percent of the total population—from 12 to 24 million persons—was viewed as a reasonable estimate (ICLD, 1987). Referring to the number and characteristics of persons affected by learning disabilities, the ICLD report to Congress (1987) noted that "Prevalence may vary when (1) different case definitions of the condition are used, (2) different populations are studied, or (3) studies are done at different ages or different points in time" (p. 107). It is clear that the study of learning disabilities is characterized by all three inconsistencies from the wide variation in asserted prevalence rates.

Most cases of learning disability are identified through measures of discrepancy in performance. However, there are numerous choices involved in the process of measuring discrepancy between ability and achievement, and these choices affect the number of children with educational differences who will be found to be learning disabled. Because all humans exhibit variable patterns of strength and weakness, the more functional areas that are included in an initial screening, the greater the number of persons who are likely to be identified as having learning disabilities. For example, the ICLD report (1987) pointed out that if listening, speaking, reading, writing, reasoning, mathematical, and social skills all were tested, a higher prevalence of learning disabilities in a given population would emerge than if only reading skills were tested. The second step in the identification process is the application of more specific measures to exclude children who were screened in by the more sweeping functional measures. Currently, there are no standard criteria for the selection of measures, either for inclusion or for exclusion.

Considerable controversy also surrounds the various procedures used to determine the level of discrepancy, and whether or not each one provides a valid basis for measurement. Commonly used measures include the number of years below grade level at which a child is functioning; expectancy formulas based both on age and on mental age; and techniques involving standard scores and regression analyses (McLaughlin & Lewis, 1986; Cone & Wilson, 1981). The inherent arbitrariness of measures involving cutoff points is clear. For example, defining as learning disabled all children whose test scores for a given skill (such as reading or arithmetic) fall below 80 percent of the mean score for the general population of children of the same age necessarily would result in higher prevalence rates than a definition setting the cutoff point at 75 percent (ICLD, 1987). Unfortunately, no general agreements have been reached that would standardize these measures. Some states have adopted 80 percent cutoff points, others have used lower percentages, and still others use different approaches altogether. Also, as the definitions of learning disabilities have changed, demographic studies have included and excluded different subsets of populations with learning problems.

Public education identification procedures for learning-disabled children present an equally confusing picture. Part B of EHA requires that data be collected annually regarding the different categories of children receiving special education services. Among the public school age population, the number of children categorized as being affected by learning disabilities has grown exponentially since the enactment of the legislation. In the 1975–76 school year, 1.79 percent of the school enrollment was served as learning disabled (U.S. Department of Education, 1986). In the 1985–86 school year, 4.73 percent of the school enrollment was so served, or 42 percent of all identified and served handicapped children. This figure represents almost 1.9 million children between the ages of 3 and 21 (U.S. Department of Education, 1987). From the 1975–76 school year to the 1984–85 school year, the number of learning-disabled students rose 119 percent, while the total number of students enrolled in special education increased by only 16 percent (Gartner & Lipsky, 1987).

The largest proportion of increase was in the 3- to 5-year-old and 18- to 21-year-old groups. All other categories of handicapping conditions showed a decrease in absolute numbers during this period, particularly the category of the mentally retarded. Referring to this as the result of "classification plea bargaining," Gartner and Lipsky (1987, p. 373) observed that parents prefer the learning-disabled label to that of mental retardation. In addition, local school districts can establish their own inclusionary and exclusionary cutoff criteria for classification, further confounding the goal of achieving a count based on uniform national standards. As Gartner and Lipsky noted, prevalence data and classifications become suspect when some states have large learning-disabled populations and very few mentally retarded students, while other states have very few learning-disabled, and many mentally retarded, students.

Most children counted as having learning disabilities are in regular classrooms (77.27 percent in 1984–85), 21.21 percent are in separate classes, 1.33 percent are in separate schools, and 0.18 percent are in other environments. When analyzed by age group, the 3- to 5-year-olds tend to be served in more restrictive settings—those providing more supportive services—than 6- to 17-year-olds. This pattern might reflect the availability of fewer regular education programs (Gartner & Lipsky, 1987). These statistics do not tell the whole story, however. Another group of students is able to compensate for their learning problems in schools that are flexible enough to tolerate their pace and style. These students remain in regular educational classes and are not evaluated or counted, even though they may have learning profiles similar to those of children in special education (ICLD, 1987).

An additional group of children who are not counted among the handicapped includes those whose abilities are in the superior range but whose performance is only average for their age and grade level. These children may function at grade level because they have developed good compensatory skills and put in the time necessary to produce adequate work—if they were to receive special remediatory help in the areas of their deficits, however, they would be able to perform at a level commensurate with their abilities. Considerable controversy surrounds the identification of such students as among those entitled to receive the supportive services enumerated by EHA. These students' performances meet general age and classroom standards, so by conventional standards they are ineligible. Only if measures of discrepancy focusing on developing these children's optimal ability and performance are used do their needs become undeniable.

Although gifted children may represent a very small fraction of the total numbers of learning disabled, they are a group whose true abilities go unrecognized and whose education is meeting their needs only minimally. The frustration, the possibility of chronic high stress levels, and the development and reinforcement of maladaptive coping strategies due to neglect of their needs have not been

15

addressed (Jones, 1986). The loss to society caused by this group's inappropriate education has not been given sufficient attention.

VARIABLES INFLUENCING LEARNING
DISABILITIES DEMOGRAPHY

The overrepresentation of culturally diverse students and those of low socioeconomic background in special education classes (Brosnan, 1983; Tucker, 1980; Argulewicz, 1983), specifically in classes for learning disabilities, is a statistical fact. The overriding definitional problems make it risky to explore the variables that influence the demography. Any consideration of apparent causal factors must allow for the possibility that some of the variables may represent a complex mix of influences and associations.

A number of health and environmental variables have been identified as influences on the prevalence of learning disabilities in the population. One of the most striking associations is that existing between learning disabilities and children's health factors correlated with low socioeconomic backgrounds. Even if children from these backgrounds are overrepresented in special education classes, they are a group vulnerable to numerous high-risk factors in their immediate living environment. Children from low socioeconomic circumstances are especially vulnerable to low birthweights, high blood lead levels, lasting hearing impairments, and congenital infections. The developmental impacts of these conditions have been associated with behavioral or learning difficulties (Alberman, 1973; Schorr, 1983). A second, striking association involves gender—studies showed a frequency of learning disabilities that was three to five times higher among males than among females (Broman et al., 1985), which may support McEwen's (1983) finding that the development of the cerebral hemispheres appears to be vulnerable to differential effects of sex hormones.

Genetic factors are believed to represent a multifactorial predisposition to learning disabilities (Pennington & Smith, 1983). A variety of different chromosomal patterns are currently under investigation. Finucci, Guthrie, Childs, Abbey, and Childs (1976) and Finucci, Isaacs, Whitehouse, and Childs (1983) found that a high number of first-degree relatives of learning-disabled children also had some specific reading disabilities. However, no single genetic link was involved. Another recent study revealed that parents who reported having reading difficulties were significantly more likely to have children with reading problems (Volger, DeFries, & Decker, 1984). Similar patterns of reading problems have been found between siblings. Some genetic disorders are known to impair development and academic ability and behavior if not treated, such as phenylketonuria (PKU) (Holtzman, Kronmal, van Doorninck, Azen, & Koch, 1976; Levine, 1987). Extensive research has been devoted to the linkage between developmental lags and chromosome irregularities. Distinct chromosomal patterns have been linked to difficulties in visual-spatial perception, specific language development, and conceptual faculties (Levine, 1987).

An increasing amount of research documents associations between various factors suspected of causing learning disorders. Advances in understanding the complex mechanisms underlying central nervous system development have led to exploration in medical, environmental, and nutritional areas. Although studies in these areas usually are discussed in the context of the search for causes, the studies also can be considered in terms of their demographic implications. Most of the studies involved small, fairly discrete populations, which raises serious questions about whether findings can be generalized. Also, most of these studies only identify high-risk factors. It is essential to remember that not all children who have the characteristics of those studied will show evidence of impaired learning ability.

Prenatal Risk Factors

Studies of congenital sources of learning impairment have focused on the complex interrelationship among the developing brain, hormones, mood, and environment of the fetus. A number of prenatal maternal infections, such as rubella and toxoplasmosis (Desmond et al., 1978; Sever, 1982); illnesses, such as high blood pressure, kidney disease, and toxemia; metabolic disorders, such as diabetes; addictive drugs; prescription drugs (Nichols & Chen, 1981); alcohol (Hesselbrock, Stabenau, & Hesselbrock, 1985); x-rays early in pregnancy; smoking; and environmental toxins, particularly lead (McMichael et al., 1988) are known to affect the fragile central nervous system of the embryo or fetus, and to affect nutritional status and growth. All of these factors are thought to give rise to a continuum of effects that can range from miscarriage, through retardation or subtle neurological dysfunctions, to no effect at all. Of all these areas, the role of alcohol and the impact of different degrees of alcoholism in the mother have received the most intense scrutiny (Shaywitz, Cohen, & Shaywitz, 1980; Dorris, 1989). Increasingly, definitive research is showing that causal connections can be established.

There also is increasing evidence that the mother's use of drugs other than alcohol has a direct influence on the unborn child's growth and development (Brody, 1988). For example, research is now showing that even brief use of cocaine by a pregnant woman may cause subtle impairments in the development of the nervous system in a fetus. Infants born to cocaine-using mothers often are premature, and have easily overloaded nervous systems that make them hypersensitive to their environment. Difficulties in the mother-child relationship may ensue, because these babies often cannot be comforted by the usual means, and their incessant crying may elicit increasing parental frustration, even rejection. Subsequent neurological problems, such as learning disabilities and attentional problems, have been observed in these children when they reach school age.

17

A recent survey of cocaine use by pregnant women in 36 U.S. hospitals found that an average of about 11 percent of women surveyed were exposing their unborn children to drugs. The hospitals studied were in urban, suburban, and rural areas, and patient populations included all income groups. In some hospitals, as many as 27 percent of the mothers surveyed were using illicit drugs (Brody, 1988).

Perinatal and Postnatal Associations

Certain events occurring during the period immediately preceding birth (including labor and delivery) and the period immediately after birth are suspected of directly influencing a child's development. During these periods, the stage is set for future developmental problems by an injury or other obstetrical trauma to a normally developed fetus. This can result from poor professional service (Friedman, Sachtleben, & Wallace, 1979) or from unexpected complications, such as breech delivery with delay in delivery of the head (Muller et al., 1971). Most of these problems are associated with interference to the fetal or maternal respiratory or circulation systems, resulting in physical damage to the fetal nervous system and a lack of oxygen to the fetal brain (Tobel & Lambert, 1981).

The influences of the larger environment are more difficult to assess. Children born in poverty are more vulnerable than others to the impact of deficient prenatal care and any perinatal risks (Breitmayer & Ramey, 1986). Lack of community health resources, poor nutrition, and emotional stress, such as that suffered by an abused or neglected teenager who becomes pregnant, may all be factors contributing to the low health status of both mother and fetus. Existing vulnerabilities in the growing child may be exacerbated, or new ones created. For example, when the variables of prematurity and low birthweight are considered (Drillien, Thomson, & Burgoyne, 1980; Eilers, Desai, Wilson, & Cunningham, 1986), and poor postnatal care is added, the vulnerable child may exhibit various learning dysfunctions. The additional variables of low socioeconomic and demographic status appear more closely linked to the appearance of learning disabilities in some longitudinal studies (Werner, Bierman, & French, 1971).

Many health-related risk factors of early childhood have been correlated with learning disabilities because of their frequent associations with children's learning problems. Examples are infections of the central nervous system, such as meningitis, and frequent infections affecting hearing over long periods of time, such as otitis media (Kavanagh, 1986). Environmental pollutants and toxins of all kinds, from cigarette smoke to insecticides and mercury, also are beginning to receive serious attention. Studies of the effects of lead poisoning show a direct relationship between high tooth-lead levels and signs of attention deficits and processing problems (McMichael et al., 1988). Anemia and iron deficiency also have been identified as possible factors affecting behavior and attention. Malnutrition at early ages has been seen to have an impact on language skills, behavior, and attention span. Food additives, carbohydrates, low blood sugar, and allergies all have been tentatively linked to hyperactivity and concentration problems. However, systematic review of existing research has concluded that, although these factors may be relevant for some small groups of children, the numbers are nowhere as high as those who suggest a causal linkage claim (Levine, 1987).

The role of abuse and neglect in the emergence of developmental disabilities was reviewed by Snyder, Hampton, and Newberger (1983). For many children, abuse in the home is a fairly frequent and predictable event (Straus, Gelles, & Steinmetz, 1980). Abuse can range from shaking, which may cause subdural hematomas in infants (Caffey, 1972), to severe battering, which causes serious internal injuries. Disturbed adult–child relationships may have been triggered by preexisting neurological impairment in the child (Friedrich & Boriskin, 1976), such as the frustrating behavior and responses related to prematurity (Hunter, Kilstrom, Kraybill, & Loda, 1978). In other situations the violence or neglect may have injured a child with a previously intact central nervous system. Negative effects of abuse on the child's development and growth range from language delay (Newberger & McAnulty, 1976), through cognitive deficits and motor dysfunctions (Kempe, 1987; Solomons, 1979), to the most extreme physical damage to the body (Snyder et al., 1983). Families at all income levels abuse and neglect their children. However, in poor and minority families the results of abuse are more likely to be reported as abuse than in middle-class families, where a report of accidental injury (Gelles, 1975) is more likely. The socioeconomic stresses of unemployment, poor housing, large family size, and lack of access to child care are correlated both with abuse or neglect and with poverty.

Group studies of children with head injuries, particularly those in which the child was unconscious for a long time, have shown a frequent association between such injuries and problems in school that have many of the characteristics of learning disabilities. However, as with other health risks, other variables must be considered. There may have been preexisting neurological vulnerabilities (Levine, 1987). There also is a statistical likelihood that children who have had severe head trauma also have suffered other, environmentally related, deprivations affecting their learning (Rutter, Chadwick, & Shaffer, 1983).

Many variables have been identified tentatively as influences on the learning patterns of children. However, the small size of most of the studies, the variability in the sample definition and the measurements used to determine the presence of learning disabilities, and the frequent clustering of high-risk variables make it difficult to establish actual causal linkages. Nevertheless, even tentative associations may be useful in understanding certain recurring patterns of prevalence of learning disabilities. Although clear causal relationships between a child's environment and learning disabilities have not been proven, the interaction between biological predisposition and environmental high-risk configurations of child and family temperaments is indisputable. Children from certain biological, familial, and community situations—often those associated with low socioeconomic backgrounds—are profoundly vulnerable.

This discussion of the demography of learning disabilities has focused on children, identifying environmental influences and high-risk situations that can be altered. Although most studies of the prevalence of learning disabilities and of predisposing factors have involved preadolescent populations, the adult population should not be neglected. Follow-up studies of learning-disabled children show that, as adolescents and young adults, many members of this population appear to have continued problems in independent functioning (Gittelman, Mannuzza, & Shenker, 1985). Some adolescents and adults with learning disabilities suffer hyperactivity and attention deficits; others have deficits in perceptual or communication skills (Rawson, 1977; Weiss, Hechtman, & Perlman, 1978). An increasing number of longitudinal studies show that learning-disabled adolescents are at high risk for early school dropout, drug abuse, and juvenile delinquency (Dunivant, 1982; Murray, 1976). Adults with learning disabilities who have acquired maladaptive coping strategies continue to be at risk to themselves and others. Adults also may suffer marital instability, chronic unemployment, and psychiatric disorders. Accordingly, the emphasis here on the demography from birth through elementary school age should not obscure the fact that there are identifiable groups of learning-disabled persons in all age brackets. These groups also must be considered in any assessment of the prevalence of learning disabilities.

IMPLICATIONS FOR SOCIAL WORK INTERVENTION

Despite the problems of identifying and measuring learning disabilities, the demography of these disabilities provides some direction for social work intervention. The diversity of associations among prenatal, perinatal, and postnatal risk factors and conditions that affect normal developmental processes indicate a necessity for early social work intervention during pregnancy and for follow-up work with families and children after hospital discharge. Many of the factors are simply predispositions and high-risk factors, rather than causal links leading inevitably to learning dysfunctions. Socioeconomic status and high-quality post-natal care may help to overcome the negative effects of birth complications (Werner & Smith, 1982; Sameroff, 1979). Early intervention is critical in preventing unnecessary associative emotional and social problems. Even if the social work intervention cannot be timed for maximum prevention, improving nutritional and environmental factors may reduce or mitigate negative influences.

Practitioners should work with children and their parents to eliminate as many risk factors as possible. Even without a diagnosis of learning disabilities, social workers can identify and target early intervention strategies directed at maternal nutrition, health, and behavior during pregnancy. Special parental supports for the low birthweight and premature infant, parenting education for the first-time parent, and responsive health care monitoring during the preschool years are prerequisites for the healthy growth and development of all children.

The knowledge that, given the same sets of developmental problems, children from low socioeconomic backgrounds already are more vulnerable than others gives social workers clear priorities in developing creative interventions to moderate the influences of home, school, and community inadequacies. Although prevention may not be possible, creating a setting where vulnerable children are not always struggling with an inhospitable environment may make some of the unavoidable developmental variation less of a threat.

Early identification of learning disabilities has proven helpful in alleviating some of the disabling consequences of developmental dysfunctions, but does not obviate the need for lifelong support in some cases. Learning disabilities do not end with childhood and are not limited to performance in school—they constitute a "life disability" (Silver, 1979, p. 606). Because learning disabilities affect all aspects of daily life, a holistic viewpoint is essential in planning services and structuring intervention for a child. Also, despite the critical importance for society and for individuals of early intervention, the increasingly visible populations of adolescents and adults with learning disabilities cannot be ignored or left unserved. The problems these individuals pose for their families and for society are undeniable on the policy-making level. The distress these people encounter as adults—competition in the workplace, underemployment, social isolation—must be met with compassionate help.

REFERENCES

Alberman, E. (1973). The early prediction of learning disorders. *Developmental Medicine and Child Neurology, 15,* 202–204.

American Psychiatric Association. (1980). *Diagnostic and statistical manual of mental disorders* (3rd ed.). Washington, DC: Author.

American Psychiatric Association. (1987). *Diagnostic and statistical manual of mental disorders* (3rd ed., rev.). Washington, DC: Author.

Argulewicz, E. N. (1983). Effects of ethnic membership, socioeconomic status and home language on LD, EMR and EH placements. *Learning Disabilities Quarterly, 6,* 195–200.

Association for Children with Learning Disabilities. (1963). *Bylaws.* Pittsburgh, PA: Author.

Breitmayer, B., & Ramey, C. (1986). Biological non-optimality and the quality of post natal environment as codeterminants of intellectual development. *Child Development, 57,* 1151–1165.

Brody, J. E. (1988, September 20). Cocaine: Litany of fetal risks grows. *New York Times,* p. Cl.

Broman, S. H., Bien, E., & Shaughnessy, P. (1985). *Low achieving children: The first seven years.* Hillsdale, NJ: Erlbaum.

Brosnan, F. L. (1983). Overrepresentation of low socioeconomic minority students in special education programs in California. *Learning Disabilities Quarterly, 6,* 517–525.

Brown, D. (1989, January). Learning disability not learning difference. *Newsbriefs.* Pittsburgh, PA: Association for Children with Learning Disabilities.

Caffey, J. (1972). On the theory and practice of shaking infants: Its potential residual effects of permanent brain damage and mental retardation. *American Journal of Diseases of Children, 124,* 161–169.

Chalfant, J. C. (1987). Learning disabilities: Problems in definition of . . . . In C. R. Reynolds & L. Mann (Eds.), *Encyclopedia of special education* (pp. 925–929). New York: John Wiley & Sons.

Coles, G. (1988). *The learning mystique: A critical look at learning disabilities.* New York: Pantheon Books.

Cone, T. E., & Wilson, L. R. (1981). Quantifying a severe discrepancy: A critical review. *Learning Disabilities Quarterly, 4,* 359–361.

Desmond, M. M., Fisher, E. S., Vorderman, A. L., Schaffer, H. G., Andrew, L. P., Zion, T. E., & Catlin, F. I. (1978). The longitudinal course of congenital rubella encephalitis in non-retarded children. *Childhood Journal of Pediatrics, 93,* 584–591.

Dorris, M. (1989). *The broken cord.* New York: Harper & Row.

Drillien, C. H., Thomson, A. J., & Burgoyne, K. (1980). Low birthweight children at early school age: A longitudinal study. *Developmental Medicine and Child Neurology, 22,* 26–47.

Dunivant, N. (1982). The relationship between learning disabilities and juvenile delinquency (Executive Summary). Williamsburg, VA: National Center for State Courts.

Education for All Handicapped Children Act, Pub. L. No. 94–142, § 5, 6, 89 Stat. 773–796 (1975).

Eilers, B. L., Desai, N. S., Wilson, M. A., & Cunningham, M. D. (1986). Classroom performance and social factors of children with birth weights of 1250 grams or less: Follow up at 5 to 8 years of age. *Pediatrics, 77,* 203–208.

Epps, S., Ysseldyke, J. E., & Algozzine, B. (1982). *Public policy implications of different definitions of learning disabilities.* (Research Report No. 99). Minneapolis: University of Minnesota, Institute for Research on Learning Disabilities.

Finucci, J. M., Guthrie, J., Childs, A., Abbey, H., & Childs, B. (1976). The genetics of specific reading disability. *Annals of Human Genetics, 40,* 1–23.

Finucci, J. M., Isaacs, S., Whitehouse, C., & Childs, B. (1983). Classification of spelling errors and their relationship to reading ability, sex, grade placement, and intelligence. *Brain and Language, 20,* 340–355.

Friedman, E. A., Sachtleben, M. R., & Wallace, A. K. (1979). Infant outcome following labor induction. *American Journal of Obstetrics and Gynecology, 133,* 718–722.

Friedrich, W. N., & Boriskin, J. A. (1976). The role of the child in abuse: A review of the literature. *American Journal of Orthopsychiatry, 46,* 580–590.

Gartner, A., & Lipsky, D. K. (1987). Beyond special education: Toward a quality system for all students. *Harvard Educational Review, 54,* 367–395.

Gelles, R. J. (1975, April). *Community agencies and child abuse: Labeling and gatekeeping.* Paper presented at the Conference on Recent Research on the Family of the Society for Research in Child Development, Ann Arbor, MI.

Gittelman, R., Mannuzza, S., & Shenker, S. (1985). Hyperactive boys almost grown up: Psychiatric status. *Archives of General Psychiatry, 42,* 937–947.

Hammill, D. D., Leigh, J. E., McNutt, G., & Larsen, S. C. (1981). A new definition of learning disabilities. *Learning Disabilities Quarterly, 4,* 336–342.

Health Research Extension Act, Pub. L. No. 99–158, §9, 99 Stat. 820, 882–883 (1985).

Hesselbrock, V. M., Stabenau, J. R., & Hesselbrock, M. N. (1985). Minimal brain dysfunction and neuropsychologic test performance in offspring of alcoholics. *Recent Developments in Alcoholism, 3,* 65–82.

Holtzman, N. A., Kronmal, R. A., van Doorninck, W., Azen, C., & Koch, R. (1976). Effect of age at loss of dietary control on intellectual performance and behavior of children with phenylketonuria. *New England Journal of Medicine, 314,* 593–598.

Hunter, R. S., Kilstrom, N., Kraybill, M. D., & Loda, F. (1978). Antecedents of child abuse and neglect in premature infants: A prospective study in a newborn intensive care unit. *Pediatrics, 61,* 629–635.

Interagency Committee on Learning Disabilities. (1987). *Learning disabilities: A report to the U.S. Congress.* Washington, DC: National Institute of Child Health and Human Development.

Jones, B. H. (1986). The gifted dyslexic. *Annals of Dyslexia, 32,* 301–317.

Kavanagh, J. F. (Ed.). (1986). *Otitis media and child development.* Parkton, MD: York Press.

Kavanagh, J. F., & Truss, T. J., Jr. (Eds.). (1988). *Learning disabilities: Proceedings of the National Conference.* Parkton, MD: York Press.

Kempe, R. S. (1987). A developmental approach to the treatment of the abused child. In R. E. Helfer & R. S. Kempe (Eds.), *The battered child* (4th ed., pp. 360–381). Chicago: University of Chicago Press.

Keogh, B. K. (1987). Learning disabilities in defense of a construct. *Learning Disabilities Research 3,* 4–9.

Kutchins, H., & Kirk, S. (1988). The future of DSM: Scientific and professional issues. *Harvard Medical School Mental Health Letter, 5,* 3.

Lerner, J. W. (1987). The regular education initiative: Some unanswered questions. *Learning Disabilities Focus, 3,* 3–7.

Levine, M. D. (1982). The low severity-high prevalence disabilities of childhood. In L. Barness (Ed.), *Advances in pediatrics* (pp. 529–554). Chicago: Yearbook.

Levine, M. D. (1987). *Developmental variation and learning disorders.* Cambridge, MA: Educators Publishing Service.

Levine, M. D., Brooks, R., & Shonkoff, J. P. (1980). *A pediatric approach to learning disorders.* New York: John Wiley & Sons.

Lynn, R. (1979). *Learning disabilities: An overview of theories, approaches and politics.* New York: Free Press.

McEwen, B. S. (1983). Hormones and the brain. In C. C. Brown (Ed.), *Pediatric round table series: Childhood learning disabilities and prenatal risk* (pp. 9, 11–17). Skillman, NJ: Johnson & Johnson Baby Products Company.

McKinney, J. D., & Hocutt, A. M. (1988). The need for policy analysis in evaluating the regular education initiative. *Journal of Learning Disabilities, 21,* 12–18.

McLaughlin, J. A., & Lewis, R. B. (1986). *Assessing special students* (2nd ed.). Columbus, OH: Charles E. Merrill Books.

McMichael, A. J., Baghurst, P. A., Wigg, N. R., Vimpani, G. V., Robertson, E. F., & Roberts, R. J. (1988). Port Pirie cohort study: Environmental exposure to lead and children's abilities at the age of 4 years. *New England Journal of Medicine, 319,* 468–475.

Mercer, J. B. (1973). *Labeling the mentally retarded: Clinical and social system perspectives on mental retardation.* Los Angeles: University of California Press.

Muller, P. F., Campbell, H. E., Graham, W. E., Brittain, H., Fitzgerald, J. A., Hogan, M. A., Muller, V. H., & Rittenhouse, A. H. (1971). Perinatal factors and their relationship to mental retardation and other parameters of development. *American Journal of Obstetrics and Gynecology, 109,* 1205–1210.

Murray, C. (1976). *The link between learning disabilities and juvenile delinquency.* Washington, DC: U.S. Department of Justice National Institute for Juvenile Justice and Delinquency Prevention.

Myers, P. I., & Hammill, D. D. (1982). *Learning disabilities: Basic concepts, assessment practices and instructional strategies.* Austin, TX: Pro-Ed.

Newberger, E. H., & McAnulty, E. H. (1976). Family intervention in the pediatric clinic: A necessary approach to the vulnerable child. *Clinical Pediatrics, 15,* 1155–1160.

Nichols, P. L., & Chen, T. C. (1981). *Minimal brain dysfunction: A prospective study.* Hillsdale, NJ: Erlbaum.

Pennington, B. F., & Smith, S. D. (1983). Genetic influences on learning disabilities and speech and language disorders. *Child Development, 54,* 369–387.

Rawson, M. B. (1977). Dyslexics as adults: The possibilities and the challenge. *Bulletin of the Orton Society, 27,* 193–197.

Rutter, M., Chadwick, O., & Shaffer, D. (1983). Head injury. In M. Rutter (Ed.), *Developmental neuropsychiatry* (pp. 83–111). New York: Guilford Press.

Rutter, M., & Shaffer, D. (1980). DSM III: A step forward or back in terms of the classification of child psychiatric disorders. *Journal of the American Academy of Child Psychiatry, 19,* 371–394.

Sameroff, A. J. (1979). The etiology of cognitive competence: A systems perspective. In R. B. Kearsley & I. E. Siegel (Eds.), *Infants at risk: Assessment of cognitive functioning* (pp. 115–151). Hillsdale, NJ: Erlbaum.

Schorr, L. B. (1983). Environmental deterrents: Poverty, affluence, violence, and television. In M. D. Levine (Ed.), *Developmental behavioral pediatrics* (pp. 293–312). Philadelphia: W. B. Saunders.

Sever, J. L. (1982). Infections in pregnancy: Highlights from the collaborative perinatal project. *Teratology, 25,* 227–237.

Shaywitz, S. E., Cohen, D. J., & Shaywitz, B. A. (1980). Behavior and learning difficulties in children of normal intelligence born to alcoholic mothers. *Journal of Pediatrics, 96,* 978–982.

Silver, L. B. (1979). Children with perceptual and other learning problems. In J. Noshpitz (Ed.), *Basic handbook of child psychiatry* (Vol. 3, pp. 605–614). New York: Basic Books.

Silver, L. B. (1988). A review of the federal government's Interagency Committee on Learning Disabilities' Report to the U.S. Congress. *Learning Disabilities Focus, 3*(2), 73–80.

Snyder, J. C., Hampton, R., & Newberger, E. H. (1983). Family dysfunction: Violence, neglect and sexual misuse. In M. D. Levine (Ed.), *Developmental behavioral pediatrics* (pp. 256–275). Philadelphia: W. B. Saunders.

Solomons, G. (1979). Child abuse and developmental disabilities. *Developmental Medicine and Child Neurology, 21,* 101–106.

Straus, M. A., Gelles, R. J., & Steinmetz, S. (1980). *Behind closed doors: Violence in the American family.* Garden City, NJ: Doubleday.

Thurlow, M. L., Ysseldyke, J. E., & Casey, A. (1984). Teachers' perceptions of criteria for identifying learning disabled students. *Psychology in the Schools, 21,* 349–355.

Tobel, H. V., & Lambert, L. (1981). *Introduction to developmental disabilities: Characteristics and social needs.* Lexington: University of Kentucky, Human Development Program, Title XX Training Project Graduate School.

Tucker, J. A. (1980). Ethnic proportions in classes for the learning disabled: Issues in nonbiased assessment. *Journal of Special Education, 14,* 93–105.

Unruh, L. (1987). Diagnosis in special education. In C. R. Reynolds & L. Mann (Eds.), *Encyclopedia of special education* (Vol. 1, pp. 503–507). New York: John Wiley & Sons.

U.S. Department of Education, Office of Special Education and Rehabilitative Services. (1986). *Eighth Annual Report to the Congress on the Implementation of the Education for All Handicapped Children Act.* Washington, DC: Author.

U.S. Department of Education, Office of Special Education and Rehabilitative Services. (1987). *Ninth Annual Report to the Congress on the Implementation of the Education for All Handicapped Children Act.* Washington, DC: Author.

Volger, G. P., DeFries, J. C., & Decker, N. (1984). Family history as an indicator of risk for reading disability. *Journal of Learning Disabilities, 17,* 616–618.

Weiss, G., Hechtman, L., & Perlman, T. (1978). Hyperactives as young adults: School, employer and self-ratings obtained during 10 year follow up evaluations. *American Journal of Orthopsychiatry, 48,* 438–445.

Werner, E. E., Bierman, J. M., & French, F. E. (1971). *The children of Kauai.* Honolulu: University of Hawaii Press.

Werner, E. E., & Smith, R. S. (1982). *Vulnerable but invincible.* New York: McGraw-Hill.

Will, M. (1986). Educating children with learning problems: A shared responsibility. *Exceptional Children, 52,* 411–415.

142.5 33

LIBRARY
College of St. Francis
JOLIET, ILLINOIS

Ysseldyke, J. E. (1983). Current practices in making psychoeducational decisions about learning disabled students (Introduction). *Journal of Learning Disabilities, 16,* 226–233.

Ysseldyke, J. E., Thurlow, M. L., Graden, J. L., Wesson, C., Deno, S. L., & Algozzine, B. (1982). *Generalizations from five years of research on assessment and decision-making* (Research Report No. 100). Minneapolis: University of Minnesota, Institute for Research on Learning Disabilities.

Chapter 2
Nature of Learning Disabilities

Recently, a proliferation of books on learning disabilities has been selling to general, rather than special interest, audiences, demonstrating the public interest in learning disabilities and providing evidence of the highly charged atmosphere in which professionals and parents are making crucial decisions about their children. The book titles indicate the conflict and unresolved issues in the field: *When Children Don't Learn* (McGuinness, 1985), *The Learning Mystique* (Coles, 1987), *The Magic Feather* (Granger & Granger, 1986), *Turnabout Children* (MacCracken, 1986). Current participants in the debate on the nature of learning disabilities range from those who view the term as a pseudoscientific construct intended to protect middle-class children from failure and maintain the existing structure of public education (Coles, 1987; Sigmon, 1987) to those who view learning disabilities as medical problems with neurological (Cruickshank, 1972; Wender, 1971) or neuropsychological (Rothstein, Benjamin, Crosby, & Eisenstadt, 1988) origins. There also are many debate participants whose positions fall somewhere between these extremes.

CHARACTERISTICS AND PATTERNS OF LEARNING DISABILITY

The phenomena associated with learning disabilities (in a pretheoretical use of the term) embrace a wide range of developmental, cognitive, and behavioral problems that are manifested in unique but recognizable patterns. The recognizable patterns of learning disability, the compromising of performance rather than ability, and the startling discrepancies among the skills of the individual child challenge both professionals and parents. Each child is unique. It is only when an individual pace, pattern, or style of performance hinders a child in accomplishing developmental tasks that the child's variant pattern becomes a dysfunctional one. The extent to which a difference becomes a true disability depends on internal factors, such as the child's compensatory strategies and the impact of other developmental dysfunctions, and on external variables, such as the importance of the tasks affected, rigidity of expectations, and available supportive structures (Levine, 1987).

The following discussion of learning-related developmental difficulties adapted from Levine (1987) is organized according to the specific functional areas most relevant to children. Anecdotal examples illustrate the impact of these difficulties on children and on people interacting with them—parents, teachers, social workers, other professionals, and peers. The emphasis here on specific manifestations is not intended to downplay the importance of the environment on development of learning disabilities. Rather, the goal is to provide a general framework for the observation and initial evaluation of variations in functioning. This analytical assessment is a necessary preliminary to understanding a child's functional "fit" with the different environments in which he or she is learning, living, and playing.

PERCEPTUAL FUNCTIONS

Perception, the individual's experience and organization of his or her environment through the five senses (vision, hearing, smell, taste, and touch), has far-reaching psychosocial implications. For example, confidence that one's powers of hearing or sight will deliver accurate information, which then can be further processed and acted on, if necessary, contributes to a feeling of competence and independence. If children cannot trust the information they take in, or cannot organize it to be useful and retrievable, they will feel uncertainty and self-doubt, frequently even in areas of genuine strength. Children need to become aware of their strengths and to have them recognized by important adults. Every opportunity to confirm a strength, and thereby to increase a sense of competence and mastery, benefits a child's self-esteem and helps provide the necessary balance for a realistic view of his or her weaknesses and strengths.

Visual and Spatial Perception

Visual-spatial perception, the ability to orient oneself and other objects or persons in space, and to act on the knowledge of these relationships, is one of the major organizing systems for the immense amounts of information absorbed through the senses. This system is so fundamental to human existence that developmental difficulties may be manifested in problems with academic, social, and leisure time activities, affecting many of the day's tasks, with important consequences for self-esteem and emotional resiliency. Note that, although the eyes are the transmitter or vehicle through which the world is seen, a deficit in visual perception is not a problem with visual acuity or eye-muscle coordination. The simultaneous processing of visual stimuli that underlies visual perception requires a complex interaction of the skills of coordination, attention, recognition, and judgment of distance. Frostig, Maslow, Lefever, and Wittlesley (1963) developed a series of tests to evaluate visual-spatial abilities. Although the effectiveness of Frostig's tests and training methods have not been documented adequately

(Mann, 1978; Sabatino, 1985), the categories Frostig established provide a useful framework for exploring the proposed functions of visual perception.

As defined by Frostig et al. (1963), *visual-motor coordination* is the ability to coordinate vision with movements of the body or parts of the body. *Figure-ground perception* is the "ability to attend to one aspect of a visual field while perceiving it in relation to the rest of the field" (p. 464). The inability to distinguish a figure or object in the foreground as distinct from the background becomes important when judging distance, because the guideposts by which most children would gauge what is near or far are lost. Later difficulties with driving and gauging distances from other cars may be a result of figure-ground perceptual problems.

Frostig et al. (1963) defined *perception of constancy* as the "ability to recognize that an object has constant properties such as shape, position, size, despite the variability of the impression on the sensory system (shapes, numbers, or objects)" (p. 464). Dysfunctions in this area affect a variety of academic tasks. To read fluently, a child must be able to create and hold visual representations of letters and words. Poor visual discrimination skills and lack of ability to remember visual shapes affect reading fluency, even though these perceptual problems generally are not considered to be the primary cause of reading difficulties. Letter reversals (p-d, g-q, u-n, x-t) may be an indication of a child's perception of the movement of symbols in space—the instability of the symbols makes their orientation ambiguous. Shape-perception difficulties may lead to problems in spelling, math, and all areas requiring accurate perception of symbols distinguished primarily by shape, such as letters and numerals. Problems in the sequencing and organization of visually gathered data, and the consequent difficulty of retaining patterns of symbols, may emerge as spelling problems. Contrary to popular wisdom, research has shown that a synergistic combination of specific verbal deficits of language processing may be more likely to cause reading disability than are the difficulties characterized by reversals (Roswell & Natchez, 1977).

Frostig et al. (1963) described *perception of position in space* as the "awareness of an object's position in relation to the observer" (p. 464) and the perception of spatial relationship (the position of two or more objects in relation to each other). A child who asks the seemingly existential question of "Where does up end and down begin?" may be a precocious philosopher—or may be suffering from a perceptual deficit. Children who have difficulties with their orientation in space often are confused about the relationship between foreground and background, left and right, up and down, and over and under. A child aged 6 to 9, when participation in team sports becomes an important route for self-esteem, can be at a significant disadvantage if this confusion persists. For example, on the soccer field these youngsters may make a goal for the opposing team, suffering both immediate disgrace and the continuing humiliation of being the last one chosen for every future game. In adolescence, they may stand too close to others at a party and wonder why people always seem to be moving away. They may be labeled by children and adults as "spacy," a painful but evocative term, as they may indeed present themselves as though lost in space. They may have difficulty in reading maps and become disoriented in unfamiliar surroundings with repetitive design and few landmarks, such as school corridors and shopping malls. Other children with spatial deficits may look and act bewildered when they walk into a strange room. To others, their efforts to orient themselves in space often are very apparent, although usually misunderstood.

Spatial orientation, including the perception of one's body in space, is critical to effective motor functioning, or negotiating one's body's movement through space—in everyday terms, to walking through a room without tripping. Repeated accidents with furniture, and the accompanying parental anxiety, may make young children with spatial disorientation problems reluctant to explore their world. Misjudging distances, they may trip over a chair leg, bump someone's elbow, and spill their milk, in what appears to be one single disoriented movement. Such a child frequently leaves anger in his or her wake and may be referred to as naughty, clumsy, accident-prone, or even emotionally disturbed. However, this behavior is not intentional clumsiness, clowning, or a delaying tactic; rather, it is the behavior of a child who cannot perceive the position and depth of other objects in relation to his or her own body, and, because of this, cannot control or coordinate his or her body's movements on the basis of positional data.

Visual *perceptual* and visual *motor* skills are separate but related. A child may be able to take in the correct image or placement of an object in space, but be unable to reproduce the object through drawing or building. Simply perceiving shapes and forms, then copying them, requires different sets of skills—which should be familiar to all who see themselves as nonartistic. But such self-deprecating claims by adults typically are meant to refer only to an extremely narrow range of skills—reproducing, in accordance with cultural norms, an object seen or imagined. For the infant, however, early sensory motor experiences—involving "perceiving and copying" in a much broader sense—are the fundamental building blocks for more advanced mental developmental processes (Piaget & Inhelder, 1969). Although all areas of motor development that are related to perception are important, the study of learning problems has consistently placed special emphasis on visual motor perception.

In a particularly visible example, visual motor perception and discrimination problems have been identified tentatively as causal factors contributing to a child's problems with laterality, including outright failure to establish lateral dominance. Some of these children may use their right hand and their left hand alternately for writing, reaching, or throwing, or may use both when they need only one—or only one hand when both are needed (Kirk & Chalfant, 1984). Another developmental problem in this area is evidenced by a child's failure to reach the level at which the eye "leads" the hand when peers do, making play less skilled. Instead, the child remains at an earlier developmental stage, in which the hand leads the eye. Visual *spatial* perception also is fundamental to the general motor coordination skills used in hand-eye coordination. Using a pencil, playing with toys, building with blocks—all are early indicators of the child's future success in playing, or competing, with peers and mastering the developmental tasks of childhood.

Hand-eye coordination is a crucial skill for the youngster anxious to be on a neighborhood or school ball team. In many American communities, participation in organized team sports is still the critical determinant of a boy's acceptance by his peer group. A boy whose parents share this norm may suffer even greater loss of self-esteem from the lack of any socially sanctioned and valued arena in which he can excel. The anxious father who tries to force interest and skill on a child who never makes the team instead may be giving him a devastating message—that he will never measure up to his father's standards. Social norms for girls involving demonstrated hand-eye coordination generally have been less narrowly defined, although participation in such socioculturally prescribed activities as school sports, dancing lessons, knitting, sewing, or scouting groups affords ample opportunity for similar loss of self-esteem. Paradoxically, increased opportunities for, and recognition of, female athletes may have a mixed impact on young girls, by broadening the range of role models and activities available to them while narrowing the range of acceptable variation in athletic attainment. Such heightened scrutiny may make it more difficult for girls with marginal visual discrimination deficits or spatial orientation problems to negotiate the hurdles of group activities and to find ways to engage in effective social interaction. For children of both sexes with this type of learning disability, school compulsory sports and physical education activities have long been a source of inescapable failure, public humiliation, and damage to self-esteem.

Children whose initial problems involve visual discrimination sometimes are characterized as socially unobservant. A friend's significant change in hair style or attire may elicit no comment. However, the child's attention to an irrelevant detail may lead peers to wonder what is "wrong" with him or her. For some children, the inability to identify and interpret visual social cues—facial expressions, a hand gesture, or a nod of the head—means that a critical nonverbal signal requiring either a response or some modification of behavior will pass unnoticed. Although they may perceive that someone is winking or staring at them in a peculiar way, these children may not realize that these nonverbal behaviors are meant to convey a message. Their resultant inability to fine-tune their conversational and interactional responses is seen as a lack of sensitivity. As they mature, these children may become more aware that a nonverbal message is being sent, but rather than responding through a parallel nonverbal channel, they may inappropriately confront the sender with an explicit question such as "What's the matter?" and embarrass everyone present. Of course, successful manipulation of nonverbal cues involves much more than visual discrimination skills. It also requires the individual to assume, at least momentarily, the role of the other person, and to identify the behavior that may be seen as objectionable by that other person. Finally, the individual determines what kind of modification is needed (Levine, 1987). Many children and adolescents with learning disabilities lack the powers

31

of conceptual integration and planning and retrieval necessary to use nonverbal behavioral cues appropriately. Their ineptitude at nonverbal communication—an essential aspect of human interactions of all kinds—tends to set them apart, making both them and their peers uncomfortable. Not surprisingly, the nonverbal oddness that may be sensed by those around them often is found inexplicable or undefinable.

As the example of nonverbal cues suggests, visual-spatial perception problems may play a significant, and often unsuspected, role in the social problems of some children and adolescents. Even when such problems are perceived to be based on past life experiences—such as missed opportunities to acquire and practice social skills and the consequent deepening of social isolation—they are not always identified as being related to a child's visual or spatial deficits.

Researchers now are questioning the role of language processing in deficits in interpretation of nonverbal social cues (Tallal, 1987). The socialization difficulties of children with these problems typically are viewed as emotionally based, or are simply dismissed as an aspect of the children's personalities. The children themselves, often well aware of their difficulty in social situations, also tend to express this difficulty in social or psychological terms—as not being able to make friends, or as always being the object of their peers' ridicule. They may respond by withdrawing from social encounters. Alternatively, they may be bristly, socially aggressive, or always ready to lash out in response to a perceived slight.

Auditory Perception

Auditory perceptual skills are skills involved in the ability to distinguish and recognize sounds and to interpret what is heard. Deficits in any of the auditory areas have profound consequences for receptive language abilities, and predict receptive language impairment. Children with auditory perception problems may have difficulty processing speech and nonspeech sounds, distinguishing between subtle differences in sounds, processing combined sounds, or discriminating between words and sounds without meaning.

The ability to process sounds and integrate the information rapidly is essential for *receptive language skill,* or the ability to understand what is heard. Children with receptive language impairments almost invariably display oral language deficits as well, being hindered in appropriate production of utterances by their decoding/processing deficits.

Difficulty in *auditory discrimination,* or distinguishing among sounds, makes it hard for children to isolate "letter sounds" in words and to capture the sequences of sounds as groups within words. Predictably, spelling and decoding large words become difficult (Levine, 1987). Children's attempts at spelling may be so unsystematic, ill-understood, and remote from the accepted spelling of a word that a dictionary would provide no help at all.

Children with deficits in *auditory attention* or *figure/ground discrimination* are unable to screen out extraneous noises and focus on important sounds. Such children, displaying what Levine (1987) called auditory distractibility, may pay attention to the noise in the street when a parent is talking to them in the house, and may even respond to a honking car by asking, "What did you say?" When crossing a street, these children may be listening to the laughter of other children up the street instead of to the noise of an approaching car. At home, such children may require absolute quiet when doing homework, which can disrupt the normal late-afternoon activities of other family members. Hidden family resentment may build, particularly when assignments are not completed correctly even in a quiet house. Paradoxically, a predictable background noise may be used to screen out intrusive episodic sounds of the conversations of other household members.

Difficulties in auditory perceptual areas can be a great source of insecurity for a child or an adolescent, with social distancing a common outcome. The inability to make sense of rapid conversational give-and-take among peers or in the classroom may inhibit healthy peer relationships. Some children withdraw from their peers, denying themselves opportunities to use their often lagging social skills; others, recognizing that they fare better if they can control the rate of verbal interchange, tend to initiate and dominate conversation, often angering and alienating their listeners.

Children with receptive language impairments due to an auditory processing deficit generally perform poorly in all aspects of language use. This deficit interferes with spelling and sound reproduction, adding new vocabulary items, understanding what other people say, attending to classroom instruction, taking notes—all vital activities in school. Such children may appear to be of normal ability in spontaneous language production. If they initiate a conversation and keep control of its content and pace with questions or expressions of their own ideas, a listener will have few clues to the existence of a receptive language deficit. In the classroom, such children might be able to answer a question when pupils may volunteer by raising their hands but be unable to respond when the teacher calls on them without warning. Because this kind of classroom interrogation is stressful for most children, the fact that a child has an actual receptive language deficit may not be noted. Adults tend to become impatient when such children repeatedly say "what?" as they stall for time, almost audibly struggling to process information. Peers are more likely to say, "Forget it," and ask someone else, leaving the youngster with receptive language deficits even fewer opportunities to practice the necessary skills of social communication. These children often choose withdrawal, sometimes to TV, sometimes to play with younger children, where verbal demands are slower and simpler and the price for failure to understand is smaller. Although the retreat to younger playmates provides some opportunities to socialize, it does not foster a child's developmental progress.

Expressive Language

Expressive language skills—those enabling people to capture their thoughts and talk with themselves and others—are critical to forging a link between the child's

33

interior life and the outside world. By using language, growing children not only are communicating; they also are strengthening their understanding of the difference between the self and others, testing reality, and gaining tolerance for frustration (Rothstein et al., 1988). The nurturing, reinforcement, and assistance available through verbal interchange solidify positive identification with parents and, with expanded communication skills, the child can enlist an ever-larger circle of adults to provide help and support. Verbal communication is direct and fast. Through speech, children build relationships and explore the world around them, gaining mastery and control through naming objects, people, and—eventually— feelings. Verbal interchange with other people is a primary means of learning and monitoring one's own actions. Because development of verbal skills is highly influenced by practice and by the availability of articulate role models, the social distancing or isolation that is a frequent outcome of any learning disability has profound implications for language use.

Expressive language skills, sometimes referred to as *output skills,* underlie two linguistic functions, speaking and writing. Both functions involve a number of skill components and a complex array of support skills. Both involve retrieving the correct words from memory, sequencing and organizing ideas, and selecting a grammatical structure to communicate them. Children with problems here are likely to be inhibited by their difficulties in speaking, whether these arise from poor articulation, lack of fluency, poor grammar, or difficulties in finding the right words. This inhibition may cause them to appear shy, to gesticulate excessively, or to use disconnected single words. Difficulties in verbal communication can easily become a barrier to making friends or developing relationships outside of the family, and make the child the focus of considerable negative attention in the family. Avoidance, withdrawal, and other maladaptive strategies to save face and avoid humiliation are typical outcomes. As children advance in school, typically beginning in the fifth grade, requirements for written assignments shift from an emphasis on simple narrative to more sophisticated exposition. A lack of skill in expressive language becomes very evident. Writing, which our culture considers the highest and most abstract form of expressive language, becomes increasingly important to meeting academic expectations. Inevitably, writing becomes the basis for considerable stress and anxiety among older children (Shepherd & Charnow, in press).

Effective use of expressive language skills depends on smooth functioning in other areas. Problems observed in a child's use of expressive language may reflect deficits in auditory perception, sequencing, integration, abstraction, attention, or memory. If it is faulty, visual perception cannot play its normal role as an aid to receptive language processing. Children with expressive language impairments generally perform better when they are using the language they know in structured tasks, and are less adept in spontaneous situations. Cultural norms, particularly those involving the use of expressive language, the role of children in family and community, spontaneity of speech patterns and interaction, and the acceptance of divergence, may be reflected in environments that mitigate—or reinforce—a child's predisposition toward expressive language difficulties.

In Tallal's (1987) report on a large longitudinal study of language outcomes for preschool children with diverse language deficits, children suffering primarily from expressive language deficit were judged to have fared better than those with a receptive or combined (more global) language deficit. According to Tallal, this confirmed the key role of the processing deficit in determining the precise nature and extent of the children's impairment. In this context, another finding presented by Tallal is particularly significant: language-impaired children differ greatly from children developing normally in their processing rate for sensory (nonverbal) information. The language-impaired children can process information presented slowly, but their performance slips considerably at higher rates of presentation. Their ability to remember nonverbal or sensory material shows a parallel decline at higher presentation rates.

Children with expressive or receptive language impairments do not outgrow their difficulties. If anything, they grow deeper and deeper into them, as their processing deficits, which initially may be evident only in their oral use of language, later impede their access to other learning systems, including reading, spelling, and even social interaction. A series of longitudinal studies has confirmed this cumulative negative impact of language disabilities on the ability to learn and interact normally in other settings (Tallal, 1987). Although a child with receptive or expressive language difficulties can benefit significantly from strategic environmental interventions, deliberate repetition, and careful attention to the child's comprehension of what is being said to him or her, one-to-one counseling sessions may prove particularly frustrating for both the child and professional. The social worker or therapist must scale down unrealistic performance expectations and allow enough time in the session for the child to answer questions without feeling pressured or embarrassed. For some children, simultaneous involvement in a secondary activity (playing a board game or building a model) diverts attention from the tension inherent in the verbal interchange, and facilitates ease with an idiosyncratic pace of verbal expression. A fragile self-concept, one highly vulnerable to a perceived failure to communicate, is typical of the learning-disabled child. Special care must be taken to ensure that the language-impaired child feels that what he or she has to say is important, regardless of how it is said or the pace at which it is uttered.

ORGANIZATIONAL AND INTEGRATIVE FUNCTIONS

Time and Sequencing

The ability to select and organize data and activities in response to visual or verbal directions reflects *sequencing and integrative skills*. Children's learning difficulties may reflect sequencing problems in many different areas involved in the organization and channeling of data from the senses. The identification of sequencing problems is made more difficult by the fact that dysfunctions in visual or auditory perception may be present concurrently. If a child is receiving inaccurate information from the environment in the first place, his or her subsequent attempts to make sense of it and organize it will be vastly more difficult. The child who also has sequencing difficulties will be doubly handicapped. Similarly, children with word finding and sequencing problems also may appear to have difficulties with temporal sequencing.

A child's difficulties in telling time or in mastering the days of the week and the order of the months may reflect sequencing or retrieval problems or difficulties in understanding the concept of time. It usually is clear from the questions children ask and the way they organize themselves to use time whether their difficulties lie with the *abstraction* of the passage of time, with the *sequencing* of time markers, or with *retrieving* the appropriate names of time periods. For example, children who have difficulty with the idea of time's passage often ask such existential questions as "What is now?" "When was then?" or "How will later come?" The child who cannot content himself or herself with the promise of an ice cream cone later in the afternoon probably will become impatient and angry, and may be punished for misbehaving. In fact, the child's difficulty may reflect incomprehension of the regular, cyclic passage of time, and the inevitable arrival of the afternoon. Other children may be successful at planning a day's activities and organizing meetings with friends, but will forget that the events are to occur tomorrow rather than today.

In the classroom, sequencing and organizational difficulties may be manifested by children who are unable to maintain the sequence of instructions given by the teacher or the proper steps for performing a complex task. Diagnosis of this problem is complicated by the frequent presence in the class milieu of competing auditory stimuli, coexisting memory deficits, or the effects of heightened motor activity. All of these may be involved simultaneously. The frustration so often encountered in class can lead some children to rely on such ultimately maladaptive coping strategies as avoidance or clowning. These behaviors often appear to the teacher as willful inattention, or as distractibility or hyperactivity, which may then mistakenly be viewed as the primary problem.

It is at home, however, that a child with organizational and sequencing difficulties may reveal one of the most poignant and far-reaching consequences of the functional impairment: the inability to present self and activities in words. Recounting the events of one's day at work, play, or school; portraying oneself as hero or victim; and explaining a difficulty or excusing a lapse—all of these linguistic activities so fundamental to human interaction involve organizing information in a way that may be beyond the child's grasp. If these children are ridiculed at school—as they all too often are—they may be unable to narrate the chain of events coherently, and their efforts may elicit parental impatience instead of the desired sympathy. One child known to the author used to complain bitterly that he couldn't "convince" his parents of anything. He meant that he could not present what had happened to him at school, what he wanted to do, or what he wanted others to do for him. When speaking about his experiences and needs, this boy typically presented a jumble of thoughts, assumed that others would recognize the people and events he was referring to without explanation, and often began in mid-argument, as if assuming that an exchange he was having in his head was clearly audible to all. Fortunately, his parents were able both to recognize his idiosyncratic concept of "convincing," and to address the underlying issue of effective narration.

Although this boy's disordered and incomplete narrative style is characteristic of some children with language processing and sequential organizing problems, other children develop such sharply contrasting defense mechanisms as compulsivity and rigidity in direct response to their lack of internal organization. They may be upset by changes in schedules both at home and at school, and their lack of flexibility may become evident in small ways—often by their distress at an unfamiliar babysitter's bedtime routine, changes in weekend plans, an unexpected doctor's appointment, or even the sudden appearance of new furniture in the house.

Narrating past events, planning and organizing future time—whether for enjoyment or for required tasks—present pitfalls for the child with sequential organizing problems. Making or following schedules, allocating limited time among competing demands, or conceptualizing a plan of attack on a difficult, many-stepped project may seem to be insurmountable hurdles. If the skills that will be needed to execute a plan involve other areas of deficit—for instance, when math homework or an assignment to write a short story is involved—the need to harness initial anxiety, to overcome areas of weakness in planning or organizing, and finally to carry out the project itself can easily overwhelm a child.

Children struggling with these combined deficits and their potential for disastrous interaction need strategically designed support systems at all stages of their activity if they are to stay on task. It is easy for children with multiple interrelated deficits to develop secondary inattention problems, such as drifting off into daydreams or engaging in disruptive behavior, rather than focusing on the task at hand. In the classroom, the outcomes can be devastating. At home, parental frustration parallels that of the child and becomes potentially incendiary. When a child's temporal sequencing or organizing problems affect the accomplishment of an important task, structure and support in the development of a plan of action must be provided (Levine, 1987). Encouragement and recognition must continue with each step toward completing the task.

Certain warning signals help to identify temporal-sequential deficits or sequencing and abstraction disabilities. The social worker should look for early difficulties in telling time, discomfort with such time-related concepts as before versus after and now versus later, and an inability to name in sequence the days of the week or the months of the year. Of course, cultural and family style differences must be taken into account. Different cultures give different meanings to time and space relationships, and value different sequencing and organizing skills. Some families may provide little opportunity for organizing activities, structuring time, or discussing delays in activities ("We'll do it later, or tomorrow"), and the overlearning and repetition necessary for a child to compensate for a predisposition to weakness in this area may not take place at home. A child with no experience in situating actions in time inevitably will appear much more dysfunctional in the classroom than will another child who has the same vulnerability, but whose home life familiarizes him or her with the issues.

Memory

Drawing again on Levine's (1987) conceptual framework, the separate but interrelated cognitive systems that constitute memory are critical to developmental growth, academic success, and interpersonal relations. At the highest level, memory is an integrative function, drawing on five specialized subfunctions: (1) receiving and understanding information (*acquisition*); (2) putting it in an appropriately sequenced format for effective storage (*registration*); (3) allocating the information to one of three general storage areas—instant recall, short-term memory, or long-term memory (*storage and consolidation*); (4) retrieving stored information as needed (*access*); and (5) flexible application of stored data for creative new uses (*transfer training*).

This analysis of memory as involving five functions is based on work by Baddeley (1976) and is the framework for Levine's (1987) extensive discussion of the role of memory in children's learning processes and in their *productive behaviors* (those involving performance and communication based on the reconceptualization, with new information, of knowledge and skills held in memory). Memory functions play an important role in the difficulties experienced by nearly all children with learning problems. A child's original impairment may involve any one of the five subfunctions. However, the interdependency of the different levels of memory and the potential for interfering stimuli from multiple sources, both within the child and in the environment, often make it difficult to determine the specific locus of a memory problem. The following discussion draws on Levine's (1987) interpretation of work by Baddeley and other researchers in the areas of cognition and memory.

The initial process, the *acquisition* of data on which to build a basis for knowledge, involves not only exposure to experience but also the selection of salient data for retention. Perceptual problems in processing and making sense of experience also may impede the ready acquisition of new information. However, children whose exposure to external experience is limited, either in extent or in variety, may have had less opportunity to use and develop acquisition and data-selection faculties than other children whose experiential history has been richer and more diverse. (Clearly, socioeconomic factors contribute to the range of experiences available, and may play an important part in determining a child's range of sensory input.)

Registration, the second stage of memory, requires a commitment of attention in selecting an appropriate coding strategy for the new data. *Coding strategies,* which facilitate the storage of new information and relate it to information stored previously, include visual imaging, semantic naming, rehearsing, and the use of mnemonic associations. The broader a child's repertoire of coding strategies, the more likely he or she is to succeed in registering new data in memory at sufficient depth. Children who are highly distractible or who are suffering from an attention deficit will register new information in a very shallow manner, and will not retain it from one day to the next. Other children may be inconsistent in their focus on new material, tiring easily and losing their motivation.

The third processing step, involving data *storage and consolidation,* is heavily dependent on the ability to hold data in active working memory for instant recall. This interactive capacity allows information to be sorted and arranged efficiently for subsequent storage in the short- or long-term memory. A child's ability to carry out many school tasks is compromised by difficulties with instant recall and active working memory. Such multistep procedures as sounding out words, performing nested operations to clarify a complicated mathematical expression, or even multiplying numbers mentally all require an effectively functioning, active working memory. A child who understands each step involved in the overall process at the time it is discussed still may be unable to store the intermediate results effectively for eventual retrieval in the final, integrating step of solving the problem.

Short-term memory, one of the two longer-range storage areas, has a very limited capacity; only through creative coding strategies can it be stretched to hold more than seven items. Short-term memory is highly vulnerable to interference, whether due to such internal factors as emotional distress or attention difficulties, or arising from such external sources as a teacher whose instructional technique clashes with a child's learning style. Children with short-term memory deficits typically have difficulty retaining telephone numbers after calling Information, or remembering directions, instructions given by parents, or dates made with friends. Their forgetfulness, if not seen as beyond their control, may elicit verbal reproofs or more serious punishment, even abuse.

Long-term memory holds the bulk of an individual's accumulated learning. Once information has reached short-term memory, a decision, conscious or not, is made on whether to shift it into long-term memory and, if so, on what classification system will be used. Deficits in long-term memory are less common in children than are other memory problems; when they do occur, however, they are typically much more serious, creating real barriers to developmental progress. Indeed, because of their severe difficulties in retaining information, children with long-term memory problems are likely to be mislabeled as retarded.

The fourth, or *retrieval,* stage in Levine's (1987) model is perhaps the one most closely paralleling the lay concept of memory. In general, the ability to retrieve stored information is considered the only conclusive demonstration of having "learned" it; a child whose retrieval skills are slow or require too much effort inevitably will fall behind in school, unable to meet the ever-increasing demands for demonstrations—retrievals—of learned material. Frustration and loss of self-esteem are common outcomes, as the inability to recall what one knows one has learned (or at least tried diligently to memorize) brings a loss of faith in one's capabilities. For children with learning disabilities such a loss only deepens their doubts about themselves.

Frequently, the tension surrounding a request for retrieval of information, such as a classroom test or recitation in front of peers, brings such anxiety that the child's memory fails completely, leaving the child unable to remember anything on the subject at hand. A child's inability to *demonstrate* retrieval of learned information, of course, must be distinguished from his or her inability to retrieve it, and all other factors that may inhibit performance must be taken into account. For example, a child who remains mute when called upon to answer questions in class may be suffering from a retrieval impairment—or may prefer silence to an embarrassing display of a speech impediment, even though he or she has retrieved the information without difficulty. Parallel physical factors may overwhelm the child who cannot write quickly enough to demonstrate retrieved knowledge on a written test administered under severe time constraints.

The fifth and final phase of memory involves the *transferral* of stored information and its creative use in new contexts. As the most sophisticated and flexible use of memory, it requires that the storage and retrieval processes draw on a rich variety of associative linkages between new and old information. The unique relationships drawn by each individual bring a wide diversity of creative responses; a youngster with learning disabilities may excel in the unexpected, almost metaphoric, applications of information, perhaps based on unique perceptions and compensatory coding and storage strategies.

Levine (1987) correctly stressed the extreme sensitivity of all memory functions to interference from internal and external sources. Children who are depressed, preoccupied by a family crisis, or anxious because of repeated failures are unlikely to be able to make optimal use of their memory. Other children, for whom memorization—whether the task itself or the content to be mastered—is highly divergent from family or neighborhood values, may have difficulty finding appropriate coding mechanisms for information without cultural resonance. Furthermore, deficits that seem to involve memory may in fact be related to any of several other functions. A child may have difficulty organizing and sequencing visual or auditory stimuli and integrating them with information already stored. Attention deficits or high distractibility levels may impede the organization and sequencing of data stored in the short-term memory. Finally, the child's cultural environment may provide neither the values nor the experience that would foster memorization of certain kinds of material. Memorizing the Greek myths may be an excruciating exercise, whereas the latest plot on the action-packed TV sitcom may be remembered in great detail. The family and neighborhood culture reinforces one task, but provides no recognition for the other.

Complex Cognitive Processes

Children with learning disabilities often have difficulties with conceptualization and abstract thinking, both cognitive abilities that depend heavily on organizing, sequencing, memory, and retrieval skills. Children who are engaged in a desperate quest to make sense of the world around them may be giving unwitting testimony to deficits in these crucial skills. Although these children may ask question after question ranging from the totally concrete to the unanswerable, they ultimately have difficulty pulling the results of their research together. They do not understand where all the people are going during the evening rush hour, or why their parents cannot give them an answer. All of the children's books they have looked at over the years, full of pictures of individual mothers and fathers heading home from work or out for the evening, are of no use; the children have not abstracted from the stories the general explanatory theme of evening traffic destinations. The 15-year-old may still blurt out, "But where are they going?" then smile guiltily, realizing that it is a question left over from childhood—although one for which the child never found a satisfactory answer. This same youngster may have no difficulty negotiating a crowded urban bus terminal during the same rush hour, secure in space, but be unable to abstract the principle of multiple destinations or, if the youngster can later reason it out, unable to connect it to the question asked while he or she was actually experiencing the crowds.

Organizing and grouping similar phenomena, making inferences and analogies, generalizing rules, self-monitoring, and flexibility in seeking options—these are the hallmarks of the abstract thinking patterns crucial to problem solving (Levine, 1987). Such techniques free individuals from the endless accumulation of isolated concrete experiences, allowing them instead to insert each new experience into an existing order, or use it to restructure their previous array of accumulated knowledge. The child with learning disabilities may display extreme difficulty with these processes. It is a challenge for the professional to determine whether the child's problems involve the area of abstract thinking, or reflect deficits in skills related to the initial acquisition, organization, and storage of data.

Through movement to more abstract levels of thinking, children come to perceive how others may be feeling and to see the world—and themselves—from an outsider's perspective. Achieving a "social" perspective presupposes both the ability to observe and organize a multitude of details about oneself and others and the conceptual sophistication to generalize, to move from "*my* self" to "*a* self," from "*the* perceiver" to "*a* perceiver." A child's inability to grasp the perspective of another person, the assumption that he or she is the center of attention at all times, or his or her inability to modify behavior in response to feedback—any or all of these may indicate a child's failure to advance from a more concrete egocentric view of the world to higher level, secondary process thinking (Rothstein et al., 1988).

According to Flavell (1985) and Levine (1987), the interdependence of the basic and higher level cognitive processes is evident in the way in which the active working memory and sequential organization skills support more abstract levels of thinking. In turn, information becomes more succinctly organized and more easily retrievable when it is conceptualized in a more sophisticated fashion. Thus, children with dysfunctions in any of the basic cognitive areas have to work much harder when they engage in problem solving because they are working with more disparate elements, which are less fully integrated into different memory levels and less easily retrieved. Identifying, through informal and formal evaluation, the locus of a child's difficulties will allow the social worker, parent, or teacher to intervene with strategies that bypass or bridge the cognitive gaps or weaknesses to the extent possible, while exploiting existing strengths.

MOTOR FUNCTIONING

Deficits in gross or fine motor functioning bring children endless embarrassment because of their highly visible lack of control over their bodies' actions. Fear of appearing clumsy to their peers makes them self-conscious, which only heightens their awkwardness and lack of grace. Athletic ineptitude, typical of children with gross motor problems, may intensify an inclination toward social withdrawal, and reluctance to participate in group activities is common. Parents, despairing of their child's lack of physical grace, may prescribe gym classes or dancing lessons to "train" them out of their awkwardness.

Even subtle deficiencies in gross motor functioning can exert a powerful influence on self-image, self-esteem, and personality development. Of all learning disabilities, motor functioning deficits are among the most visible and the most immediately stigmatizing. Children affected by these deficits suffer from both primary and secondary effects; self-esteem already shaken, they are often overprotected because of their vulnerability to more than just the usual bumps and hurts of childhood accidents. Their inability to react quickly and appropriately makes their parents understandably reluctant to allow certain age-appropriate behaviors, thus confirming the child's perception of himself or herself as different, slow, and incompetent.

For the child with gross motor deficits, family and community values regarding competitive sports may be supportive—or devastating. Particularly for boys, excellence in sports can help to win peer acceptance, even in the presence of other areas of disability. However, when sports are the only avenue for winning parent and peer approval, a child who fails, in a dramatic display of his or her disability, may become seriously depressed. Even more than with the other areas of learning disability, a deficit in gross motor control seems to the child to be a global deficit: the body, to an extent denied by many adults, *is* the self, from the child's perspective.

Shaw, Levine, and Belfer (1982) compared levels of self-esteem in two groups of children—one with gross motor delays and learning problems and one with learning problems alone—and characterized those children with both problems as being in "developmental double jeopardy" (p. 19), because they had more self-image problems and were more emotionally fragile. Thus, during the school years, when body image and physical coordination are so closely intertwined with peer acceptance, failures in this area tend to compound the impact of any other developmental weaknesses. The common wisdom of finding specific areas of athletic endeavors in which a child with gross motor problems can excel is borne out once again. Sports that require the use of "inner spatial data" (Levine, 1987, p. 221) and are performed under the control of the individual (such as jogging, swimming, sailing, track and field events, dancing, rollerskating, hiking, skiing, biking, gymnastics, and martial arts), rather than those involving hand-eye coordination or team interdependence (and the resulting peer pressure), are most appropriate (Wall, McClements, Bouffard, Findlay, & Taylor, 1985).

Fine motor control problems, although often manifested in less striking ways, may have equally profound and far-reaching consequences. For the infant or toddler, exploration of the environment through touching and grasping objects is a primary source of knowledge. Deficits in these exploratory skills—the child's experimentation methods in his or her microcosmic "learning laboratory"—inevitably hinder the learning process by diminishing the tactile feedback available to the child. More subtly, a child's poor coordination may make him or her "accident-prone," eliciting overprotective and hovering attitudes in adults that, although understandable, may dampen the child's further efforts at exploration and mastery of the environment (Rothstein et al., 1988). Difficulties with fine motor control tend to make their initial appearance at home in a child's early attempts at dressing, fastening buttons and zippers, and tying shoelaces. In play situations, a 3- to 6-year-old child's facility at cutting, coloring, pasting, and other "finger" activities affords clues to the observer. A child's performance in school may give rise to concern once the fine motor activities related to writing, drawing, "neatness" of calculations, and so on begin to have weight in teachers' evaluations of their pupils' work. Educational philosophy, whether an individual teacher's or that of an entire school, is obviously a factor. Still common, unfortunately, is a "neatness counts" policy that may penalize a child through lowered grades not only in penmanship but also in the subject area, despite his or her mastery of the material. Social workers may need to work with parents and teachers to support a more enlightened grading policy that makes appropriate distinctions between subject mastery and presentation skills. Even in a supportive school environment, however, children with fine motor control problems become frustrated with their work very quickly, and must be encouraged to move beyond the looks of their work, however "sloppy" or imperfect, to focus on its communicative power.

ATTENTIONAL DEFICITS AND DISTRACTIBILITY

Although the syndrome known as attention deficit disorder (ADD) frequently is related to the presence of learning disabilities, the relationship is not well defined. Of all children suffering from learning disabilities or ADD, those identified as having ADD by their schools most often are those who are the most disruptive in the classroom. The resulting selective referral patterns are reflected in biased research findings, and the distinction between the two disorders has become blurred in the public mind. Two studies of children diagnosed as having ADD show that approximately 10 percent have learning disabilities as well (Halperin, Gittelman, & Klein, 1984; Shaywitz, 1986). Other studies of children with learning disabilities estimate that between 40 and 80 percent also have a physiological basis for their hyperactivity or distractibility (Holobrow & Berry, 1986; Safer & Allen, 1976; Shaywitz, 1986). The physiological basis is crucial to the definition of ADD. Although these characteristics may be aggravated by stress and anxiety, other causal factors are present (Silver, 1979).

The characteristics of ADD that are most devastating, both for the child and for those around him or her, are physical restlessness, impulsivity, aggression, and a short attention span. ADD often is referred to as a low visibility, high prevalence disorder—the fact that children with ADD tend to look perfectly normal often leads others to conclude, at least initially, that they are simply willfully disobedient. In reality, however, children with ADD are not able to organize their own activities in a productive way without outside help (Levine, Brooks, & Shonkoff, 1980). Children with ADD, whether or not hyperactivity is also present, display different symptoms at different developmental stages. Activity levels increase up to age 3 and then slowly diminish for some; others remain excessively active through early adolescence. However, the attentional deficits generally remain, continuing to interfere with learning and work in structured settings, and also with social relationships. Undue vulnerability to perceived failure may remain, and self-esteem may continue to be weak.

Girls with ADD recently have been in the spotlight as an underidentified population at risk. Several factors may be at work. Berry, Shaywitz, and Shaywitz (1985) suggested that ADD with hyperactivity (ADDH) is so strongly linked with boys, in the lay perspective, that only the most severely affected girls may be identified correctly. The same researchers postulated that less severely affected girls may be better able to tolerate the difficulties they encounter in school and are less disruptive in the classroom than their male peers. Thus, boys with ADDH, who experience greater difficulty controlling their impulses and are consequently viewed by adults as more severely impaired (Tauber, 1979), are identified and diagnosed more quickly.

Berry and his collaborators (1985) found that both girls and boys with ADDH used inappropriate and aggressive behavior in peer interaction; the girls, however, encountered more peer rejection. As a tentative explanation of the different acceptance rates, the researchers suggested that such behavior is closer to the range of accepted play patterns for boys. Girls' play, in contrast, traditionally emphasizes gentler, more language-dependent games. The aggressive behavior typical of children with ADDH, combined with the language and speech problems frequently displayed by girls with this syndrome, accordingly falls further outside the acceptable range and elicits greater rejection (Hechtman, Weiss, & Perlman, 1984).

Children constantly are refining their ability to maintain a pattern of selective attention—paying attention, for example, to the teacher's words and the writing on the blackboard rather than to their own dirty fingernails and the whispers of classmates at the back of the room. Any neurological dysfunction that interferes with concentration and focus inevitably affects the child's ability to observe and process aspects—both sensory and social—of his or her environment. Consistent growth in the ability to control attention is fundamental to the child's acquisition of knowledge and the varied problem-solving skills that are, in turn, necessary for achieving developmental maturity. Children who are highly distractible and who react indiscriminately to everything that happens around them appear constantly out of focus, as if they were trying to "catch up with themselves." They exhaust those around them, and never seem to learn from their experiences.

Children with ADD may tune in and out of selective focus, distracted from moment to moment by visual or auditory stimuli, or by thoughts of their own. Such distractibility may be aggravated by a sensory environment too rich in visual or auditory data that they are unable to screen out, select, or organize. Other children may be hypersensitive to tactile sensation: the itchiness of clothes, a light tap on the shoulder, or the feel of a chair. Before they know it, they are out of the chair, caught up in a fight, or peeling off their clothes, unable to concentrate on anything but their own overriding discomfort.

Impulsivity is both a frequent and particularly disturbing symptom for children with ADD and the people around them. Rapidly shifting attention and behavioral responses from one aspect of the environment to another, children with ADD are unable to reflect on, or to monitor, their own behavior. The inappropriate behavior of impulsive children—even when they think they are thinking things through—frequently alienates parents, teachers, and peers. Indeed, these children sometimes seem to go out of their way to select an activity or behavior that will exacerbate an already uncomfortable situation. Not surprisingly, these children rarely gather the "system advocates" they need to protect them during their growing years. They exhaust everyone. The results of their poor judgment involve them in increasingly serious difficulties the further they move from the protective base of home and school.

Closely akin to impulsivity is task impersistence (Levine, 1987). Some children with ADD may seem never to finish what they start, dabbling in one area and then wanting to move on, and others may show little more than superficial interest in anything. This impersistence is particularly distressing to parents, who shower their children with toys, hoping to catch their interest, and then watch with dismay as each new toy is discarded in minutes. Similar patterns of impersistence may be present in social situations. Friends are transitory in these children's lives, and their superficial interest in other people and inability to pay prolonged attention to others may become increasingly evident with their later attempts to develop sustained relationships in latency and adolescence.

Other children may manifest what has been called "insatiability" (Levine, Brooks, & Shonkoff, 1980, p. 56). Just as they quickly tire of a toy, they also find the tasks of daily living too bland and are forever seeking more stimulation and more excitement. Parents brace themselves when such a child comes home from school, knowing that despite their best intentions the household soon will be in an uproar. It is almost as though these children, unable to tolerate a mild emotional climate, must precipitate an emotionally charged situation in order to feel engaged, alive; those with sufficient powers of introspection will ask why nothing is "happening" at dinner, or on a picnic. By that, they mean there is no tension in the air, nothing to engage them or focus their need for change. As these children grow older, their insatiability may well exhaust their friends as well as their family.

These specific primary manifestations of ADD are only part of the problem. The difficulty many ADD-affected children have in responding to social conventions, constraints, and limits arises not only from their neurologically based impairments but also, with increasing age and an ever-growing track record of failure, from the child's anxieties at the expectations he or she may not meet. A child may talk incessantly, as if to drown out others' thoughts and defer the demands he or she fears may be made on him or her. Similarly, a sudden spate of hyperkinetic activity or distractibility may coincide with the onset of a classroom (or other group-oriented) task requiring sustained attention. Further, the child's inability to abstract the implications of specific sequences of events may well make rewards and punishments of little use in redirecting his or her behavior. A teenager who shrugs off 3 weeks' suspension from school may fail to perceive that future infractions might lead instead to expulsion. Such children have been described as "refractive to punishment" (Levine, 1987). A downward spiral of more serious punishments for more serious misbehavior is a familiar pattern, and one to which the social worker should be alert. Even in the absence of more clear-cut symptoms, ADD should be considered as a possible factor in *any* child's apparent tendency to provoke extreme punishment or repeated abuse from family members.

Both parents and professionals face a difficult task in attempting to distinguish between willful disobedience and a genuine disability arising from a child's impaired control over his or her behavior. However, an even greater challenge often follows a diagnosis of ADD: that of providing, within a family situation severely damaged by years of disruptive and frustrating behavior, the environment the ADD-affected child requires. Children who need support as well as structure, positive reinforcement for tasks well done as well as negative consequences closely tied to their own poor judgment, may find themselves handed a new script—and find that the rest of the cast, exhausted if not actively resentful, effectively has left the stage. After years of chaotic family meals, nightmarish expeditions, and siblings permanently angered by what they perceive as favoritism, there may be little family support left, as each member seeks escape in isolation and the household becomes a series of physically and emotionally closed doors.

SOCIAL SKILLS

In the preceding discussions of specific learning disabilities and their power to shape the lives of those who suffer from them, the potential for impaired self-esteem and consequent withdrawal from social contact has been a fairly constant refrain, as has the ostracism that may result from a child's failure to perform socially valued tasks acceptably. Experienced social workers have found that many, though not all, children with learning disabilities do have social difficulties, whether in peer interaction (including establishing and maintaining friendships, and, in the adolescent years, developing romantic or sexual relationships), interacting with adults, or responding appropriately to specific social situations. Speculations that such difficulties may, at least in some cases, be manifestations of a separate, *social* learning disability, rather than secondary consequences of more narrowly defined perceptual deficits, have gained tentative support from recent studies of long-term adjustment and patterns of workplace success or failure among learning-disabled adults (Fass, 1987; Van Hasselt, Hersen, Whitehill, & Bellack, 1979). Rather than having outgrown the social difficulties experienced during childhood or adolescence, subjects in these studies often displayed serious problems in adult social interaction both on and off the job. In particular, difficulties in the employee/supervisor relationship often were severe enough to result in an employee's being fired. Probing of the areas of specific difficulty showed that these learning-disabled adults tended to behave impulsively in relationships with others, had difficulty differentiating between social and work-based behaviors, or failed to pick up behavioral feedback or social cues meant to help them modify their behavior. Allowing for the necessary age-appropriate changes, these are the same problems that plague the first grader or high school student with poor social skills.

Although research on the relationship between social abilities and learning disabilities is still in an exploratory phase, much effort is being expended on the necessary preliminary tasks of identifying and defining social abilities and identifying specific learning problems that may be relevant (Levine, 1987). Although direct linkages between specific neurologically based deficits and social dysfunctions are still far from being established conclusively, leaving the definitional issue of a separate social learning disability unresolved, the work of Levine and others offers both a helpful conceptual framework for assessing a child's social development and suggestive empirical correlations that merit further investigation. Of course, regardless of definitional or etiological questions, a child's impaired social abilities can constitute a tragically handicapping condition, leaving few areas of his or her life unaffected. The child's problems are all too easily identified by parents, teachers, and peers, drawing responses of impatience, anger, misunderstanding, and rejection (Bryan & Bryan, 1981; Gresham & Reschly, 1986). These children show increased levels of anxiety and depression, and lower self-esteem, in comparison to their nonhandicapped peers (Cullinan, Epstein, & Lloyd, 1981).

Social skills have been defined by Schumaker and Hazel (1984) as the cognitive functions and discrete verbal and nonverbal behaviors that are performed during a person's interaction with others. Social competence is established through performance—in a socially acceptable manner—of a sequence of learned social skills. The words *sequence* and *learned* are highly suggestive, evoking the earlier consideration here of sequencing and organizational skills, and the relativism inherent in the definition of social competence serves as a useful reminder that interpersonal interaction, like many other human endeavors, is constrained by complex, wildly varying, and largely arbitrary sets of rules. Consciously or unconsciously, people must learn the rules that govern their individual milieus, drawing on social abilities to initiate and maintain relationships in these milieus.

Children who have been identified as having learning disabilities often experience social failure in several areas. They frequently have great difficulty making and keeping friends, they often are accused of self-absorption and insensitivity to the needs of others, and their poor judgment about the appropriateness of various behaviors affecting other individuals or society often leads them into trouble. These areas are closely paralleled by the three major themes Levine (1987) identified: (1) friendship formation, (2) understanding of others, and (3) moral development. In Levine's scenario, a child's expectations of more long-lasting, mutually supportive, trusting, and altruistic relationships grow along with his or her increasing maturity, and increased understanding of others proceeds through a conceptual advance from rigid dichotomizing of people as all good or all bad, toward a more subtle and relativistic perception that people behave differently in different circumstances. Basing his treatment of moral development on Kohlberg's (1963) conceptual framework, Levine demonstrated that the growth of moral values in children is accompanied by an increasingly sophisticated code of fair versus unfair, and appropriate versus inappropriate. Levine identified this code as fundamental to children's understanding of others' behavior in relation both to themselves and to the larger society.

Although research effectively linking specific types of dysfunctions with specific difficulties in social development is extremely limited, Levine (1987) proposed a series of tentative connections between a number of deficit areas and their possible impacts on social abilities. Attentional problems, for example, may contribute to some children's difficulties in becoming part of a social group or establishing closer relationships within it. As Levine noted, inattention to detail causes children to miss salient clues and feedback on their own behavior when they enter a social situation. The superficial and impulsive work that is characteristic of these children in school may be paralleled in their interpersonal relationships—conversations may be cut short in mid-sentence as a new thought flits across the child's mind or a new object diverts the child's interest. Preoccupation with their own needs and drives leaves little room or incentive for concern for the needs or interests of others, and no motivation to share their views in a genuine give-and-take. With continuity of exchange and returned interest so conspicuously absent, both peers and adults tend to drift away from the unrewarding engagement.

Other perceptual and cognitive deficits have been tied tentatively to specific difficulties in social development. Some children's difficulties in learning to identify and interpret nonverbal messages have been linked speculatively to problems with perceiving and organizing simultaneous gestalts of visual-spatial stimuli (subtle facial expressions indicating approval, a noncommittal attitude, impatience, or disgust; suggestive or menacing postures). The frequency with which learning-disabled children have difficulty predicting social consequences and learning from social experience—two critical developmental areas for all children—has led some researchers to posit a link between sequential reasoning deficits or specific memory disorders and trouble in these areas (Levine, 1987). Poor receptive language skills hamper many peer interactions by making it difficult for a child to interpret what is being said to him or her and, consequently, to respond appropriately. Of course, fluent command of expressive language is critical in almost all forms of social interaction beyond the most intimate. A child who cannot "get control of " a social situation except through physical means is on a dangerous path (Donahue, 1984; Levine, 1987).

Social maturation, proceeding through analysis of social situations and reflection on social problems, requires some facility at introspection and self-criticism in addition to overall interpretive abilities. Although some children who have difficulty in solving more "cognitive" problems experience similar troubles in the social arena (Levine, 1987), others seem to be able to conceptualize and abstract rules of behavior and social functioning through their ability to pick up feedback. For many children, the importance of social acceptance so far outweighs that of academic attainment that their cognitive efforts, along with other abilities and personality traits, are devoted entirely to the problem of becoming part of a social group. Their diligence in this area may provide much-needed confirmation of their own worth, and their increased sensitivity to the appropriate social behavior in different situations and their cultivation of social adaptability may become an important passport to broadened options in adult life. However, a child's abandonment of academic endeavor in favor of a full-time pursuit of social acceptance may have profound consequences. Particularly in the information-based, postindustrial society of the developed nations, such a step early in life may limit a child's future options sharply. Social workers, teachers, and parents must strive to maintain some balance in the child's life by ensuring enough academic "success" to motivate continued efforts in school-related tasks.

In recognition of the great handicapping potential of social deficits, remediatory curricula have been developed, both to teach relevant social skills and to facilitate generalization of broader behavioral patterns. Remediation typically parallels subject-oriented academic instruction and is targeted at specific deficits. There currently is little consensus on which skills should be taught or on how they should be taught and assessed. Some limited evidence exists that relatively few sessions of coaching in social skills do make a difference in peer acceptance of the socially impaired child. The opportunity to practice in a "safe," nonjudgmental environment has been found to be particularly helpful (Oden & Asher, 1977).

Efforts at social remediation raise troubling issues. Whose social skills should the child be taught? When family values—perhaps reflecting gender roles or class- or culturally related traditions—conflict with those of the community, which values should prevail? In addition, placing social deficits under a remediation "umbrella," inside an exclusively educational framework, limits the ways in which intervention is conceptualized. It is important to establish a variety of environments in which children can practice social skills and receive feedback in a protected atmosphere. Social workers, who engage children with social skills deficits in a variety of settings (home, social agencies, hospitals, and community centers, as well as schools and afterschool programs), are uniquely situated to provide this variety. Children with these deficits often have difficulty generalizing behavior from one setting to another. Offering diverse opportunities for social practice in the communities in which children live and play both underlines the transferability of social skills and ensures some congruence between the patterns taught and the child's usual environment.

REFERENCES

Baddeley, A. (1976). *The psychology of memory*. New York: Basic Books.

Berry, C. A., Shaywitz, S. E., & Shaywitz, B. A. (1985). Girls with attention deficit disorder: A silent minority? A report on the behavioral and cognitive characteristics. *Pediatrics, 76,* 801–809.

Bryan, T. H., & Bryan, J. H. (1981). Some personal and social experiences of learning disabled children. In B. Keogh (Ed.), *Advances in special education* (Vol. 3, pp. 147–186). Greenwich, CT: JAI Press.

Coles, G. (1987). *The learning mystique: A critical look at learning disabilities*. New York: Pantheon Books.

Cruickshank, W. M. (1972). Some issues facing the field of learning disability. *Journal of Learning Disabilities, 5,* 380–383.

Cullinan, D., Epstein, M., Lloyd, J. W. (1981). School behavior problems of learning disabled and normal girls and boys. *Learning Disabilities Quarterly, 4,* 163–169.

Donahue, M. (1984). Learning disabled children's conversational competence: An attempt to activate the inactive listener. *Applied Psycholinguistics, 5,* 21–35.

Fass, L. (1987). *The Arizona State University transition research project final report.* Tempe: Arizona State University.

Flavell, J. H. (1985). *Cognitive development.* Englewood Cliffs, NJ: Prentice-Hall.

Frostig, M., Maslow, P., Lefever, D. W., & Wittlesley, J. R. (1963). *The Marianne Frostig developmental test of visual perception: 1963 standardization.* Palo Alto, CA: Consulting Psychologists Press.

Granger, L., & Granger, B. (1986). *The magic feather.* New York: E. P. Dutton.

Gresham, F. M., & Reschly, D. J. (1986). Social skill deficits and low peer acceptance of mainstreamed learning disabled children. *Learning Disability Quarterly, 9,* 23–32.

Halperin, J. M., Gittelman, R., & Klein, D. F. (1984). Reading disabled hyperactive children: A distinct sub-group of attention deficit disorder with hyperactivity? *Journal of Abnormal Child Psychology, 12,* 1–14.

Hechtman, L., Weiss, G., & Perlman, T. (1984). Hyperactives as young adults: Past and current substance abuse and antisocial behavior. *American Journal of Orthopsychiatry, 54,* 415–425.

Holobrow, P. L., & Berry, P. S. (1986). Hyperactivity and learning difficulties. *Journal of Learning Disabilities, 19,* 426–431.

Kirk, S., & Chalfant, J. (1984). *Academic and developmental learning disabilities.* Denver, CO: Love.

Kohlberg, L. (1963). Development of children's orientation towards a moral order: 1 sequence in the development of moral thought. *Vita Humana, 6,* 11–33.

Levine, M. D. (1987). *Developmental variation and learning disorders.* Cambridge, MA: Educators Publishing Service.

Levine, M. D., Brooks, R., & Shonkoff, J. P. (1980). *A pediatric approach to learning disorders.* New York: John Wiley & Sons.

MacCracken, M. (1986). *Turnabout children: Overcoming dyslexia and other learning disabilities.* Boston: Little, Brown.

Mann, L. (1978). Review of the Marianne Frostig developmental test of visual perception. In O. K. Buros (Ed.), *Mental measurements yearbook* (pp. 1275–1276). Highland Park, NJ: Gryphon.

McGuinness, D. (1985). *When children don't learn.* New York: Basic Books.

Oden, S., & Asher, S. R. (1977). Coaching children in social skills for friendship making. *Child Development, 48,* 495–506.

Piaget, J., & Inhelder, B. (1969). *The psychology of the child.* New York: Basic Books.

Roswell, F. G., & Natchez, G. (1977). *Reading disability: A human approach to learning.* New York: Basic Books.

Rothstein, A., Benjamin, I., Crosby, M., & Eisenstadt, K. (1988). *Learning disorders: An integration of neuropsychological and psychoanalytic considerations.* Madison, CT: International Universities Press.

Sabatino, D. A. (1985). Review of Marianne Frostig developmental test of visual perception, 3rd ed. In J. V. Mitchell, Jr. (Ed.), *Ninth mental measurements yearbook* (pp. 892–893). Lincoln: University of Nebraska Press.

Safer, D. J., & Allen, R. P. (1976). *Hyperactive children: Diagnosis and management*. Baltimore: University Park Press.

Schumaker, J. B., & Hazel, J. S. (1984). Social skills assessment and training for the learning disabled: Who's on first and what's on second? (Part 1). *Journal of Learning Disabilities, 17,* 422–431.

Shaw, L., Levine, M. D., & Belfer, M. (1982). Developmental double jeopardy: A study of clumsiness and self-esteem in learning disabled children. *Journal of Developmental and Behavioral Pediatrics, 4,* 191–196.

Shaywitz, S. E. (1986). *Early recognition of educational vulnerability: A technical report*. Hartford, CT: State Department of Education.

Shepherd, M. J., & Charnow, D. (in press). *Comprehensive textbook of psychiatry* (5th ed.). Baltimore: Williams & Wilkins.

Sigmon, S. (1987). *Radical analysis of special education: Focus on historical development and learning disabilities*. Philadelphia: Falmer Press.

Silver, L. B. (1979). Children with perceptual and other learning problems. In J. Noshpitz (Ed.), *Basic handbook of child psychiatry* (Vol. 3, pp. 605–614). New York: Basic Books.

Tallal, P. (1987). Developmental language disorders. In J. F. Kavanagh & T. J. Truss (Eds.), *Learning disabilities: Proceedings of the national conference* (pp. 181–272). Parkton, MD: York Press.

Tauber, M. A. (1979). Parent socialization techniques and sex differences in children's play. *Child Development, 50,* 225–234.

Van Hasselt, V. B., Hersen, M., Whitehill, M. B., & Bellack, A. S. (1979). Social skills assessment and training for children: An evaluative review. *Behavior Research and Therapy, 17,* 413–437.

Wall, A. E., McClements, J., Bouffard, M., Findlay, H., & Taylor, M. J. (1985). A knowledge-based approach to motor development: Implications for the physically awkward. *Adapted Physical Activity Quarterly, 6,* 21–42.

Wender, P. H. (1971). *Minimal brain dysfunction in children*. New York: John Wiley & Sons.

Chapter 3

Evaluation of Learning Disabilities

A crucial assumption is made in the process of evaluating learning disabilities—the assumption that the diagnostic picture that emerges must reflect both a thorough psychosocial and developmental history and a "snapshot" evaluation of current functioning that focuses on the interaction between the child and his or her environment. This insistence on a broad-based evaluative approach, stressing both history and current performance, has both theoretical and pragmatic roots. An understanding of the child's past experiences is essential for proper interpretation of his or her current performance. In addition, a clear picture of the child's milieu must precede an intervention strategy, in which changes in the immediate environment may be as important as formal remediation techniques. The social worker must integrate the two dimensions of assessment to produce the optimum circumstances for the child's healthy growth and development in the future.

The evaluation process serves a number of diverse purposes beyond the primary one of identifying conditions that require intervention. The evaluation provides an understanding of the neurological correlates of a child's behavior and cognitive functioning, offers a formal framework for professional and program intervention, and develops a baseline against which to assess future progress. Finally, the evaluation provides the documentation necessary to determine whether the child is eligible under federal law for special programs and services to be provided at public expense (Levine, 1987). The recommendations that emerge from a full evaluation provide the basis for planning strategic intervention on all fronts: in family interaction and home routines, in the classroom and in other formal programs, and in available socialization opportunities.

Federal laws governing the process of learning disability evaluation include the Education for All Handicapped Children Act of 1975 (P.L. 94–142) (EHA) and the EHA Amendments of 1986 (P.L. 99–457) (primarily Section 303.65). The EHA Amendments of 1986 embrace two age groups. The provisions concerning the 3- to 5-year-old group are considered to be an extension of the original EHA mandate with the same general evaluation guidelines. The other population, ranging in age from newborn to 2 years old, is covered under the Early Intervention Program for Infants and Toddlers with Handicaps, which mandates that an evaluation must include a comprehensive, multidisciplinary evaluation of the child's level of functioning in cognitive development, physical development, language and speech development, psychosocial development, self-help skills, and family strengths.

CURRENT ISSUES IN ASSESSMENT

"Evaluation" is a charged word for children with learning disabilities. Assessment may mark a turning point in a child's life, by leading to positive intervention and to increased access to services and opportunities, or it may provide a stigmatizing label that leads to a downward spiral of limited options. It is said that children with learning disabilities reveal their vulnerabilities very quickly, and their strengths over a much longer period of time. The saying encapsulates the major challenge in evaluation of these children. Identifying the unique pattern of problem-solving strategies that children with learning disabilities use to gain mastery over their environment is time-consuming—but this pattern provides the major clues to the most effective intervention. Only through close observation of an individual child's behavior over time will his or her "style" be revealed. History, description, observation, engagement, and testing are all critical facets of the multilevel and multidisciplinary evaluation process. Only a balanced approach combining standardized formal testing with analysis of the child's learning conditions, life experiences, and opportunities—and their continuing impact—will provide an accurate profile of his or her learning needs. Too often, the most important parts of the evaluation process are dealt with summarily, and the formal test results become the basis for classification and placement.

The strong emphasis on test results has particular perils for children with learning disabilities. Any testing process represents a sample of behavior in a particular situation, in response to a series of demands, at a specific point in time, at a particular developmental stage. Unless the testing situation is appropriately known to, and controlled by, the tester, the results will be of dubious validity. For the learning-disabled child, any number of disruptive events just before and during the testing process may crucially alter the demand and response. Typically highly sensitive to variables in the environment, the learning-disabled child may be distracted by lack of sleep, a fight with family at breakfast, or by no breakfast at all. Expectations (the child's or the parents') of performance, family tension about the assessment process, and generalized anxiety may lead to highly unreliable testing results. Many children, feeling defeated from the start, do not even try to do their best.

Even without prior anxieties, an unfamiliar testing situation may foster a fear of making mistakes, causing the child to freeze, unable to focus on the task at hand. Unintended environmental conditions in the testing room may be distracting. For example, in one case a child appeared to be totally unable to concentrate during a series of tests. The educational evaluator intuitively felt that something specific was distracting the child, and finally decided that the room might be a bit warm. The temperature in the room was 85 degrees. Some children, showing what would perhaps be deemed appropriate, "normal" assertiveness, might have voiced a complaint. The anxious child, fearful that everything he or she is doing will be wrong, might not even identify the added discomfort of an overheated room. In this case, the conscientious evaluator requested that the results be invalidated and another test scheduled.

The language used in the directions, or in the test itself; the nature of the tasks the child is expected to do; the mechanics of the way answers are recorded—all are factors that may interact to produce a testing experience that imperfectly represents the learning-disabled child's strengths and overemphasizes his or her weaknesses, creating a globally exaggerated picture of impairment (DeLawter & Sherman, 1979). Inconsistency is a common trait in children with learning disabilities. One day they will know the sequence of the months; the next day, they will leave two months out of the list. Under stress, their inconsistencies are magnified and their stock of knowledge and their available skills appear even more limited.

Hidden in many formal tests are performance expectations that may invalidate results. The life experience of children with learning disabilities, whatever their cultural or economic background, differs from that of other children, and their fund of "general knowledge" may accordingly be limited. Children with learning disabilities may not perceive certain complexities of their environment, or may be unable to establish connections between events. Their ability to organize experience into a conceptual whole, store it, and retrieve it at will may be deficient. These factors inevitably contribute to a "different" set of perceptions about the world and their place in it, which may well include "different" perceptions of the testing situation itself.

Children also may be penalized for patterns of test performance that reflect language, life-style and opportunity, or cultural milieu, rather than learning capabilities. Class, race, and ethnic background may become subtle bases for discrimination (Coles, 1978; Gliedman & Roth, 1980). Class- and culture-dependent test items weighted toward white, middle-class referents put children from other backgrounds—whose contact with such cultural artifacts may have been minimal or negative—at a clear disadvantage. More broadly, such culturally transmitted patterns as self-perception in relation to others, the child's expectations for family or personal relationships, types of organizational and problem-solving skills, and style of perseverance may all affect the child's involvement with the testing situation, and his or her score on the test itself.

Language issues pose a particular set of problems for appropriate educational assessment. In evaluation sessions conducted in standard English and relying on standard English test materials, children who are bilingual or from language communities not using standard English are at a disadvantage (Cartledge, Stupay, & Kaczala, 1988). Some inappropriate placements in special education may be due simply to the lack of appropriate testing resources to distinguish language differences from language deficits (Harber, 1980). The two groups that have suffered most severely from lack of familiarity with standard English grammar and syntax are black children, approximately 80 percent of whom speak black English (Dillard, 1972), and Spanish-speaking children (Garcia & Yates, 1986). Areas in which black English diverges from standard English include verb and pronoun paradigms and the interpretation of double negatives. As Cartledge et al. (1988) observed, performance on any test item turning on the recognition of nonstandard grammar will be misleading for children raised to speak black English. Because they are not native speakers of standard English, these children will be at a disadvantage in any task requiring them to identify as "wrong" an item not in accordance with standard English grammatical patterns. According to Cartledge et al., virtually all currently available tests to assess language capabilities include subtests and individual items that are flawed in this way.

Assessment of the bilingual child suspected of learning disabilities is equally challenging. Although basic intelligence tests are available in many languages, the standard tests for the evaluation of learning disorders are just beginning to be translated effectively into other languages. Care must be taken to ensure that future translations are sensitive to both linguistic and cultural nuances in the target language community (Ortiz & Maldonado-Colon, 1986). A translated test that retains its orientation toward white, middle-class American experience may be no more culturally relevant or useful in practice than the English-language original (Padilla & Wyatt, 1983). Professional evaluators from the child's primary language and culture are essential to ensure an appropriate, culture-sensitive interpretation of test questions and findings. Otherwise, misleading test outcomes and misinterpretations of behavior will become part of the child's overall record and will be used, with the potential for great harm, in diagnosis and educational placement.

In nonlinguistic tasks as well, children from economically or socially impoverished—or simply nonstandard—circumstances may lack the experiential background envisioned by the test instrument. Children who have had no access to very particular experiences might appear deficient because of this lack of exposure. Many of the incidental skills needed to respond to typical testing expectations reflect a culturally narrow perspective. For example, development of fine motor dexterity skills in early childhood may be related to the child's opportunity for, and encouragement in, such activities as holding a pencil, working with a pair of scissors, or using tableware—all of which constitute practice opportunities. Children who wear sandals may not be able to tie shoes. Other children who have encountered life situations and upheavals significantly different from stable, middle-class experiences will reveal correspondingly divergent values, choices, and interpretations of events. The funds of knowledge that these children have acquired may be rich, but unrelated to middle-class expectations. Specific competencies developed through necessity may have few parallels in standardized tests, placing these children at further disadvantage. (The coping skills developed by homeless children are perhaps the extreme example of these unvalued competencies.) The important task of identifying strengths as well as weaknesses through the testing process may be vastly more difficult in these instances.

Finally, family and community expectations regarding a child's behavior may either further or minimize his or her use of expressive language, exploration of the environment, and general curiosity. In some cultures, young children are not expected to do much for themselves. Adults are always ready to do things for them. Such children may appear to have problematic delays when they may simply lack practice. Again, adults may be trusted or feared, and relationships with adults outside the home may be many or few, for primarily cultural reasons. These variables influence the child's performance in a testing situation, but may not be known or given proper weight unless a detailed social history of the family life-style and culture is made part of the assessment process. The social worker's role is crucial here. Through family and community contact, the social worker may be the only professional in a position to study and assess the strong influence of culture and experience on the child.

It is important for all professionals who are working with children at significant disadvantage to develop an accurate and complete picture of the strength, resilience, and creativity that often are shown in adverse circumstances. A strong social history narrative and description, based on extended interviews, must complement the often bleak picture that emerges from test results alone. For all children, the process of evaluation for learning disabilities is biased toward identification of deficits, because the immediate objective is almost always the introduction of appropriate supportive approaches and structures. All of the disciplines involved in the evaluation process have the stated goals of identifying both strengths and weaknesses. However, strengths tend to become obscured. For example, divergent thinking, sensitivity to others, and sociability—three skills that may be related to overall success in the world—are not measured (Levine, 1987). Artistic and musical skills, and other creative modes of expression and communication, are not readily quantifiable. However, these less easily identified strengths may provide clues to a style of thinking, expression, and communication that could be incorporated profitably into the intervention strategy that is selected (Levine, 1987). In particular, these skills may form the basis for maintaining self-esteem in the face of repeated failures in other areas. Accordingly, the evaluation should include an assessment of nonacademic skills paralleling its rating of skills more directly relevant to performance in the classroom.

For all children, whether or not they are learning disabled, the family is the most powerful environmental influence. In the assessment of learning disabilities, social work practice traditionally has placed strong emphasis on the motivation, capacity, and opportunity of the family as well as of the child. Family strengths and liabilities must be evaluated clearly. However, at the same time that families are being evaluated, they also are acting as partners in the overall assessment process, providing indispensable input into the biopsychosocial history being developed of the child. This dual role inevitably creates a wide range of tensions in the relationship between parents and professionals. Social workers, who are responsible for recording the child's history and for assessing the family, school, and community as resources, have a particularly sensitive secondary task—that of ensuring that families feel empowered, rather than diminished, by their dual role.

INITIATION OF THE ASSESSMENT PROCESS

The area of early intervention has been a controversial one, due to fears of premature tracking and labeling of children with developmental delays. The tremendous developmental variation that occurs in the preschool years requires that caution be used. However, the importance of early assessment and intervention cannot be underestimated for children with developmental delays that may significantly impair their performance in cognitive or behavioral areas.

Sometimes, family members are the first people to suspect very young children have developmental difficulties. Pediatricians and preschool teachers have varying responses to parental concerns and may recommend a waiting period before initiating a formal process of evaluation. Although there are many reasons to be cautious about early diagnosis, too often early signs of learning disabilities are ignored (National Joint Committee on Learning Disabilities, 1985). For example, subtle language delays often are neglected until primary school, despite the availability of relatively simple testing proceesses. Such areas as gross and fine motor coordination, visual-spatial perception, expressive and receptive language, time and sequencing organization, selective attention, and higher cognitive processes all can be assessed at this age (Levine, 1987). It has been estimated that at least one-third of the children with early language delays and disorders have difficulty with reading and spelling in early grades and greater difficulties in later years (Wiig, 1984). Other children may have specific delays that do not show up until later, and still others spontaneously catch up with their peers. In other instances, astute professional observation is ignored by parents who may be unwilling to admit that there are problems and that their child may need special help.

Typically, children with learning disabilities present a wide variety of symptoms that eventually lead the adults around them to suspect that there may be a learning disorder. In general, when a child fails to meet developmental, cognitive, or behavioral expectations at home, in the classroom, or at a routine medical appointment, parents, school personnel, or a physician should rule out possible impediments to normal development. Family norms and values, school standards and expectations, physician knowledge of developmental variations and significance of signs of delay, and the age of the child all play a role in when and how a child with problems first comes to the attention of the appropriate professional persons.

Social workers are likely to become involved at many early stages in a child's life. If a child is identified as an infant at risk, there may be social work follow-up through the hospital pediatric outpatient clinic. Children in preschool or Head

Start programs may have access to an on-site social worker if they show evidence of developmental delay or behavior differences. If a child has been identified as having emotional or behavior problems in school, there may be a referral to a school social worker even before a learning disorder is suspected. Alternatively, a child may be receiving services from a child welfare agency or be in foster care, receiving ongoing monitoring for developmental progress. If parents are involved in family therapy or parenting workshops, a social worker skilled in identifying the behavioral impact of children with developmental differences on family functioning may be aware of learning problems at an early age.

GAINING PARENTAL COOPERATION

According to EHA and the EHA Amendments of 1986, parents must give their consent before an evaluation process is initiated. The National Association of Social Workers presented strong testimony before the U. S. Department of Education requesting that parental consent be required before an evaluation process is initiated (M. G. Battle, personal communication, February 16, 1988). The testimony stressed the importance of not coercing families into participation. The nature of the relationship between very young children and their parents requires maximum cooperation between professionals and parents.

To foster parental cooperation, whenever possible, parents should be encouraged to observe their child unnoticed in a situation that will illustrate the problem areas identified by school personnel. This may involve having parents sit at the back of a classroom or watch a play group through a one-way mirror or doorway. Interpretation could focus on the child's discomfort at not being able to join in with what the others are doing. Attention should not necessarily be drawn to the fact that the child is not competitive with the others, but to the feelings that may be expressed by the child through behavior and activity when he or she is left out. For example, one young child in a play group always sat in a corner reading when the others were playing games. Although the parents were delighted at the interest in reading, the behavior also was indicative of the child's way of dealing with difficulties in social situations with her peers. Ten years later, this child still had major difficulties dealing with her peers and chose the same way of removing herself from social interaction. The child's parents would have benefited from early discussion with the available professionals about the social skills gap already evident for this child at a prekindergarten level.

Parents also may be sensitive to variations in teacher style, classroom atmosphere, expectations, and to continuity or discontinuity with family and home. Such system discontinuities are disturbing to most children, but children with perceptual problems have more difficulty with them than others (Fish & Jain, 1985). A social worker may be able to work with parents and teachers to identify some of the discordant expectations and to modify parent or teacher behavior.

It is much more difficult to structure the same kind of observation experience for parents of younger children. If the parents have other children, they may be able to recognize differences more easily. However, a significant number of handicapped infants are born to single teenage mothers whose own resources and educational backgrounds may not prepare them for the complicated tasks of parenting. At times, the parents also have problems similar to those of their children. Parents' own learning problems or high level of distractibility may interfere with their attention to their children's needs. Parents may have a limited level of sophistication, or may be particularly vulnerable to denial, anger, or guilt. Professionals must be alert to these situations. Appropriate early intervention may involve helping the parents to identify their own parallel problems.

Early assessment enhances opportunities for parents and preschool teachers to work with children in unintrusive ways, through games and exposure to experience, to challenge the more slowly developing abilities. Frustration and failure at developmental tasks can be prevented by using appropriate early intervention strategies. Children who receive this early attention may not suffer the incremental effects of developmental delay. Stanovich (1986) and Levine (1987) suggested that a circularity of negative impacts may occur when a preexisting developmental delay inhibits the development of a skill, which then has the consequence of impeding some other developmental process. Thus, the systemic influences of developmental delay become evident, and demonstrate the need for early intervention whenever possible.

Although there are believed to be neurodevelopmental components to most learning disabilities, there also is a complex interrelationship between underlying genetic, biochemical, or organic predispositions and the environment of the child (Levine, 1982). Children who grow up in stable surroundings, with parents who are focused on their child's needs and capacities, may be more likely to have developmental difficulties identified at an earlier age. Parental high expectations can lead to early identification of problems. On the other hand, low parent and teacher expectations not only produce self-fulfilling prophecies, but also may result in delay in early intervention. Early attention increases the potential for protective structuring and stimulation of home, school, and social learning experiences. Children from unstable homes, teenage parents preoccupied with their own maturational needs, or families at low socioeconomic levels in disadvantaged communities may be less likely to receive focused attention and targeted intervention.

Social workers must be particularly aware of the discrepant access patterns resulting from these factors. Children living in homes with parents or parent surrogates who are not willing or able to be their advocates must receive the attention that they need and deserve. The social worker may have to become involved in working to gain family trust, bridging cultural gaps, ensuring linguistic comfort, and attempting to make the child's needs a priority, while respecting the integrity of family values and decision-making processes. Other families with more resources also may need help in negotiating the complicated evaluation process.

Each major area of assessment overlaps and contributes to understanding of other areas. The areas of cognitive, emotional, social, neurological, and health processes are not separated easily. The evaluation process may be initiated in any one of these areas, but should cover all of them. Often, a professional skilled in one of these areas will perform some basic exploratory tests in other areas to identify other sources of impairment that may be impinging on the functional area of focus. For example, a learning specialist may perform a series of ability and aptitude tests and include some basic projective personality tests. The pediatrician may include some basic neurological tests in the health examination. Often, these tests will provide indications of whether more extensive neurological or psychological batteries are needed.

Usually, the area in which the child's difficulties were noticed serves as a starting point for the formal assessment process. For example, if the parents bring their concerns to their pediatrician, there may be a recommendation to a pediatric neurologist, after a thorough physical exam. If the teacher has identified difficulties in cognitive processes, a recommendation for testing by a learning specialist may follow. If the child shows behavior problems, is distractible, and bothers other children in the class, there may be an initial recommendation to a psychologist, social worker, or family counselor. If the child is in a public school, and the problem has significant ramifications in the classroom affecting the pace of learning, or is behavior that precludes learning, the teacher may make a referral for a formal multidisciplinary assessment to be carried out by the special education assessment team. This usually includes an educational evaluator, a school psychologist, a social worker, and a parent representative.

Parents may seek out, or be encouraged to use, other specialists to further refine the problem area and diagnosis. For example, if a child has language, communication, or auditory attention problems an audiologist will be recommended to assess hearing (particularly if the child has had numerous ear infections). An otorhinolaryngologist may be called upon to assess the involvement of the nose, throat, or ears, or a speech-language pathologist may be involved. If there appear to be visual or spatial difficulties, an ophthalmologist will test for vision acuity, distance, motility, color vision, and evidence of near- or farsightedness. Or an optometrist specializing in identifying refractive errors of the eye and developmental vision inefficiencies may be called in. Psychologists are called on to evaluate cognitive, behavioral, and affective areas through the use of intelligence, achievement and personality tests, and informal interviews. Although psychologists are most familiar with quantitative methods of evaluation, other professionals, such as learning disabilities specialists, also may be performing and interpreting intelligence and achievement tests in addition to providing an indepth assessment of academic skills, learning style, visual and auditory processing deficits, and other perceptual problems. Psychiatrists and social workers may be involved in evaluating the affective, emotional, and social levels of functioning.

61

Although most specialists are partial to, or familiar with, certain types of interventions that relate to their particular area of expertise, other specialists may announce that they have cures and new systems of intervention. There is much that is still unknown about the causes and cures of learning disabilities. Parents, and those counseling them, should be wary of engaging in lengthy, expensive, and possibly intrusive processes that have not been researched in available literature. Allergists, nutritionists, specialists in orthomolecular medicine (chemical imbalances), and developmental optometrists, to name a few, tend to promote cures as they diagnose causes. On one hand, families with children with learning disabilities often feel they are bounced from specialist to specialist with great expenditures of time and money. On the other hand, some families search the popular press for mention of new and alternative approaches. Although they are aware of success stories, parents do not always have a broad frame of reference that includes a knowledge of failures, the expense involved, and the lack of substantiated research in many of the cases for which the most spectacular successes have been reported.

Parents need support in exploring new options, while retaining a healthy skepticism for instant panaceas. A delay in the timely design of a comprehensive educational and social plan for a child may lead to far-ranging difficulties in social, emotional, and academic areas. Increasingly, major hospitals and some universities are offering learning disability clinics that provide a multidisciplinary diagnostic and therapeutic team. Families should be encouraged to take advantage of these services. These programs simplify the sequence of steps in a full evaluation, provide recommendations of resources for more specialized procedures if necessary, provide the resources for follow-up, and permit the maximum integration of the findings. Because the costs of a broad, multidisciplinary assessment are prohibitive for many families, there is likely to be a sliding fee scale based on family income.

Alternatively, families may obtain a free evaluation through the public school system based on their own request or a recommendation from a teacher or other school-based personnel. The identification of learning disabilities in school-age children has been spotlighted as the most difficult of the diagnostic categories mandated by EHA. The difficulty lies not just in the breadth of the learning disabilities definition, but also in the complexity of characteristics, sociocultural variations, and the skill and knowledge required to select appropriate evaluation instruments and interpret them appropriately. In school systems, it has been documented that the specialists designated to evaluate children with learning disabilities often are the most poorly trained and least skilled at doing so (Bennett, 1981; Bennett & Shepherd, 1982). Additional problems, such as budgetary pressures, availability of resources, or unspoken quotas of children in each disability area also can affect the objectivity of the school-based evaluation process.

When social workers are involved at the preevaluation stage, they may play an active role in helping families select an overall strategy toward the assessment process. Choices must be made that are consistent with family resources and needs and take advantage of available professional resources. If there is no local learning disabilities clinic, the social worker can serve as case manager, assisting parents in determining where to start and when to stop the seemingly endless processes of diagnosis and evaluation. Families may need assistance with asking probing questions, anticipating the bias of the professional evaluator, knowing what to expect from different types of evaluation, and integrating the knowledge gained.

Almost any text on learning disorders provides a discussion of the sequence of steps to follow in the development of an in-depth assessment. Levine's (1987) model is extremely useful because of his stress on interdisciplinary collaboration, on the integrative function of the psychosocial history, and on the concentration on description, rather than labeling, of the individual child.

AREAS FOR IN-DEPTH EVALUATION

Initially, a comprehensive assessment should determine the parameters of the child's problems, as seen by parents, teachers, and the child himself or herself both currently and in the past. The initial exploration should provide a basis for establishing priorities for subsequent areas of assessment. There are six basic areas for evaluation: (1) psychological, (2) social, (3) physical, (4) developmental, (5) cognitive, and (6) educational functioning.

Psychological and Social Assessment

The social worker is often the professional with the major responsibility of taking the social history. When social workers are involved, they are in an excellent position to coordinate the observations of parents, children, teachers, other professionals, and the various agencies, such as mental health clinics or child welfare services, that may be involved in a child's overall history. There may be marked differences between the learning-disabled child's behavior at home and at school. Home is familiar—routines are known, the anxiety in dealing with unknowns usually is absent, and there may be many areas of successful achievement of developmental milestones. Additionally, assessing the child's functioning at home provides the opportunity to view developmental variations in a cultural context. Indicators of social adjustment with peers and adults may be assessed differently in a setting where a child feels more comfortable than in the tension-filled setting of the school. In the school, linguistic differences may interfere with the development of a good teacher-pupil relationship. Unfamiliar classroom norms and structure may be confusing. Developmental delay and the resulting behavior by the child may be negatively interpreted (Sugai & Maheady, 1988). School challenges may promote very different behavior and performance standards, particularly if the child has become accustomed to failure in school. These differences in home and school behavior, as viewed by parents, teachers, and the child, are very important and may provide clues to strengths that can be transferred to the classroom.

A visit to the school to observe the classroom, the teacher's style, the general atmosphere, the degree of divergence of learning style and pace allowed in the classroom, and the teacher's attitudes toward children receiving special education services all provide clues about the pressures and potentials of the classroom. For example, in one classroom it was observed that there was a marked increase in whispers and noises when a youngster left a math class to go to the resource room. The child being evaluated was very fearful of being singled out in a similar manner. It was obvious to the social worker that if use of the resource room was recommended it would be important to work with the teacher on the attitudes conveyed in the classroom about children who had to leave for special instruction.

Before any formal testing, the child's teachers should have an opportunity to share their observations about the problems the child is having in the classroom. Teachers generally have a strong fund of descriptive knowledge about their pupils' learning style, areas of difficulty, and ways of handling frustration. It is important that this resource be tapped to guide in the selection of evaluative tests. It is equally important to return to the teachers after the testing is completed, to add to the teachers' knowledge about a particular child, and have the teachers' hunches confirmed or disproved. If the child is to remain in the same classroom, this visit provides the basis for a continuing dialogue with the teacher about appropriate learning strategies.

Social workers have the opportunity to observe the child's behavior at home and in recreational settings, and to gain an understanding of the parents' investment in community norms. In some communities, academic success is a form of status. Parents' attitudes may provide clues about the pressures on the child to conform and the sense of disappointment that is conveyed for deviance. Discussions with parents can elicit information about how the family spends its leisure time and to what extent their child is expected to conform to expectations of the local community. For example, in many communities participation in Little League, the local tennis team, or the 4-H club may provide the key network for friendship and acceptance. If a child is not comfortable competing in these areas, it may be important to assess the alternatives for socialization opportunities that are available, such as swimming, biking, hiking, or sailing. These are all sports that do not require being chosen for a team, and do not emphasize competition. In urban areas, consider the child's susceptibility to peer pressure. Too often, children with learning disabilities are swept into antisocial activities, where competition is minimal—but risks are high. Alternatives must be sought.

Other than social workers, few professionals have the opportunity to see children interacting with their environment and to assess the fit between the needs and capacities of the child and the resources of the environment. As stated by Vigilante (1983), "The subtle and complex manifestations of learning disabilities touch every aspect of a child's and family's life. Social workers have the skills to discriminate between the problem and its impact on functioning; to perceive its effects upon parents, siblings, peers, and teachers; and to help parents selectively in their roles in supporting the child, as well as in advocating for the child" (p. 429). The social worker's observational skills and sensitivity in raising issues relating to differential interpretation of the child's behavior are critically important for effective multidisciplinary assessment. Social workers must raise these issues for other professionals, to ensure the broadest possible understanding of the child's situation.

Because there are increasing links being made between parental behavior during pregnancy and learning disability, a thorough family history should begin with a discussion of any possible behavior that might have influenced conditions in utero or at birth. The family history should include the parents' perception of any problems that they or other members of the family have had in the areas of learning and attention, slow development of speech, or reading skills. Discussions with relatives also can provide clues to familial inherited tendencies, and to attitudes about the problems being encountered in the child.

Specific emphasis on developmental milestones and clusters of skills that relate to such areas as gross and fine motor coordination, language acquisition, and independent self-help skills provide important clues for further evaluation. Early behavior patterns and the personality of the child as seen by the parents should be documented. Studies of behavioral style show a marked consistency of temperamental style from early childhood throughout life. Adaptability, coping patterns, ability to persist with difficult tasks, dealing with frustration, and adapting to change all have been shown to emerge very early in life and to continue to greatly affect school performance and social acceptance (Thomas & Chess, 1980).

Although this material also may be covered in a health examination, the social work approach also focuses on the emotional response of the parents, as they reflect on possible influences on the developmental course of their child. Self-blame, guilt, and anger may emerge in the discussion, and these feelings can be dealt with and assessed for possible impacts on family and child relationships. For example, parents may need to be reassured that they were not neglectful because they failed to identify problems at an early age, or that they are not bad parents if they do not recall developmental milestones. Many children show a perfectly normal developmental history until some particular level of complex response is necessary in their academic work, and then suddenly they may not be able to cope with the new demands.

It may be useful to ask parents about the skills that the child uses at home. The social worker then can assess the child's acquisition of age-appropriate skills in the context of the cultural expectations of the family. The social worker should recognize that, as pointed out earlier, in some cultural groups young children are not expected to do things for themselves and, therefore, do not get the practice they need to dress themselves, tie their shoes, use a knife at the table, or tell time, to name just a few common examples. In some families, children are not encouraged to talk to adults, ask questions, or show independence. If a child in this kind of home has a developmental delay, parents may not recognize a problem, and may note that this is a particularly "good" child. In other families, the child's difficulties would be caught quickly, and extra practice and stimulation would be offered. Home observation also provides clues to strengths that may not be immediately visible in school, as well as providing reasons why a child performs more poorly than expected. Without an assessment of family and home environment, appropriate strategies for intervention cannot be developed.

Parents may sense that the developmental course of their child has been different even though they may not be adept at identifying the exact nature of the differences. For example, parents' struggles with discipline may be clues to a child's cognitive difficulties, such as impulsivity, disorganization, or attention deficits. In particular, the child who always breaks things may be a child with difficulties in integrating spatial relationships or with poor motor functioning, and the child who talks all the time may be seeking to control the situation to protect himself or herself against verbalized expectations of others that he or she cannot understand (Strang & Rourke, 1985). The apparently unsocialized child who does not respond to nonverbal cues may be a child with visual-perceptual or processing problems that inhibit the understanding necessary for successful social interaction (Ozols & Rourke, 1985). Some parents view this behavior as part of the child's personality, labeling a child as "stubborn," "disrespectful," "thoughtless," "clumsy," or "absent-minded." Parents and teachers will describe the adaptive defenses the child uses, such as avoidance, as "sneaky," "manipulative," or "lazy." For the child, these defenses are temporarily adaptive, because they help him or her save face. Above all, they are protective choices.

Parents need help with understanding the contradictions that they see in their child's functioning (Rothstein, Benjamin, Crosby, & Eisenstadt, 1988). One child may be very good at negotiating a complicated urban bus terminal, but may be unable to set the table correctly—both skills that appear to rely upon visual skills. However, experiencing the dimensions and placement of a building in space is different from the abstract notions of judging left and right in undifferentiated space. A second child may not remember what the parent has just told him or her to do but is able to recount yesterday's school class picnic in detail. The child has experienced the event and draws on long-term memory to reconstruct the details. The verbal instructions the mother gives require auditory processing, attention, and short-term memory skills. A third child may not appear to hear a parent call, but can hear the neighbors fight next door. Subtly differentiated skills may be at play that impede an even profile of a child's functioning. At the evaluation stage, it is important to help parents air their sense of puzzlement and begin to partialize their child's problems in functioning with specific details. A child with learning disabilities also can be stubborn or lazy, but blanket generalizations regarding personality are not helpful to a differentiated diagnosis.

Gaining Children's Cooperation. Children with learning disabilities have their own generalizations and stereotyped views of themselves, often gleaned from parents, peers, and fragments of overheard conversations. It is important to find out how the evaluation process has been explained to the child. It also is important that the children be talked with directly, so that they can have an active sense of participation in unraveling the puzzle of their difficulties. As Rothstein and her coauthors (1988) observed, involvement demonstrates a respect for the child, and conveys the belief that his or her difficulties can be looked at objectively. Children often have unique perceptions about their problems, and can be stimulated to look at them in a new way through the evaluation process. Additionally, the social worker gains an idea about the child's receptivity to different kinds of intervention. Finally, an understanding of the child's view of the problems gives the social worker guidelines about the best way to interpret the findings to both the child and the parents. The evaluation presents an opportunity for the child to share hidden fears about his or her problems. The most frequent fear is a diagnosis of mental retardation, because that is the label peers frequently will choose to explain behavioral or academic differences.

Although the use of questionnaires is not common in psychosocial assessment, the ANSER system (Levine, 1980) provides an example of how questionnaires can be used to help obtain specific information and to serve as a springboard for discussion. The ANSER system consists of parent, teacher, and child self-administered questionnaires for different age groups. Although a social worker may not want to use the questionnaire method to obtain information, the breadth of areas covered and the structured balance to ensure the assessment of strengths, as well as weaknesses, may be useful. For example, in the teacher and parent questionnaires there are specific sections listing up to 20 different areas of potential strength. Interviews can be guided to stimulate parents and teachers to consider these areas. Examples of strengths include having an even disposition, enjoying new experiences, being affectionate, not complaining much when sick, confiding in others about worries, or having a sense of humor, imagination, or creativity (Levine, 1980). As Levine noted, if a teacher cannot identify any strengths in a child, questions should be raised about whether the classroom atmosphere is appropriate for the child. Similarly, if the parent cannot identify any strengths, questions about sources of positive feedback for the child become critically important for further exploration.

The questionnaire for learning-disabled children (age 9 or older) asks for a response to a series of questions about their perceptions of their problems, strengths, and interests. Included in the questionnaire are some comments made by other learning-disabled children. Sometimes, children with learning disabilities cannot express the way they are feeling about themselves. It can be difficult to know whether this relates to difficulties in identifying feelings, word-finding problems, embarrassment, or depression. Seeing in print, or hearing, statements made by other children can reduce the sense of isolation, free verbal expression, and begin the process of legitimizing feelings about hurt and failure without judgment. Formal, tangible, and active inclusion in the process of under-standing the problems has been shown to encourage children with learning disabilities to actively engage in dialogue with parents and teachers and counselors (Levine, 1980).

The best psychosocial assessment becomes an educational process for all participants. The outcome should be a shift from the conceptualization of a child as having a problem to a broader picture—a child with developmental strengths and weaknesses, interacting with an environment that is more or less supportive to successful learning and growth. Clear issues for further exploration and intervention are identified. Strategies and interventions are planned, based on a knowledge of the child's limiting factors and of the opportunities available through family and community resources. For example, a teenaged parent who has not finished high school may have very little parenting experience and poor system-negotiating skills. This parent would require a different level of intervention than the older, more resourceful parent with broader education and experience.

Through their development of the biopsychosocial assessment, social workers make an important contribution to the comprehensive picture of the child's current functioning and history. This exploration of the interacting influences of home, school, and community environment provides a baseline for the ongoing evaluation of the fit between the child's abilities and the resources used and needed.

Physical Evaluation

Unless parents mention academic or behavioral difficulties during their child's check-up, the pediatrician may be left out of the learning disabilities evaluation process. The astute pediatrician who sees a child regularly should notice behavior patterns that may indicate problems. For example, a series of complaints for which no physical basis can be found may be school avoidance behavior. Such common problems as the Monday through Friday headache or abdominal pains may be signals of school-related distress that should be brought to a parent's attention. A closer look at the school situation, as well as a check for possible underlying health problems, such as mononucleosis or ulcers, may be needed.

Pediatricians are becoming more alert to the different medical conditions that may relate to or aggravate a developmental dysfunction. The family doctor is a familiar person to the child, and may be able to engage the child in a discussion about worries regarding size, growth, academic and social failures, and habits that are of concern. It can be extremely helpful to parents to have feedback about their child as well as a thorough medical review in a familiar atmosphere when there are initial problems with school. However, there are pediatricians who do not believe in learning disabilities. These doctors can be extremely insensitive to the emotional vulnerabilities and fears of learning-disabled children. For example, one pediatrician questioned a learning-disabled, school-age child about the multiplication tables until the child was almost in tears. The physician refused to believe that such a bright child was being anything but stubborn and rude by not providing answers. It would be impossible for this pediatrician to assess this child's strong fears of failure in school. Parents must be encouraged to trust their intuition about whether their pediatrician deals appropriately with their questions and their children's vulnerabilities.

Developmental Evaluation

Pediatricians can be good sources for referrals to a pediatric neurologist. However if the pediatrician does not want to make a referral, parents should get a second opinion or seek a referral through the social worker or other professional. A pediatric neurologist usually is the most appropriate person to perform a full medical exam with a special focus on the nervous system. This exam includes an assessment of motor strength, coordination, balance, reflexes, sensation, vision, and hearing. Neurological examinations can be divided into two broad areas. The goal of the standard neurological exam is to rule out *hard signs*, or indicators of major developmental dysfunctions, such as cerebral palsy, epilepsy, or muscular dystrophies. Hard signs are indicators that would be seen in patients, regardless of their age, and that do not change in significance over time. The second type of exam is a search for minor neurological indicators, often referred to as *soft signs*, that document maturational delays or persistent inefficiencies in central nervous system functioning. Soft signs tend to appear inconsistently and are not always correlated with other problems.

One subgroup of soft signs includes indicators that are seen in all young children but that normally disappear with increasing age. For example, balancing difficulties, hyperactivity, short attention spans, erratic eye movements, or mixed laterality, such as right-handed and left-eyed preference, are examples of findings that, found alone, or at early ages, are not of concern. *Perseveration,* which is starting a movement, behavior, or thought pattern and having difficulty stopping and moving to the next task, also can be viewed as a soft sign. However, this difficulty also can be caused by anxiety, or by reluctance to take a risk with a new activity. When soft signs appear in clusters as children grow older, they may be associated with other performance problems, and add to the comprehensive picture of the child's difficulties in functioning. The significance of many of these soft signs is a source of considerable controversy in the medical community.

Another subgroup of soft signs includes mild neurological signs that are inappropriate at any age. For example, involuntary or jerky movements of limbs or facial muscles, tremors, clumsiness, general awkward posture and gait, borderline abnormalities, or asymmetries of muscle tone are some of the more common of these indicators. One of these soft signs is not sufficient to indicate a brain injury or learning disabilities. However, clusters often are present when these conditions exist (Levine, Brooks, & Shonkoff, 1980).

Parents may be afraid to have their child undergo a neurological examination because of fears of intrusive procedures or a diagnosis of brain damage. The old terminology of "minimal brain damage" has left parents with an image that the child will have irreversibly depressed capabilities. Parents may need to be reassured that the goal of a neurological examination is to reveal any persistent inefficiencies, which, in combination with the rest of the assessment, complement the understanding of the child's functioning (Levine, 1980). Under usual circumstances, the standard neurological examination explores the child's functioning in the areas mentioned above, and does not involve any intrusive procedures. The activities children are asked to engage in seem simple, such as walking on the sides of the feet, separating certain fingers, or identifying right and left sides of the body. However, if a child is having difficulty, parents must be alert to this and ensure that the exam does not magnify the child's feelings of failure, particularly in the area of motor functioning.

Although the neurological examination rarely makes possible definitive conclusions regarding central nervous system involvement, useful information about the child's level of functioning is gathered, which may provide useful insights for parents and teachers. The examination may reveal vulnerabilities that have been plaguing the child, but that have had no name. For example, clumsy children often are frustrated by their inability to do things better. Teased by peers, reprimanded and punished by adults, these children suffer unnecessarily. Once it has been established that the behavior is not purposeful, but due to delayed motor control, parents and teachers are encouraged to restructure the child's environment to meet the child's needs and promote more opportunities for success.

When clusters of soft signs are present, it can be assumed that organic factors are playing more of a role than are environmental factors in a child's learning problems. However, the multiple impacts of the environment (both historical and current) cannot be discounted. Adding to the complexity of diagnosis is the strong possibility that the child with these neurological dysfunctions may be more sensitive than other children to ordinary environmental stresses, and may react in less appropriate ways owing to faulty compensatory skills (Kandt, 1984). At times, a child's extremely dysfunctional emotional and educational responses to minor neurological deficits mask the larger dimensions of the difficulties that may exist at home or school.

In other situations, the interplay between neurological impairment and developmental psychological processes may present a superficial picture of mental illness. Some children have been misdiagnosed as having childhood schizophrenia, or borderline personalities, or mental retardation, when they actually had patterns of neurological impairment that indicated a learning disorder (Palombo,

1982; Voeller, 1981). Vigilante (1985) noted that, because the relationship between the neurological impairments and the development of ego functions is not understood fully, professionals should be cautious in defining the behaviors of these children as pathological.

Once a child reaches age 12 or 13, some of the neurological lags that may have impeded the completion of earlier developmental tasks may no longer be present. However, the overlay of emotional responses to earlier failures and the lack of earlier acquisition of age-appropriate skills provide clues to possible earlier neurological delays. Other children have seemingly slight neurological impairments that are not fully identified until the teenage years. Failure to master the more complex developmental and performance tasks of adolescence forces a focus of attention on possible physiological causal factors. It may be useful for some teenagers to have a neurological evaluation. If organic sources of problems are found, the emotional burden of repeated failures may be lessened and the child may find renewed energy to develop more constructive, compensatory strategies. Families can begin to adapt their approaches to be more helpful to their teenage child.

Cognitive Evaluation

Intelligence levels, indicated by language, conceptual abilities, and creativity, can be observed throughout the assessment process. However, individual intelligence tests have been used routinely in the abilities assessment process since the establishment of the EHA in 1975. These tests attempt to identify the child's mental age, or his or her innate cognitive abilities and talents. There has been considerable controversy about the fairness of intelligence testing. Charges of test bias, which may have led to racial differences on test scores and disproportionate placement of black children in special education or in classes for mentally retarded or learning-disabled children (Lynch & Lewis, 1982), have lead to several important court cases (*Larry P. v. Riles,* 1972; *Parents in Action on Special Education v. Hannon,* 1980).

In *Larry P. v. Riles,* the California State Court banned the use of individually administered intelligence tests for black children being considered for placement in classes for mentally retarded children. In the other case, the tests were deemed fair. The controversy still continues, and there is continuing analysis of possible discriminatory impacts of intelligence tests. Generally, experts agree that intelligence tests measure acquired knowledge as well as innate abilities. The question is how much of the score is determined by the acquired knowledge base of the child, and to what extent children from other cultures, a different language base, or non-mainstream (that is, non-middle-class) experience are penalized. All tests must be administered in a child's native language, according to the EHA mandate. However, as mentioned earlier, unless the content is adapted appropriately to the

71

cultural context of the child, the benefits derived from the translation are not optimal.

There are three intelligence tests now being used widely. The Stanford-Binet test, the oldest, has been revised several times, most recently in 1986. It measures intelligence in people ages 2 through adult. Children begin work at a level where answers are very easy and progress to a level where they fail all the subtests. The new version has four subtest categories: (1) verbal reasoning, (2) visualizing and visual reasoning, (3) quantitative comprehension, and (4) short-term memory. Rather than one overall score, the new version yields several scores that are comparable to the children's version of the Wechsler Intelligence Scale (WISC-R). The Stanford-Binet revision has received mixed reviews in a wide variety of areas (Gordon & Reed, 1987). The WISC-R has three versions, one for preschool and primary levels, one for children, and one for adults. WISC-R is used widely and has been viewed as very reliable, with a good normative sample (Gordon & Reed, 1987).

The Kaufman Assessment Battery for Children (K-ABC) was designed for ages 2 through 12, drawing on recent research in neuropsychology and cognitive psychology. Rather than emphasizing verbal and nonverbal content, like the Stanford-Binet and WISC-R, the subtests are designed to highlight the processes required to solve problems. *Intelligence* is defined as the ability to integrate and synthesize information sequentially and simultaneously. A relatively new test, K-ABC is sensitive to minority and learning disability issues and is viewed by professional evaluators as having promise (Narrett, 1984; Vance & Kutsick, 1983). Nevertheless, it has received criticism for its culture-bound items, and there have been cautions that it should not be used as an intelligence test (Gordon & Reed, 1987).

Drawbacks of a Popular Test

Each of these testing instruments is designed to examine many different functions, and each provides a scoring formula used to arrive at an intelligence quotient, which is defined as the ratio of mental age to chronological age. The WISC-R is used most frequently and provides an example of the issues that emerge in intelligence testing with learning-disabled children. The WISC-R has a verbal scale, which reflects a series of verbal subtests intended to measure the child's ability to use language for cognitive processes; a performance scale, which reflects a series of subtests to highlight motor abilities and visual-spatial processing; and a combined full scale.

WISC-R Verbal Subtests. The Information Subtest is designed to measure the basic fund of factual information. This test may reflect a child's ability to retrieve words from long-term memory (Levine, 1987). Questions include, What is the number of days in a week? What does the stomach do? How many eggs make a dozen? Long-term memory, sequencing and organizing skills, and time orientation are evaluated. Experience in the dominant culture also is assumed. The Similarities Subtest is designed to measure verbal reasoning through the ability to form abstract concepts. Actually it tests categorizing ability, from concrete to more abstract levels, through analogic reasoning, with scoring weighted to give more abstract questions more value. This subtest reflects the ability to capture an abstract idea in one or two words that form a category and requires some simultaneous processing language facility and recall skills. Some examples are cat-mouse, anger-joy, beer-wine, scissors-copper pan. Children from different cultures may have a different frame of reference that might change their perceptions of similarities and affect their final scores.

The Arithmetic Subtest asks children to listen to oral arithmetic word problems and to provide the answers. Its objective is to measure the capacity to pay attention and concentrate. However, auditory memory is critical here, providing some information about a child's active working memory. Therefore, this subtest is not considered very reliable (Levine, 1987). Some children cannot remember the required information long enough to compute the answers. The added pressure of a timed test may increase their difficulties. Results should be compared with written arithmetic subtests, and answers given after the time limits should be examined. An example question is, "If I cut an apple in half, how many pieces would I have?"

The Vocabulary Subtest deals with defining words, starting with the concrete, such as "nail," and moving toward the more abstract, such as "affliction." This subtest is supposed to measure vocabulary knowledge. It also is reflective of skills in expressive language, efficiency of language use, word-finding skills, simultaneous processing, and long-term memory. The Comprehension Subtest is supposed to evaluate perceptions of social situations and to test reasoning and judgment abilities. It begins with interpersonal situations and moves toward the role of societal institutions. This subtest actually measures higher level receptive and expressive language abilities, memory, and exposure to certain types of cultural experience. Examples are: What should you do when you cut your finger? Why is it better to give money to a well-known charity than to a street beggar?

The Digit Span Subtest often is seen as an optional subtest, but is particularly useful when learning disabilities or attention deficits are suspected. Orally, the child is given a short series of numbers to repeat both forward and backward. This is supposed to measure sequential memory, and additionally requires short-term memory and focused attention. Levine (1987) noted that a poor score on this test alone does not provide enough evidence that a child has problems with verbal sequential memory. Problems may relate to attention deficits, anxiety, or other deficits in auditory processing.

WISC-R Performance Subtests. The Picture Completion Subtest offers the child individual pictures, each of which is missing an important element (for example, a woman's face missing a mouth, a cat missing whiskers). The objective is to evaluate attention to visual detail and comprehension of part–whole relationships. The test actually requires good word-finding skills and long-term memory. However, because attention and visual perception also are needed skills, these functions either may mask visual retrieval problems or may accentuate them (Levine, 1987). The Picture Arrangement Subtest requires the child to arrange a series of pictures to tell a sensible story. Visual sequencing, planning, relations between people and events, and overall social awareness are critical skills evaluated. There are many different ways children accomplish this task. Some leave out key ingredients. Often, children are asked to verbally review each picture in their story and describe the process they have used, even if they get the correct order. They may have missed subtleties or have relied on visual cues, rather than on complete comprehension of the situation. Here, too, culturally divergent experience may play a role in different responses. This is a timed subtest. Any timed test tends to create anxiety.

The Block Design Subtest asks children to copy designs, using blocks with different color sides. The goal is to measure visual-spatial awareness, perception, and visual-motor integration, requiring analysis and synthesis of spatial part-whole relationships and construction skills. The overall focus is to assess the child's ability to form concepts and solve problems in a nonverbal area. This test is particularly difficult for children with visual-spatial deficits. It is a timed subtest. The Object Assembly Subtest asks the child to put together four puzzles of common objects. It is supposed to measure visual-motor integration. Actually, it draws on visual memory of the whole and on visual sequential memory, to determine which part relates to which. This test offers some indications of long-term visual recall skills. It also includes visual perception and attention skills. If the latter are weak, this detracts from the child's performance, and if attention is strong, it may camouflage a visual retrieval weakness. It too is a timed test.

The Coding Subtest asks the child to draw symbols, which correspond to specific numbers that are designated in a key. The objective is to measure the ability to engage in new role learning, visual-motor coordination, fine motor efficiency, and short-term visual memory. The subtest actually also draws on the child's ability to follow tasks spatially and sequentially and to focus, maintain attention, and follow through. It provides some insight regarding the active working memory, but is not reliable on its own (Levine, 1987). The Mazes Subtest is considered optional. In this, a child has to find the way through mazes with paper and pencil, avoiding the dead ends. For the young child, this test is used for visual-motor skills and visualization. Traditionally, this subtest is considered to measure planning, anticipation, and directionality. It also uses visual memory, attention, and focusing skills. It is particularly difficult for children with visual-spatial deficiencies (Rothstein et al., 1988).

It is easy to see how children may achieve similar full scale scores with widely different individual profiles of strengths and weaknesses. For this type of test to be of maximum usefulness, the examiner must be aware of the patterns and themes that repeat themselves throughout the different subtests. These may relate, for example, to verbal processing, visual-spatial functioning, short- and long-term memory, sequencing, and reasoning. Also, there must be an analysis of the processes through which the child arrives at answers. Only through analysis of these strategies will a broader understanding of the cognitive issues facing the child be possible. For children of divergent cultural backgrounds, it is important to group the subtests that use acquired knowledge and to scrutinize items that presume mainstream cultural familiarity. Additional observations regarding affect, anxiety, depression, and reaction to the authority of the tester should be noted. Some learning-disabled children may appear to be exhausted. These children sometimes do burn out their concentration rather quickly with the effort of attending to task and need frequent breaks.

Some children will not show a discrepancy between subtests of the intelligence tests, but will have relatively uniform scores throughout. This does not necessarily mean that there is no learning problem. The test may not show the problem, or the whole series of subtest scores may be lowered, owing to a pervasive underlying dysfunction. Children may do poorly on intelligence tests such as the WISC-R for many reasons. It has been noted that certain key elements of language are not identified through WISC-R subtests: the ability to understand and form complex sentences, the ability to adjust language to specific situations depending on audience, the ability to monitor one's own use of language, and conformity to grammar rules (Levine, 1987). In another area, testing for visual and spatial perceptions often includes a request for the child to copy shapes and images. Problems in fine motor coordination may cause a child to appear to have visual-spatial perception problems, when the problems actually lie elsewhere. An even more potent problem involves intelligence tests comprising many subtests. WISC-R commonly is referred to as an intelligence test designed to produce measures of innate ability. Memory, organization, and the ability to abstract are skills that cut across the performance and verbal parts of intelligence tests. When test results are grouped or averaged to get the intelligence quotient (IQ), the child may be penalized several times for the same deficit, such as a poor short-term memory. Thus, strengths that may be present are obscured.

Many professionals and parents recognize that the WISC-R is really more of an achievement test than an intelligence test. However, the WISC-R still has the power to open or close doors of opportunity. Intelligence tests still are used widely by schools for classroom placement. Parents are devastated when scores are low. Teachers may change the level of their expectations. Appropriate target services may not be offered to groups of children because they may be judged erroneously to be working up to their potential, due to poor test results. Historically, many children with poor test results have been put into classes for mentally retarded children (Levine, 1982; Mercer, 1973). More recently, some of these children have been placed in bilingual classes. Straddling two linguistic cultures between home and school, many children have limited vocabularies and skills in both languages. The culturally specific skills and fund of knowledge of these children are not assessed. They are penalized for demonstrating knowledge that does not conform to the requirements of the testing situation. The fact that they may have knowledge based in two cultures is not assessed anywhere as a potential strength (Cummins, 1984, 1986).

On the other hand, the gifted child with learning disabilities may be able to score very high on the WISC-R, demonstrating a mental age far exceeding physical age. If these children are working at grade level, the fact that they are underachieving, given their potential, may not be seen as an issue by a school administration. Parents may have to pressure for services or provide them outside of school. The gifted learning-disabled child often is identified late, if at all, after many years of compensatory efforts. Often, these students receive repeated criticism of their "laziness" because they are so obviously highly intelligent. The discrepancy between what they think they should be doing and their actual level of performance can lead to depression, excessive anxiety, withdrawal, or disruptive behavior. Among the most misunderstood, these children often elude identification and require a highly individualized assessment (Jones, 1986).

Other Abilities Tests. Tests of specific developmental abilities should not be used to obtain a general intelligence level because they do not always correlate with other intelligence tests. For example, the McCarthy Scale of Children's Abilities often is used with younger children. The tasks on the battery are similar to those of the classroom, which makes it easier to transfer findings in ways that are helpful to teachers. However, children with learning disabilities have been found to score as many as 20 points lower on this test than on the Stanford-Binet or WISC-R. If this test is used mistakenly as a general intelligence test, children could be misdiagnosed as mildly retarded and be placed inappropriately. Also, unusually gifted children will not show their true range of abilities, due to the lack of a sufficiently high ceiling for scoring (Gordon & Reed, 1987).

Other tests used to explore specific developmental abilities are the Illinois Test of Psycholinguistic Abilities (ITPA), the Detroit Test of Learning Aptitude (DTLA), the Cognitive Abilities Test (CAT), and the System of MultiCultural Pluralistic Assessment (SOMPA). Each test has its advocates, who cite special areas of strength, and each has detractors, who identify missing areas, poor design, questions of validity, cultural bias, or problems with assessment of subpopulations. (A full discussion of these tests, and references for further follow-up, may be found in the *Encyclopedia of Special Education* by Reynolds & Mann, 1987.) Tests to highlight specific underlying abilities should be selected carefully. There are many options available. Existing tests are always being revised, and not always for the

76

better. The skilled evaluator will be able to explain the strengths and weaknesses of the tests that are selected for each child. Ultimately, it is the skill in use and interpretation by the evaluator that makes any test of value.

Testing Educational Achievement

Achievement tests determine a child's level of understanding of academic content in the key areas of reading, math, and writing. Achievement tests differ from general intelligence and ability tests in that they are designed to measure acquisition of specific, uniform class content that all students at the grade level being tested would have received, rather than knowledge gained through diverse prior experiences. In schools, achievement tests serve four functions: (1) basic screening, (2) determining whether a child is eligible for special education classes, (3) assessing strengths and weaknesses for specific teaching level placement, and (4) evaluating educational outcome (Salvia & Ysseldyke, 1981). Specific tests may assess a wide variety of skills related to academic achievement, such as word recognition and analysis, reading fluency and rate, comprehension and memory, spelling in different contexts, math facts, computation and problem solving, writing under different situations, organization, and study skills (Levine, 1987).

Achievement tests may be administered to a group or an individual. Decisions about placement of individual students never should be made solely on the basis of group-administered achievement tests. These are usually *norm referenced,* or scored to relate the individual child to a peer reference group. If the group tests are used for screening, and discrepancies are found, then specific, individually administered achievement tests that are *criterion referenced,* or designed to measure whether or not a child has mastered a specific skill, should be given. The test results always should be evaluated in the context of the work the child currently is doing in the classroom.

For most children with learning disabilities or attention difficulties, the group testing environment generally is the least beneficial. They may be easily distracted, comparing their pace with others', or watching chair movements, legs swinging, or pencils dropping. Timing of the tests puts an added pressure on performance that only makes the learning-disabled student more anxious and prone to error. There is another group of children with learning disabilities who perform at an appropriate level on achievement tests, but who are unable to function adequately in the classroom due to deficits of auditory attention and sequencing, skills that are not demanded by standardized written group tests.

An educational evaluation is not complete without informal assessments of the child's work in the classroom, through informal teacher inventories, analysis of sample work tasks, and observations that take into account amounts of actual academic engagement, appropriateness of the student's curriculum, and the effectiveness of the instructional methodologies (Sugai & Maheady, 1988). If the child's primary language is not English, assessments should help determine whether the same learning problems are seen when the child is using his or her own native language (Ogbu, 1978). For ability and achievement tests to have real value in the educational process, the emphasis must be on the identification of the child's learning style, patterns of problem solving, and specific strengths and weaknesses as they affect particular learning tasks. The findings must be translatable to teachers, for incorporation in the daily work plan for their pupils. The results also must be made understandable to parents and children, not as percentiles and ranks, but as insights that will help in understanding the child's difficulties.

Assessing Children's Personalities

Assessment of the child's personality as it relates to overall functioning is being done throughout the testing process. However, specific projective personality tests may offer special insights into underlying preoccupations and emotional issues and conflicts. Rothstein et al. (1988) suggest that "assessment of personality functioning is an essential component of comprehensive evaluation of the learning disordered child, even when there is no previous evidence of psychopathology" (p. 156). Generally, the tests used offer visual-perceptual stimuli to the child, who must process what he or she sees and give a verbal description of it. The tests used are usually Rorschach, Thematic Apperception Test (TAT), and CAT. They include figure drawings of the body, responses to unstructured shapes, and completion of partially drawn pictures. Although Rothstein and her coauthors warn evaluators about interpretation of these tests with children with deficits in the learning disabilities range, essentially they view these tests as useful additions to the assessment process. There are differences of opinion about the utility of these tests with children with learning disorders, however. The picture that is gained is fragmentary, and the interpretations are highly subjective. It has been observed that children with language difficulties may produce unusual responses and impulsive answers and offer disjointed sequences of ideas, leading to diagnoses of psychopathology where none exists.

IMPLICATIONS FOR SOCIAL WORK

Whether working as a member of a multidisciplinary evaluation team in a school or clinic, an agency-based social worker, or a public service agency case manager, social workers must be sensitive to the counseling, educational advocacy, and coordinating functions they may be asked to perform.

In some agency settings, social workers will be encouraged to assume all of these functions as they are needed or required by individual families, to ensure a positive outcome for the assessment. In other agencies, there will be an emphasis on one or another of the functions, to the exclusion of others. It is imperative that social workers recognize the importance of these functions so that they can help families find the professionals they need to perform evaluations, if the social worker is constrained by agency mandate. These functions are particularly important for families who are less comfortable negotiating assistance systems, whether because of language, class, or sociocultural differences.

When the social worker is a member of a multidisciplinary team, there usually is a heavy emphasis on collaboration, because team members are challenged to develop an integrated plan. Depending on the setting—school or mental health or learning disabilities clinic—members of the evaluation team may include psychologists, psychiatrists, special educators, learning specialists, pediatric neurologists, audiologists, physical therapists, or speech therapists. Effective work on an interdisciplinary team requires an understanding of different professional areas of expertise, turfs and biases, and expectations and constraints. Social workers must be aware of the concerns of each discipline and of the major evidence used by each professional to make a diagnosis. However, the social worker's biopsychosocial perspective may differ from the perspectives of the other professionals involved with the evaluation of learning-disabled children. Social work recommendations do not focus on remediation approaches, practice in specific behaviors, medical prescriptions, or physical exercises. Social work intervention focuses on redistributing resources to support the child's normal maturational processes and needs. In addition to the child's needs, family needs are addressed. Social workers depend on a wide range of variables, frequently not in the control of any one institution. These variables often require environmental change and the allocation of scarce or nonexistent resources. Changes in the structure of the educational or home environment may be recommended to provide a more hospitable situation to support the child in taking educational risks and engaging in new learning. Individual, family, or group therapy may be presented as a way to help the child achieve changes in self-concept, motivation, and social abilities. Assessment of community opportunities may bring parents and professionals into new collaborative relationships.

Social workers in multidisciplinary settings often are viewed by others (and view themselves) as the client's "in system" advocate. Nevertheless, the ability to perform an advocacy role in the team may have costs that limit the effectiveness of the social worker as a team member. The dilemmas of internal advocacy are well known, and challenge social workers to keep a focus on their primary goal of ensuring that the child and family receive the appropriate services (Dane, 1985; Mailick & Ashley, 1981). The issues impeding effective social work advocacy are exacerbated when learning disabilities are diagnosed. Overlapping knowledge domains, unproven interventions, and limited resources add to the tension and difficulty of determining the best plans of action. The extent to which a social worker chooses to act as the advocate for the child with learning disabilities must be determined individually. If the social worker feels too constrained by peers or by the organizational hierarchy, the ethical response is to help parents find other community advocates to press for necessary resources.

As an agency-based practitioner in a child welfare/family services agency or mental health clinic, the social worker usually has a broad institutional mandate for work with families and their learning-disabled children. The social worker may perform as family therapist, case manager, informal advocate, or educator before, during, and after the assessment process. Because social workers are not allied with any of the disciplines performing the standardized tests in neurological, psychological, or educational areas, they are less likely to have a bias based on professional allegiance. They can help parents maintain their sense of balance; guide them in terms of what to expect from different specialists; support them in asking appropriate questions before, during, and after the testing process; interpret findings; and help set priorities for the child in terms of family needs.

Case management is one of the most important functions of a social worker during the overall evaluation process. There has been considerable attention to case management as an essential element of good clinical work in social work practice. Generally, the focus is on ensuring that the client's needs are met in the existing program of services (Weil, Karls, & Associates, 1985). Discussions about case management and the needs of families with a child with learning disabilities must have a different focus. The pervasive impact of learning disabilities on both family and child and the gaps in services in most communities require that the case management function have a broad mandate. Ideally, each family should function as its own case manager. Indeed, while raising a child with learning disabilities, most families do take on this role, with greater or lesser success.

Recognition of the complexities of choice, priorities, and accompanying stresses that emerge with the initiation of the learning disabilities assessment process has brought many recommendations that a formal case manager position be created (Ochroch, 1981). The changing needs and stresses, the inevitable impact on other children in the family, the increased pressures on marital relationships, and the financial and psychological drains all may require different types of supportive intervention. Initial steps taken by social workers performing a case management function during the evaluation process serve as a role model for families and establish a pattern for later collaborative family-professional case management.

There are seven basic principles that create a good testing situation and should form a basis for the social worker's discussion with parents about the overall evaluation process. The social worker should help parents accept the legitimacy of discussing the following issues in the first meeting with a new professional evaluator:

1. *Each professional performing an evaluation should maintain a holistic view of the child, despite the focus on the expertise of his or her specialization.* The perspective of the specialist can be determined in the consultation interview by the type of questions asked, and by the responses to the parents' and child's questions. If possible, parents should have access to the experiences of other families who have gone through the process. The social worker may act as liaison or facilitator in this process.

2. *There should always be more than one kind of test given.* This enhances the possibility of getting a broader and more inclusive view of a child's strengths and weaknesses. Sometimes, only one test is recommended, to save parents money. Parents should be encouraged to refuse this option and to seek advocacy help.

3. *The professional orientation of the evaluator should be clarified explicitly before the testing is agreed upon, and reinforced at the end of the testing.* Parents must be reminded to remain aware of the perspective of the professional and the possible denial or exclusion of other contributory factors to the child's situation.

4. *The evaluator should share with parents what he or she will tell the child about the process of the testing so the parents can reinforce and support the child with consistent information.* Parents should feel comfortable in interviewing the evaluator about preparation of the child for the testing process. It is difficult for parents to understand the role that testing plays in the fantasies of children with learning disabilities. They may think they are crazy, retarded, slow, or stupid. This may be what they have been told by peers, playmates, and sometimes by teachers.

5. *The same tests that are used to identify the weaknesses and vulnerabilities in a child's cognitive, perceptual, and behavioral areas of functioning also can be used to explore the child's potential* (Levinger & Ochroch, 1981). For example, many standardized tests are designed to bring a child to the point of failure on up to five consecutive items to assess the child's current limits. This can be very upsetting to children trying to do their best. The evaluator must stress continually that the child is not expected to answer all of the questions. If the social worker or parent finds that the evaluator is not protecting the child from experiencing failure in the testing situation, a different evaluator should be found.

6. *The evaluator's role with parents and child when testing is completed should be discussed in the initial consultation interview.* The evaluator can share a great deal of information about the tests in describing the results to the child without contaminating future tests. Parents must be encouraged to seek out professionals who have a reputation for being able to communicate results to both children and adults.

7. *Parents should be prepared for and insist on repeated assessments as their child matures.* Manifestations of dysfunctions change with maturational development, shifts in the environment, and the application of appropriate interventions. A diagnosis and label may persist long after they have outlived their usefulness, and the label alone may foster neglect of the changing needs of the individual child. Earlier assessments must be updated to reflect ongoing parent and teacher observations.

Intervention after Evaluation

After evaluation, activities take on a different focus. Social workers often take a primary role after the assessment process. An important goal of the assessment process is the demystification of the problems children are encountering. Parents often harbor many fears about the future and their role in influencing their children's lives. At the same time, the process has introduced new variables and hints of the struggle that may lie ahead. Social workers have the responsibility to ensure that the parents and children gain the maximum information from the experience. If they start working with a family after a child has been tested, social workers should obtain a clear understanding of the tests used and the nature of the experience for both parents and child. The residue of a testing experience can affect parents' relationships with their children greatly. Social workers can help parents recognize the legitimacy of their strong emotions as they go through the process of mourning and grieving for the loss of their perfect child. The fragmentation of the child into functions—incompetencies, weaknesses, immaturities, lags, and delays—as a result of the slow journey through the assessment process can heighten the sense of loss. Families have to be helped to become reunited with their whole child after this process.

It is particularly important to determine how the testing process was handled by parents and evaluators with the child. Children develop their own rationales for testing, usually tuning in to their own deep self-doubts about their competency. When children are included in an honest manner, they often get great relief from the isolation of their problems, and take the first steps toward self-acceptance and assuming responsibility for their own learning and behavior. Social workers should ensure that children have a chance to discuss the outcomes of the evaluation in terms that they can understand. If parents seem to be uncomfortable with talking with their children, the social worker can serve as a model in initiating the discussion. The explanations will vary depending on the child's age, sophistication, and specific area of impairment. For example, a child who is very comfortable with visual pictures might benefit from an illustration of links and circuits that still have to grow into place in the brain. Explain that the child will need some special help while the circuits, or links in the chain, are growing stronger. Another child might respond to a very different presentation, perhaps a story about a child with learning disabilities.

The evaluation process should not be another mystifying experience for the child. Children with learning disabilities already find much of their world to be confusing. Because they may be sensitive to signs of parental anxiety and stress before and during the evaluation process, it is important that children not escalate their own fears. Lieberman (1979) suggested that the particular deficits should be discussed in a matter-of-fact way. Nevertheless, despite clear and unemotional discussion, many children with learning deficits are very much aware that something is very wrong with them, and go through their own parallel grieving process even though they may not be able to express this verbally (Cohen, 1984). Parents may need help in recognizing the signs of their child's grieving, to expand their tolerance for unusually disruptive or withdrawn behavior or preoccupations with bodily injury.

Parental disagreements about the meaning and implications of the various tests and selection of appropriate priorities for action may be exacerbated by fears of cost and the drain on family finances. The social worker may become involved with parents in reviewing the results of the evaluation process and helping them to partialize their responses and frame their priorities. The results of the evaluation should be shared with the child's teachers, both with those who were involved before the evaluation and who shared information, and with new teachers, if the child has been moved into another class. The social worker serves an important bridging role, because many times teachers do not receive timely reports.

Social workers must support parents in the rejection of predictions or prognoses of the limits of their child's future options. Parents sometimes press professional evaluators of different disciplines for reassurance about their child's future. The wise professional does not issue pronouncements of this nature. However, some evaluators do make such judgments. They rarely are warranted and usually are destructive in their impact. The focus of the evaluation mechanisms relates to performance in a wide range of areas, but by no means all of the areas necessary for successful and creative adult lives. As Levine (1982) stated:

> What may be called a disability in childhood actually could contribute to the subspecialization of a brain. In adult life such targeted strength is more likely to be rewarded, and may in fact evolve into a significant advantage. Children, however, often are expected to be generalists, to be fairly good at everything, so that areas of weaknesses or disinclination may be viewed as problems rather than demarcations of individuality. When one deals with subtle handicaps, one strays into a borderland between true deficiencies and individual styles. (p. 534)

There is much knowledge missing in the current efforts to understand the complex factors that join during the maturational process of children in their movement toward productive and satisfying adult lives. The immediate challenge lies in the coordination of efforts of professionals, parents, and the children themselves toward a healthy, growing environment. The fact that a child has a learning disability often is not known at the onset of many school difficulties. However, once identified, learning disabilities are frequently isolated as a "school problem." There is an assumption by parents that the problem will be handled by the school through special programs or classes. Home behavior is not always seen as linked with the manifestations of the learning disability at school. On the other hand, children with behavior problems are often seen by school personnel as having emotionally based problems that are unrelated to the demands of the educational setting. In these situations, parents are identified as major contributors to the difficulties. Parallel problem-solving approaches can result in the search for separate cause-and-effect relationships, wasting the time and resources of families and schools. More important, however, is the damage to the child, who undergoes misplaced therapies and remediations that do not fully meet needs.

Social workers must use their broad-based knowledge of developmental variation in children, their understanding of the impact of family context on attitudes toward educational achievement, and the constraints and opportunities available in educational systems to create a supportive environment for the child with learning disabilities. The evaluation process provides an important beginning for social work intervention with child, family, and school. The information obtained must be used judiciously. School-based professionals often have a harsh view of reality, colored by their awareness of limited services and resources and by their lack of knowledge of the variables in each situation. They may not be aware of the individual child's constitution and personality, or of the family's creative strength in structuring the environment of their child through the use of home support, institutional intervention, organizing for community resources, and political advocacy (Dane, 1985). Social workers must recognize that parents are the lifelong advocates for their children, and as such, have a commitment far beyond that of any professional helper. At the evaluation stage, the social worker must begin to support parents in the many new roles that they will assume as parents of a child with learning disabilities.

REFERENCES

Bennett, R. E. (1981). Professional competence and the assessment of exceptional children. *Journal of Special Education, 15,* 437–446.

Bennett, R. E., & Shepherd, M. J. (1982). Basic measurement proficiency of learning disability specialists. *Learning Disability Quarterly, 5,* 177–184.

Cartledge, G., Stupay, D., & Kaczala, C. (1988). Testing language in learning disabled and nonlearning disabled black children: What makes the difference? *Learning Disabilities Research, 3,* 101–106.

Cohen, J. (1984, March 23). *Learning disabilities and childhood: Psychological and developmental implications.* Paper presented at the Orton Dyslexia Society Meeting, New York City, NY.

Coles, G. S. (1978). The learning disabilities test battery: Empirical and social issues. *Harvard Educational Review, 18,* 313–340.

Cummins, J. (1984). *Bilingualism and special education: Issues in assessment and pedagogy.* San Diego, CA: College Hill Press.

Cummins, J. (1986). Psychological assessment of minority students: Out of context, out of focus, out of control? In A. C. Willig & H. F. Greenberg (Eds.), *Bilingualism and learning disabilities* (pp. 3–11). New York: American Library Publishing.

Dane, E. (1985). Professional and lay advocacy in the education of handicapped children. *Social Work, 30,* 505–510.

DeLawter, J., & Sherman, B. W. (1979, October). Skirting the perils of testing: How standardized tests affect children is up to you. *Learning Magazine,* pp. 98–102.

Dillard, J. L. (1972). *Black English: Its history and usage in the United States.* New York: Random House.

Education for All Handicapped Children Act. Pub. L. No. 94–142. 20 U.S.C. 1401 et seq. 89 Stat. 773 (1975).

Fish, M. C., & Jain, S. (1985). A systems approach in working with learning disabled children: Implications for the school. *Journal of Learning Disabilities, 18,* 592–595.

Garcia, S. B., & Yates, J. R. (1986). Policy issues associated with serving bilingual exceptional children. In A. C. Willig, & H. F. Greenberg (Eds.), *Bilingualism and learning disabilities* (pp. 113–134). New York: American Library Publishing.

Gliedman, J., & Roth, W. (1980). *The unexpected minority: Handicapped children in America.* New York: Harcourt Brace Jovanovich.

Gordon, B. N., & Reed, M. S. (1987). A guide to tests commonly used in the evaluation of children with learning disorders (Appendix). In M. Levine, *Developmental variation and learning disorders* (pp. 527–575). Cambridge, MA: Educators Publishing Service.

Harber, J. (1980). Issues in the assessment of language and reading disorders in learning disabled children. *Learning Disabled Quarterly, 3*(4), 20–28.

Jones, B. (1986). The gifted dyslexic. *Annals of Dyslexia, 32,* 301–317.

Kandt, R. S. (1984). Neurologic examination of children with learning disabilities. In S. Shaywitz, H. J. Grossman, & B. Shaywitz (Eds.), *The pediatric clinics of North America* (Vol. 31, No. 2, pp. 297–315). Philadelphia: W. B. Saunders.

Larry P. v. Riles, 354 F. Supp. 1306 (D.C.N.D. Cal. 1972).

Levine, M. D. (1980). *The ANSER system.* Cambridge, MA: Educators Publishing Service.

Levine, M. D. (1982). The high prevalence-low severity developmental disorders of school children. In L. Barness (Ed.), *Advances in pediatrics* (pp. 529–554). Chicago, IL: Medical Year Book Publishers.

Levine, M. D. (1987). *Developmental variation and learning disorders.* Cambridge, MA: Educators Publishing Service.

Levine, M. D., Brooks, R., & Shonkoff, J. P. (1980). *A pediatric approach to learning disabilities.* New York: John Wiley & Sons.

Levinger, L., & Ochroch, R. (1981). Psychodiagnostic evaluation of children with minimal brain dysfunction. In R. Ochroch (Ed.), *The diagnosis and treatment of minimal brain dysfunction in children* (pp. 101–123). New York: Human Sciences Press.

Lieberman, F. (1979). *Social work with children ages 6-12.* New York: Human Sciences Press.

Lynch, E. W., & Lewis, R. B. (1982). Multi cultural considerations in assessment and treatment of learning disabilities. *Learning Disabilities, 1,* 93–103.

Mailick, M., & Ashley, A. (1981). Politics of interprofessional collaboration: Challenge to advocacy. *Social Casework, 62,* 131–137.

Mercer, J. B. (1973). *Labeling the mentally retarded: Clinical and social system perspectives on mental retardation.* Los Angeles: University of California Press.

Narrett, C. M. (1984). Test review: Kaufman assessment battery for children (K-ABC). *Reading Teacher, 37,* 626–631.

National Joint Committee on Learning Disabilities. (1985). *Learning disabilities and the preschool child: A position paper.* Baltimore, MD: Orton Dyslexia Society.

Ochroch, R. (1981). The "case" for the case manager. In R. Ochroch (Ed.), *The diagnosis and treatment of minimal brain dysfunction in children* (pp. 127–135). New York: Human Sciences Press.

Ogbu, J. (1978). *Minority education and casts.* New York: Academic Press.

Ortiz, A. A., & Maldonado-Colon, E. (1986). Reducing inappropriate referrals of language impaired minority students in special education. In A. C. Willig & H. F.

Greenberg (Eds.), *Bilingualism and learning disabilities* (pp. 37–50). New York: American Library Publishing.

Ozols, E. J., & Rourke, B. P. (1985). Dimensions of social sensitivity in two types of learning-disabled children. In B. P. Rourke (Ed.), *Neuropsychology of learning disabilities: Essentials of subtype analysis* (pp. 281–301). New York: Guilford Press.

Padilla, E., & Wyatt, G. (1983). The effects of intelligence and achievement testing on minority group children. In G. Powell (Ed.), *The psychosocial development of minority group children* (pp. 417–437). New York: Brunner/Mazel.

Palombo, J. (1982). Critical review of the concept of the borderline child. *Clinical Social Work Journal, 10,* 246–264.

Parents in Action on Special Education v. Hannon, 506 F. Supp. 831 (D.C. Ill. 1980).

Reynolds, C. R., & Mann, L. (Eds.). (1987). *Encyclopedia of special education.* New York: John Wiley & Sons.

Rothstein, A., Benjamin, L., Crosby, M., & Eisenstadt, K. (1988). *Learning disorders: An integration of neuropsychological and psychoanalytic considerations.* Madison, CT: International Universities Press.

Salvia, J., & Ysseldyke, J. E. (1981). *Assessment in special and remedial education* (2nd ed.). Boston: Houghton Mifflin.

Stanovich, K. E. (1986). Explaining the variance in reading ability in terms of psychological processes: What have we learned? *Annals of Dyslexia, 35,* 67–96.

Strang, J. D., & Rourke, B. P. (1985). Adaptive behavior of children who exhibit specific arithmetic disabilities and associated neuropsychological abilities and deficits. In B. P. Rourke (Ed.), *Neuropsychology of learning disabilities: Essentials of subtype analysis* (pp. 303–341). New York: Guilford Press.

Sugai, G., & Maheady, L. (1988). Cultural diversity and individual assessment for behavior disorders. *Teaching Exceptional Children, 21,* 28–31.

Thomas, A., & Chess, S. (1980). *Dynamics of psychological development.* New York: Brunner/Mazel.

Tucker, J. (1980). Ethnic proportions in classes for the learning disabled: Issues in nonbiased assessment. *Journal of Special Education, 14,* 93–105.

Vance, B., & Kutsick, K. (1983). Diagnosing learning disabilities with the K-ABC. *Academic Therapy, 19,* 102–112.

Vigilante, F. W. (1983). Working with families of learning disabled children. *Child Welfare, 62,* 429–436.

Vigilante, F. W. (1985). Reassessing the developmental needs of children with learning disabilities: Programmatic implications. *Child and Adolescent Social Work Journal, 2,* 167–180.

Voeller, K. (1981). A proposed extended behavioral, cognitive, and sensorimotor pediatric neurological examination. In R. Ochroch (Ed.), *The diagnosis and treatment of minimal brain dysfunction in children* (pp. 91–100). New York: Human Sciences Press.

Weil, M., Karls, J. M., & Associates. (1985). *Case management in human service practice.* San Francisco: Jossey-Bass.

Wiig, E. H. (1984). Psycholinguistic aspects of learning disorders: Identification and assessment. In S. Shaywitz, H. J. Grossman, & B. Shaywitz (Eds.), *The pediatric clinics of North America* (Vol. 31, no. 2, pp. 317–330). Philadelphia: W. B. Saunders.

Chapter 4

Developing a Supportive Environment

There are concurrent, intersecting needs for professional intervention with the learning-disabled child, the family, and the representatives of schools and other community institutions. Mental health professionals long have been familiar with the need for multiple targets for intervention in their work with children and adolescents with serious learning and behavior problems. However, psychological stress and behavioral difficulties may not be recognized immediately as related to a central nervous system dysfunction in children with less severe learning disorders. The complex roles of social workers in these situations have not been fully addressed.

Large numbers of children with learning disabilities identified when the Education for All Handicapped Children Act of 1975 (P.L. 94–142) was enacted are becoming adolescents and young adults. There is growing evidence of the lasting psychological scars of their struggle for mastery and competence even when their cognitive and behavioral deficits appear to be minor. Despite the early introduction of supportive resources, children with learning disabilities still have a significantly more difficult maturational passage than do other children. Although their academic problems usually do not disappear, intrapsychic conflicts, feelings of social and intellectual inadequacy, and depression become sources of serious distress and alienation during adolescence (Cohen, 1985). The serious consequences of early and continuous academic and social failure are just beginning to be recognized. According to the director of the Adolescent Division of the Los Angeles Suicide Prevention Center, the leading single variable accounting for suicides among youths under age 14 is learning disabilities (S. Gardner, 1983). At the least, family, peer, school, and work relationships frequently are turbulent and disruptive, at a time when the adolescent with learning disabilities most needs support.

TIMING OF INTERVENTION

Timing of social work intervention is based on perceptions of how severe a problem must be to constitute an interference with a child's optimal pace of growth and development. As Levine (1987) observed, "a variation in development need not be a dysfunction; a dysfunction need not create disability; and a disability may never become a handicap" (p. 3). Expectations related to age and sex of the child, family and community culture, and availability of resources all may play significant roles in the determination of what constitutes a problem, and when and how intervention should occur.

Professional knowledge of the way that neurological development interrelates with social and emotional functioning also guides the timetable for intervention. Controversy and a lack of clarity cloud the debate about whether learning disabilities reflect temporary neurological lags, or are central nervous system deficits that may change in manifestation but whose basic features remain. The two perspectives actually may be part of a single continuum, but the lack of definitive knowledge and the infinite variety of learning disorders make this only a conjecture. Professional and lay responses have been influenced by these different interpretations of neurological involvement.

The concept of a neurodevelopmental lag or delay emerged in the 1970s (Kinsbourne, 1973; Rosenthal, 1971; Ross, 1976) as a means of understanding children who function at the level of chronologically younger children, but who continually make progress. By ages 12 to 14, these children no longer show neurological indicators indicating delay, and proceed with a more or less normal development (Rosenthal, 1971; Weil, 1978). Many maturational lags, however, are actually multiple functional disturbances of the central nervous system that do not disappear with neurological maturation, and continue to affect developmental patterns negatively, even though the irregularities may not be visible in a neurological examination (Levine, 1982).

Whether these central nervous system deficits remain "developmental variations" contributing to an idiosyncratic mix of strengths, vulnerabilities, and talents or become dysfunctional, disabling, or handicapping depends on the unique growth pattern of the individual child. Additional factors of genetic inheritance, biochemical or organic disturbance, environment, and culture all will play a role in how the child is perceived, and to what extent deviations from a norm are seen as worthy of attention and intervention by parents, professionals, and societal institutions.

The considerable ambiguity of professional response to learning disabilities is largely due to lack of definitive knowledge about the context of neurological involvement and its course as children mature. As with any of the terms associated with the complex phenomenon of learning disabilities, either concept—"lag" or "deficit"—may be used too loosely. Early evaluation and testing may result in premature labeling of deficits and dysfunctions. Key adults in the child's life, particularly parents and teachers, then may lower their expectations of performance. Historically, many children have been labeled mentally retarded or severely emotionally disturbed at a very early age and tracked into inappropriate settings, producing self-fulfilling prophecies. On the other hand, appropriate evaluation highlights areas of vulnerability, promotes understanding of idiosyncratic behavior, and permits targeted parent and professional intervention.

In other circumstances anxious parents may be told, "It's just a developmental lag. Come back when she's 7 or 8." Some of these children will catch up or appear to catch up, reassuring their parents that everything is now normal. Indeed, some will go on to more or less tranquil school careers, whereas others will have more severe academic, social, or emotional problems as school work becomes more demanding and peer relationships more complex. Still other children may flunk first grade and develop a lasting fear and distrust of school. The reassurance that "it's just a lag" may meet the parent's need to deny that there are developmental issues that need attention. When a child's problems have been defined as a maturational lag or delay, relieved parents may be blinded to the stress their children may be experiencing and the at-times collusive behavior of their children in reassuring parents that everything is fine. Children may not reveal that they are socially isolated, or that they must spend many more hours on school work than do their peers. Fearing discovery, these children often believe that their achievements are not real. Confusion about their capabilities and discomfort with their self-concept and judgment contribute to shaky self-esteem.

Viewing themselves through the discerning eyes of their peers, children with learning disabilities often sense their differences very early. This peer feedback sometimes takes place even before parents and teachers have identified problems formally in preschool or early school years. Silverman and Zigmond (1983) found that, beginning as early as age 7 or 8, learning-disabled children believe that they are damaged, inadequate, and vulnerable. The danger of premature, inappropriate action is offset by the loss caused by late intervention. Child time, in developmental terms, moves very quickly.

Early intervention directly with the child, the family, and the school promotes the child's perception of home and school environments as supportive and welcoming. Feelings of helplessness, confusion, and frustration can be limited or prevented. Effective early intervention has positive multiplier effects on other maturational activities. Because of the interdependence of developmental functions, lack of growth and consolidation in one area may inhibit growth in another. A child who does not get the necessary stimulation at early cognitive levels will not be able to build toward more complex cognitive, social, and emotional integration of experience (Levine, 1987). Deferring intervention may cause unanticipated impacts as children with learning disabilities try to cope with demands that exceed their capacities. The conflict of desire and expectations with the lack of internal resources to achieve creates an overwhelming sense of incompetence, frustration, and powerlessness.

PSYCHOSOCIAL DEVELOPMENT

The emotional and social development of children with learning disabilities has been a focus of concern for a small group of mental health professionals for the last four decades. Rothstein, Benjamin, Crosby, and Eisenstadt (1988) noted that in much of the psychoanalytic literature learning disorders have been attributed to psychodynamic factors. As Rothstein and her coauthors observed, this led to a search for solutions in a narrow psychoanalytic sphere.

Other researchers have focused on the interaction between the neurological and psychological developmental processes, leading to a conceptualization of the major role played by the central nervous system (Levine, 1982; Cohen, 1985; Silver, 1979b). This conceptualization has supported an expanded view of the interplay of biological, organic, intrapsychic, and environmental influences. In this perspective, many variables are seen as influences on the biopsychosocial development of the child. For example, the continuous interaction of strengths and vulnerabilities with social and cultural environments, and with the individual's temperament and psychological responses, makes it difficult to identify causal relationships with any certainty. Vigilante (1985) has stressed that children who have central nervous system developmental irregularities move through maturational stages more slowly than do other children. Their academic performance is uneven, and their ego development and social functioning may not follow a regular path. Vigilante (1985) and Rosenberger (1988) cautioned that deficits in ego functioning and problematic behavior may result in an inappropriate label of psychopathology, when the responses are actually transitory reactions to highly stressful situations when the ego is not sufficiently mature and few adaptive coping mechanisms are readily available.

This broad-based view of the factors influencing the development and course of learning disabilities permits a more complex approach to intervention. Integrating work with the child and key adults and institutions in his or her environment builds a comprehensive framework of support. Researchers and practitioners are exploring the impacts of learning disability on intrapsychic development, proposing that there is a framework of anticipated and predictable patterns of response to developmental challenges, rather than an enduring pathology.

Kagan (1984) stressed that the relationship between the processes of psychosocial and neurological (cognitive) growth begins very early in an infant's life. For the infant with central nervous system disturbances, the differentiated perceptions of the mother, the self, and the surrounding environment may remain fragmented and disconnected. Bonding may be impaired. The infant may not communicate consistently with early nurturers, and may not have basic needs met. Ineffective early communication attempts between child and parent may lead to subtle emotional distancing. There may be long-lasting effects of these early failures on both child and parent. Early perceptions of safety and security, or the lack of these, affect the later ability to form trusting relationships. If the environment is experienced as unpredictable and hostile, later assumptions about the world as a predictable and responsive place are jeopardized.

The usual process of integrating new knowledge about the environment involves taking in new perceptions, then reorganizing already-stored information to accept the new data. Ideas, concepts, and beliefs change as children become more sophisticated at integrating cognitive processes with experience. For children with learning disabilities, distorted perceptions and missing chunks of information lead to flawed reasoning and faulty conclusions. Unreliable and inconsistent cognitive functioning leads many of these children to mistrust all of their perceptions and their reasoning capacities. The growing realization that their self-monitoring processes may be just as unreliable as their original attempts to integrate and use new knowledge is particularly devastating. This leads these children to rely on overly simple formulas and to rigidly adhere to past patterns of functioning as the safest course of action. Thus, a vital feedback loop for learning and the integration of new knowledge and experience is not in place.

Ego Functioning

The ego functions deal with perceptions of reality. When reality is not correctly grasped due to cognitive and perceptual dysfunctions, reality testing, memory, tolerance for frustration, and the establishment of object relations may be affected from a very early age (deHirsch & Jansky, 1980; Vigilante, 1985). Because of the interdependence of the basic ego functions, difficulties in one area may affect another area. The combined deficits affect the overall functioning of the child. For these reasons, ego functioning among children with learning disabilities rarely is intact. Vigilante (1985) captured the breadth of this problem:

> A child's incorrect perceptions will affect reality testing that requires accurate perception of the internal and external world. Judgement, the ability to choose among actions based on understanding implications and consequences of behavior, also depends upon correct perception. The control of drives, affects and impulses involves the capacity to tolerate anxiety, frustration, anger and depression. The control of motility concerns patterns of activity manifested in behaviors. The appropriateness of the range, kind and amount of activity will affect the child's social and educational adjustment. Closely related to the control of motility is control of stimuli. Excessive internal or external stimulation may interfere with the development of the self-regulating mechanisms. . . . Appropriate object relations requires integration of these ego functions in order to achieve mature and sustaining interpersonal relationships. The thought processes require that thinking and speaking be organized and logical and that inner and outer stimuli are controlled, and that recall and reason are intact. Mastery competence, a composite of one's abilities including coping and adaptation, depends upon positive feedback from peers, family and teachers. (pp. 175–176)

Unless the social worker understands the interrelationship of the impacts of neurological system impairments on cognitive and psychological development, it is difficult to identify the extent to which the child's problem-solving process is at question, the data the child is working with are wrong, the emotional stress and history of failure have produced maladaptive coping strategies, or all of these factors are contributing to the child's distress. In any case, the child's often desperate efforts to make sense of the world lead to both psychic and physical exhaustion. Even mild neurological impairments can create these problems for a child. To parents and professionals not familiar with the broad implications of different learning disability conditions, a child's behavior, moods, and social interaction may seem extreme and wildly out of proportion to the documented and "tested" disability. For children, the same perplexing issues arise. Children and their parents may be able to identify specific problems in school work, but not understand the complex links to everyday functioning at home. The frustration of not being able to do things right and not being able to trust oneself quickly erodes self-esteem and feelings of competence unless there is timely and appropriate intervention.

Self-esteem and Self-concept

Issues of self-esteem and feelings, attitudes, and values about self-worth emerge for all children in early childhood. Most of the ideas children have about themselves come from the way others reflect their achievements and failures. All children experience successes and failures in the context of the academic and social expectations of the adults and children with whom they interact. At home, at school, and on the playground there are numerous opportunities for positive or negative feedback and comparison with others. Children with learning disabilities get more contradictory messages from peers and adults than do other children. A child who is a good runner but who cannot hit a ball may be referred to as clumsy. Poor mathematical abilities may put the child in the section with "the dummies," despite other academic strengths. Continued failure to accomplish developmental and school-related tasks becomes a major contributor to low self-esteem and a pervasive sense of helplessness (Licht & Kistner, 1986), which, if reinforced, becomes a "learned helplessness" response even to challenges the child could master with effort or practice.

Children with learning disabilities acquire a growing awareness and sensitivity to the extent of their differences from others and to their difficulties in measuring up to their own and others' performance expectations. Winning approval and respect and creating strategies to protect against humiliation and ridicule are pre-occupations of all children from the time they enter school (Levine, 1987). Children with learning disabilities must fight this battle more diligently than others. They are betrayed by their faulty perceptions, incomplete thinking processes, poor communication skills, and, at times, physical awkwardness. Their vigilance and strategies must match the unpredictable emergence of their deficits. This struggle tends to lead to a preoccupation with self-protection, rigid responses, and a heightened anxiety about any new activity or change in routines.

Given the powerful feelings engendered by repeated failures in important areas, it should be no surprise that some of these children describe strong feelings of self-loathing (Rome, 1971; Palombo, 1979). As many as 10 to 20 percent of children with learning disabilities show signs of depression (Stevenson & Romney, 1984).

These children may describe themselves as "sad, depressed, low, down, down in the dumps, empty, blue, very unhappy or bad feelings inside" (Puig-Antich & Rabinovich, 1983). A critical time for the onset of low-level chronic depression in children with learning disabilities appears to be between the ages of 7 and 8 (Cohen, 1984). When queried, children in Cohen's study described the loss of a part of the self, which they referred to as the "head/brain." Cohen, speculating on the reasons children mourn the loss of a part of themselves, suggested that the intermittent nature of the manifestations of learning disabilities gives children fleeting glimpses of what it is like to be free of the dysfunction, stimulating a recurrent sense of loss. Cohen suggested that the unexpected emergence of depression at this early age may be explained by the significant maturational surge that occurs between ages 7 and 8 (Shapiro & Perry, 1976) providing the child with the tools to look at his or her experience in new ways.

This surge coincides with second and third grade, when school expectations shift dramatically. The classroom becomes more competitive and becomes an increasingly important part of the child's world. At this age, children with learning disabilities may be able to list what other children in class can do and what they cannot, making them exquisitely aware of their deficiencies. For professionals as well as parents, such children are perplexing indeed. Unable to do the work, they can identify what it is they cannot do, demonstrating at times a sophisticated awareness of detail and the extent to which they fail the teacher's expectations. Parents ask how these children can be "stupid." Of course, they are not stupid, but they do not know this unless strong counterinfluences are exerted by parents and other significant adults. Even with this support, self-esteem rarely is strong and the self-concept constantly is battered by the paradoxes of erratic performance.

The Prevalence of Anxiety

The high levels of anxiety exhibited by children with learning disabilities have been observed by parents and professionals. Parents notice the constantly worried expression, the barrage of questions, increased perseveration, frantic activity, unnecessary mistakes, and temporary loss of existing competencies. Professionals focus on the dynamics of the effects of stress on intrapsychic processes. Vigilante (1985) noted that "perhaps the most significant and observable characteristic of a child with learning disabilities is anxiety. It would appear only logical that a child who is experiencing failure in critical areas of life should display significant anxiety based on these experiences" (p. 174).

Similarly, Palombo and Feigon (1984) found that "the deficit contributes to a failure in the child's capacity to maintain a sense of cohesion and in his capacity to avoid recurrent fragmentations. This lack of cohesion may be understood as an undercurrent of chronic and overpowering anxiety with which he lives" (p. 30). It is during latency that these feelings are particularly heightened. The tasks of latency, as outlined by Erikson (1963), are learning to win recognition and approval through the "pleasure of work completion by steady attention and persevering diligence . . . becoming an eager and absorbed unit of a productive situation. . . ." (p. 259) and often are well beyond the learning-disabled child's level of cognitive and physiological maturational capabilities. This imbalance leads to feelings of inadequacy, discouragement, and loss of status with peers.

The impacts of a heightened state of anxiety on daily functioning are documented by recent research on latency-age children and adolescents. Cohen (1984, 1985) has found a tendency for any anxiety or distress about performance felt by a learning-disabled child to move quickly to a panic anxiety level. This escalation inhibits the mobilization of areas of strength, the selection of bypass strategies, and appropriate alternative options for handling the stressful situation. Cohen interpreted this rapid escalation of panic as indicative of a developmental failure to modulate anxiety.

The effects of this response on the behavior of children with learning disabilities can be devastating to their educational efforts and social relationships. Perceptions of helplessness and ineffectuality may be heightened. The child's anxiety frequently is exacerbated by the corresponding anxiety of significant adults in the child's life—the teacher whose ability to teach is thrown into question, the parent whose own parenting skills seem to fail. In these circumstances, too often the identified cause of failure becomes the child, who does not learn or respond in a way sanctioned by conventional teaching and parenting approaches. Unless there is appropriate intervention to change adults' perspectives and reframe their notions of the problem to include changes in their expectations and interactions, the pressures on the child with learning disabilities will escalate further, causing ever more restrictive and self-protective behavior patterns.

Protective Strategies

The world of children with learning disabilities is fraught with hidden dangers. These children will try to evaluate quickly any new experience in terms of past successes and failures. Because successes may have been few, the threat to the self-esteem and anticipated loss of control implicit in novel situations often bring reliance on a limited range of the "tried and true" responses. To the extent that these strategies protect the child from being flooded with anxiety, while allowing reasonable contemplation of the task at hand, they are adaptive. However, the same strategies can become counterproductive very quickly if they impede the functioning necessary for risking new learning and growth. New experiences that might have been appropriate if positive coping skills had been allowed to develop are made ever more risky, and often are avoided, to the great detriment of the growing child.

Vigilante (1985) suggested that the use of defenses presents a particularly difficult set of problems for children with learning disabilities. "Adaptive defenses protect from anxiety while permitting optimal functioning," she found.

"Maladaptive defenses protect from anxiety at the expense of optimal functioning" (p. 176). She cited the need for children with learning disabilities to draw heavily on defenses that help them to maintain stability in the face of demands they see as overwhelming. Developing self-protective but maladaptive coping patterns in response to learning environments perceived as hostile or threatening, these children struggle to preserve their self-image even as they create barriers to their own cognitive and psychosocial growth.

Increased understanding of the intrapsychic burdens of the child with learning disabilities leads to a respect for the ways in which a limited number of defenses are used. Constant vigilance to support a beleaguered sense of self against humiliation requires an almost automatic recall of protective strategies. Demands for performance as varied as classroom recitation, response to classmates' dirty jokes, or remembering directions to the dentist may trigger feelings of incompetence and anticipated humiliation. Internal distress sounds the alarm, and the child selects a strategy that will minimize the risks of the situation. The risk could take the form of dealing directly with the demand for performance, or the risk could be in the form of adopting a new style of coping. No matter how the risk is defined, dealing with uncertainty, and the lack of structure that any risk entails, provokes anxiety too great for many children with learning disabilities. Mastering new skills requires trial-and-error learning, practice, and experimentation. Vigilante (1985) elaborated on the essential dilemma for the child with learning disabilities:

> Rigid and pervasive use of defenses is considered maladaptive for most children. However, for the child with learning disabilities, rigid use of defenses is a means of coping with confusion and anxiety. . . . Because of the deficits in ego functioning and the rigidity of the defenses, children with learning disabilities face a potential crisis every time adaptation is required. It is paradoxical that their very useful coping mechanisms become dysfunctional when new learning takes place. (p. 176)

Professionals and parents benefit from an awareness of the coping strategies that are most frequently used by children with learning disabilities. Because they are used almost without regard to the situation and limit the exploration of new options and actions, they are deemed maladaptive. Careful analysis of patterns of behavior that deflect attention from mastering the task at hand provides valuable clues to the areas in which these children feel most vulnerable. Although almost any defense may be used excessively and become counterproductive, there are some frequently seen, often used defenses that are particularly inhibiting to healthy developmental progress. Among these are avoidance, regression, somatization, and clowning.

Avoidance. Many children with learning disabilities are quick to find ways to avoid new activities or tasks when they think they will be shown up as stupid or incompetent. In school, they drop their pencils, become fidgety, are easily distracted, run to the bathroom, or forget their homework. Every teacher has confronted this behavior. However, if the activity or task is one in which the youngster is interested and has achieved earlier success, the behavior may diminish considerably. Avoidance is a psychological defense. It protects the child from negative assaults on self-esteem, while offering release from failure. Paradoxically, when used as a strategy, avoidance exacerbates an underlying general anxiety and confirms incompetence. Cohen (1985) noted that children in his studies who used avoidance excessively as a coping strategy tended to have a negative concept of themselves as avoiders and manipulators, keeping their secret of incompetence from others. Avoidance through withdrawal of interest or affect is a familiar pattern. This behavior often is seen in younger children, who withdraw from involvement on the playground or in school very readily if rebuffed by failure, ridicule, or heavy criticism.

Older children are quick to drop new hobbies that require too much practice, or new friends who make specific demands. They may say the activity is boring, or the rejected friends are too "uptight," engineering a rejection before it happens to them. Many learning-disabled youngsters do not experience the connection between practice and mastery. Often attributing their successes to luck, they may never have experienced their role in the mastery of a skill. They view new experiences with dread, only as chances to demonstrate their stupidity or clumsiness. Avoidance of the challenging situation, even though the avoidance may bring a negative confrontation with adults, deflects the primary assault to their fragile self-image.

Excessive use of avoidance as a coping strategy has been noted among children with learning disabilities in families that rigidly shun any expression of conflict (Spacone & Hansen, 1984) and in controlling families in which the parents accentuate a fear of the environment (Kohn & Rosman, 1974). The young teenager who disavows any interest in school, who is "turned off" to education, is particularly hard to convince that it could be different if his or her family has negative feelings about school. This is the situation exemplified in the compelling book *Reading, Writing and Rage* (Ungerleider, 1985). The character explains, "I started thinking about how I felt that first day at the high school. It just blew me away cause I realized I kept thinking why am I having to go here? I'm not gonna learn anything. It's just gonna be all these new people and I'm gonna have to prove I can't do it again . . . school is the only place I've felt really worthless" (p. 185). The character's mother, despite the fact that her teenage son can neither read nor write, lets no one know that the son has a learning disability. She states, "It's more important to me than anything in the world that people say good things about Tony . . . and all his friends do" (p. 29). It took considerable work by the educational therapist to gain the trust of this teenager and his parents, and to break through the long-standing pattern of avoidance and withdrawal. Most children who use avoidance require a consistent, strong supportive figure to reinforce a belief in their capability, and to provide strategies to accomplish seemingly insurmountable tasks.

Regression. The average course of childhood maturational growth is rarely even or without setbacks. Children with learning disabilities tend to have an even more tumultuous maturational path. Adding to this irregular growth pattern is the overuse of regression as a coping strategy. The return to an earlier, and presumably more successful, stage of functioning allows a child protection and a temporary retreat to consolidate earlier gains before attempting new challenges. However, as Vigilante (1985) noted, for many children with learning disabilities regression is too perilous to use because it violates their rigid, yet fragile, sense of control of earlier developmental gains. When these children do use regression it is with a sense of the futility of engagement, and an almost panicked retreat ensues.

Parents also have fears that regression may signal a perilous spiral backward and a loss of hard-won earlier gains. Their anxiety and overreactions to their child's temporarily more immature behavior tangibly confirm the child's perception of retreat and loss of control, adding to the parent-child tension (Vigilante, 1985). The presumption of helplessness, and the lack of ability to cope communicated by regression, can lead to a regular pattern of learned helplessness. This tendency may be exacerbated by the irregular, and often slower, movement of the child through developmental stages, requiring parental intervention long after other children are functioning independently. The intensity of the parental involvement in the successes and failures of a child with learning disabilities can lead to enmeshed family relationships. In fact, regression has been identified as a familiar maladaptive coping strategy in families in which there already is an enmeshed parent-child relationship (Spacone & Hansen, 1984).

For families with a child with learning disabilities, monitoring the balance of parental support, without encouraging regression and learned helplessness, remains a challenge well into the child's adulthood. Subtle reminders of dependency reoccur at critical transition points—such as making the transition to first grade, moving into junior high school, negotiating a job, applying for college, or selecting a first apartment. Shifting relationships, unfamiliar expectations, or increasingly serious consequences of failure bring out hidden lodes of anxiety when the child or young adult feels unequipped to cope with a new level of institutional and societal complexity.

Somatization. Many of the coping mechanisms children with learning disabilities rely on relate to their difficulties in negotiating the academic and social demands of the school environment. Psychosomatic illnesses—the familiar Monday morning headache or stomach pains—may be real. Particularly for children with undiagnosed learning disabilities, the continuing humiliation that is encountered in school and the lack of teacher and parent understanding can precipitate stress, leading to diverse physical complaints. For some children, peer rejection and social ostracism can be more devastating than academic failure. Extended school absence also serves to lessen or sever the investment in school as other, less-threatening, home-based activities take up what had been the school day. It becomes increasingly difficult to get children using this coping strategy back into school. In such situations there must be a careful look at the child's social and educational needs, as well as at the school environment. Individual evaluation or intervention with teachers through changes in teaching style and classroom programming may be tried. Special efforts to help the child make and keep friends may be necessary. If these strategies are not successful, a change of school may be in order. However, even when the school experience is a poor one by adult standards, and a child appears to suffer daily humiliation, introducing school change during the school year may bring unexpected reactions. For example, one second grader, told that he would have to leave a beloved school in the middle of the year and move to a school that would be more socially and academically comfortable for him, developed pneumonia in the planned 2-week break between schools, extending the break to 7 weeks. This was a youngster who previously was never sick and hated to miss school, even though he was always in trouble and had difficulty with virtually every classroom activity. The mourning process that took place during his 7-week break was critical to his adjustment to the new school. The bout with pneumonia allowed the stages of mourning to take place under the protection of an identifiable illness in a nurturing atmosphere—home. The child experienced bewilderment, denial, and anger. Eventually, some level of acceptance was reached as he eventually began to ask questions about the new school. His curiosity demonstrated a readiness to engage in the new school experience.

Clowning. Other children take an aggressive approach, seeking to master stressful situations through clowning and distracting behavior (Silver, 1974). This strategy serves a variety of functions, including an attempt to control elements of the anxiety-provoking situation. Clowning draws attention away from poor academic functioning and substitutes some element of a personal choice not to learn, which does not betray the fear of failure. Initially, classmates are impressed with their peer's willingness to flout authority and to clown. However, these benefits soon are lost as classmates realize that the whole class suffers and the teacher's interactions deteriorate (Burka, 1983). In situations like this, the child's behavior, rather than the underlying learning or social problems, may become the focus of intervention. For example, in a classroom of latency-age boys with learning disabilities observed by the author, Jim (known as the class clown) spent considerable energy making fun of the attempts of others to play a rather complicated game. He could not be induced to join and only ceased his antics when another child finally dissolved in tears and the game stopped. The teacher reprimanded Jim for goading his classmate, but made no attempt to focus on the repertoire of skills necessary to participate in the game, or to examine the pattern of Jim's disruptive behavior. Thus, even when learning disabilities are recognized, there must be attention to social, as well as academic, arenas in which the children may need targeted assistance.

A child's choice of the defense of clowning and mocking sometimes is supported by a family structure in which there are parental disagreements over the importance of educational achievement, or by one parent's endorsement of the clowning behavior of the child (Spacone & Hansen, 1984). In one family, the parents of the child with learning disabilities consistently made fun of the school personnel and the school rules. By condoning disrespect for the school's rules and procedures and belittling the authority of the staff, the parents appeared to support their son's inappropriate behavior. Although the parents curbed their behavior in front of the school staff, their son did not have the judgment necessary to differentiate between appropriate home and school behavior. He incorporated his parents' attitudes into his clowning at school, with disastrous effects. The whole family was seen as disruptive, and the faculty responded with minimal attempts to deal with the child's special needs.

Defenses: Personal Style and Self-concept

Learning disabilities are a "life space" issue, because they can create problems in every facet of a child's life (Silver, 1979a). Learning disabilities also can be viewed as "an organizer of development" (Cohen, 1985). Cohen painted a broad picture of a child's unfolding personality in which "the ongoing effect of the disability itself and the meanings attributed to it is a biopsychosocial process that organizes experience by being a determinant of strengths, interests, weaknesses and the development of adaptive strategies" (p. 187). Cohen suggested that the kinds of compensatory strategies that a learning-disabled child may adopt (such as refining social, athletic, artistic, or nonverbal skills that are outside the areas of weakness or working slowly) become generalized coping strategies closely inter-related with psychological defenses, making up the pattern of personality or identity of the maturing child.

Children with learning disabilities perceive many internal and external threats to their fragile self-control. Fear of internal or external chaos leads to the desire for structure and predictability. Frequently, these children exert their own form of control by relying fairly exclusively on one or two coping strategies. As these strategies become characteristic and are ritually used to respond to unknown or risky situations, they become interwoven with the character or personality of the individual, pervading many facets of behavior (Cohen, 1985; Rosenberger, 1988). Regression, somatization, and clowning often are coping strategies that serve the overall goal of avoidance. While these children are working overtime in self-protective maneuvering, they are missing critical maturational challenges.

Not all children with learning disabilities respond to challenges by using maladaptive patterns of defenses. Cohen (1985) offered the illustration of a child who was poor at reading but developed the determination to master the problem and become an excellent reader. Numerous examples of this focused attention on overcoming weaknesses occur in the sports world. Reinterpreting problems as challenges to be mastered, when realistically possible, permits the child with learning disabilities the ultimate victory, a true sense of competence.

What variables help children to choose this path? What roles can parents, mental health professionals, and teachers play? These become tantalizing and important questions. Individual constitution, tolerance for frustration, and existing areas of cognitive strength undoubtedly play major roles. However, external factors also are key. There must be flexible teachers and supportive and resilient parents who provide interpretive feedback in the areas of the child's vulnerability and find outlets for the pursuit of strengths. As Rosenberger (1988) noted, the relationship between strengths and weaknesses must be remembered. Creative efforts must be made to strengthen weaknesses, and to support existing strengths, in a way that maximizes congruence of the different bases for self-esteem and promotes perceptions of a cohesive self. If this is achieved, a child has both internal and external supports to draw on when undertaking new challenges.

From this perspective, social work intervention with children with learning disabilities takes on an added urgency. All children respond to difficulties with adaptive and other, less adaptive defense mechanisms. However, children with learning disabilities are likely to become more set in their defensive behaviors at a younger age. More tasks are more difficult at earlier ages, when discouragement and failure are more piercing to the self-concept. Learning-disabled children's slower maturational pace puts them out of synchronization with traditional expectations for their age group, reinforcing their negative images of themselves. Parental and school-based pressures may exacerbate the already existing tension around mastery of developmental challenges.

Children with learning disabilities have the potential to be creative in their responses to new learning if they are supported and not ridiculed for their slower and often unusual approaches to new experiences (Dane, 1986). Building in benchmarks of tangible successes and recognition for effort, as well as accomplishment, responds to the child's need for confirmation of self and his or her investment. Social work intervention must attend to the ways that children compensate for their deficits and to the ways that others, particularly parents and teachers, interpret supportive intervention. Keeping constant a view of the whole child, important adults must develop an understanding of what each child requires at different life stages. The breadth of choice of compensatory strategies and coping mechanisms that a child with learning disabilities has readily available contributes to the potential for positive adaptive responses to challenge and opportunity for new learning.

FOUR GOALS OF INTERVENTION

All children are entitled to the optimal environment in which to engage in appropriate developmental tasks. Although the specific intervention strategies will vary, depending upon the age and stage of development of the child, there are a number of constant features and objectives for intervention that apply throughout childhood and adolescence. The rigidity with which children with learning disabilities cling to nonadaptive defenses calls for a goal of defusing risk situations, to allow for testing of new coping skills and strategies. A realistic assessment of strengths and weaknesses, and helping the child to articulate these, is an important first step toward identification of self-advocacy skills as a more positive way of coping with threats. Clarification and validation of experience begin a process of helping children see themselves as actors—not merely as "acted upon"—in situations.

Recent work in self-psychology stresses the relational component of intrapsychic development, particularly in the development of self-cohesion and self-esteem. The mirroring of the child's experiences offered by parents or other adults provides an interpretation of the child's experience in ways that must validate the child's growing sense of self. For the child to develop the internal resiliency to maintain a positive self-image in the face of numerous defeats, the adults in the child's life must remain hypervigilant to the child's own view of the events that happen to him or her (Rosenberger, 1988). Children cannot be expected to provide this self-validating interpretation on their own. The sooner they are helped to develop strategies to appropriately interpret their experiences, the sooner they will develop a vocabulary to request what they need to be successful in stressful situations.

Social workers must attend to the dynamics of the primary adult relationships of children with learning disabilities. Negative experiences must be reframed and interpreted to provide steps for new learning. The powerful adults in the child's world—parents, teachers, relatives, and special friends—must be helped to recognize the child's efforts to pursue small successes and achievements. Risk-taking and accepting challenges must be encouraged. There must be adult acceptance of a readiness to find ways to fill gaps in ego functioning when necessary. Vigilante (1985) offered some specific ways that an understanding of the deficits in ego functioning and awareness of the potential use of less adaptive defenses can permit strategic support by caring adults:

> Intervention at this level must continually demonstrate for the child the processes of critical judgement, of decision-making, of problem-solving, of managing relationships, of managing a range of feelings, and of coping with authority. For example, it is necessary to interpret the reasoning and logic behind rules. Cause and effect need to be linked (spelled out) for the child. Addressing deficits in specific functioning accelerates perception and links problem to solution. These interventions assist in accelerating the rate of reduction of maturational lag. In a way, the parent becomes the child's ego, while demonstrating good ego functioning. Usually there is little obvious or immediate comprehension. But at some unexpected future time, the child will understand a new situation in a new way, demonstrating integration of the concept. The growth at this point is frequently quite dramatic. For example, a child who could not associate studying, as a cause, with good academic performance, as a result, after continued and repetitive experiences

in which his attention was called to many cause and effect phenomena by parents, teachers, and tutors, suddenly linked the cause-effect phenomena. (p. 177)

Motivation and Expectations

Children with learning disabilities must believe that change is possible, and that they can achieve change through their own practice and efforts, not just through luck. Self-concept and beliefs about abilities play critical roles in the motivation to achieve. Motivation does not come solely from within, but is affected by expectations in the external environment. Cultural influences, individual family patterns of belief about the ability to influence the environment, school attitudes, and class and social stereotyping all may play a role in the individual child's level of motivation. Intervention also must focus on understanding what the child with learning disabilities believes about the causes of success. If the child believes that luck is the critical determinant, he or she needs the opportunity to engage in some concrete activities that can demonstrate otherwise. He or she needs to test out the role of skill and practice in changing performance and determining outcomes (Cohen, 1986). Whether a game, a learning exercise, a group project, or a home task is used, there must be goals that do not require too much delay or effort (Levine & Zallen, 1984). Above all, there must be opportunities to challenge established patterns of behavior and lowered expectations. The negative feedback that many children with learning disabilities receive daily must be countered with numerous structured experiences that provide another reality.

Social workers play key roles in interpreting the intrapsychic impacts of failure on children to the adults who work with them in different settings. Parents also may need this assistance, and may, in turn, become the interpreters to teachers and others. Appropriate responses for teachers may include separating the skills necessary for writing a story—such as correcting only the grammar or spelling, but not both at the same time, or minimizing the number of error marks on a child's homework. In the same way, social correction, or corrective action at home, may be limited to one aspect of the task. For example, one parent was observed at a party repeatedly curbing her child's tendency to interrupt others' conversations, and consciously refraining from reminding him to say "thank you," despite the disapproval of other guests at the child's "lapse" of manners.

The multiple difficulties, the inconsistent behavior patterns, and the immense effort necessary to learn even basic skills are confusing to children and the adults who work with them. Rosenberger (1988) suggested that the experience of being learning disabled must be looked at from the child's point of view. However, it is critical that the chaotic picture that these children present not be reflected back to them by parents or others. The mother who in fury says to her daughter, "I give up, I don't know what to do with you, you're a mess!" is adding to the child's own fears of being out of control and indicating that the rest of the world will be of no help. This kind of negative feedback is hurtful to any child, but it is particularly devastating to a child with learning disabilities who already may believe that all is lost.

Competence

The development of the feelings of being personally competent comes in response to the successful accomplishment of age-appropriate emotional, social, and academic tasks. Children with learning disabilities may have experienced failure in any one or more of these areas, contributing to their feelings of low self-esteem. Here, social work intervention should focus on the development of strategies to solve problems in a more flexible way, so that the rigid use of maladaptive coping strategies does not impede the child's emotional growth. Strategies of analyzing tasks and actions, and of considering a variety of solutions, can be used as effectively in discussion as they are in completing school work.

Fears of being incompetent or humiliated, which fill all children's fantasies, all too often are realized by the child with learning disabilities. Steinberg (1986) suggested that, in individual work with these children, it is important to help them identify the specific conditions under which they function most poorly and become anxious. For example, some children are particularly upset by becoming overly tired, overstimulated, or hungry, or by time pressures or idiosyncratic conflicts. Children need help in anticipating their bouts with panic-producing anxiety and assistance in developing skills to bypass the situations that immobilize them. This awareness and the ability to articulate their needs can lead to changes in the environment in which they work and play.

Self-advocacy

Children with learning disabilities feel powerless much of the time. Decisions are made for them. Other people explain what their problems are. Protected environments are created for them in special classrooms. Often, they do not really understand the nature of their problems, nor do they understand how to negotiate for the help that they need. A consistent goal in work with these children must be to introduce them to concepts of advocating for themselves. Learning how to describe their learning disability and the circumstances in which their difficulties may be most evident helps them to gain control and lays the groundwork for a realistic appraisal of their abilities. Self-advocacy can begin at a young age. When a child first says "Uh-oh, there's my problem remembering again—too many things in a row. That's why I am getting mixed up," this is the beginning of self-advocacy. As the cognitive skills of children with learning disabilities grow, it is important that the children have the opportunity to talk about the areas in which they experience difficulty. Giving names to specific areas of dysfunction assists children in separating their having a problem from a sense of being the problem. In other words, children with learning disabilities have to know what their disabilities are and how to describe and name them in ways that others will understand. This enables children to become partners in the learning process and to realize that their point of view is valued.

In a similar fashion, strengths, areas of interest, and positive features of personal style must be identified, so that the ability to present a full picture of themselves, to themselves as well as to others, becomes a possible way to save face and self-esteem in dealing with the inevitable name-calling. As children begin to understand themselves as learners with strengths and vulnerabilities that coexist, this understanding helps them improve their sense of self-worth and permits them to act more effectively as advocates for themselves in different settings. At each age, the arenas for self-advocacy will be different, as will the content of discussion.

ISSUES IN INDIVIDUAL INTERVENTION

Children with school problems in behavioral and academic areas often are referred to social workers or educational specialists. Too often, there is an initial rush to explain a child's problems in either educational or psychological terms, and to move on to single treatment solutions. Unless a full evaluation is done, treatment plans and intervention strategies may focus inappropriately on one or another area of a child's difficulties, neglecting the subtle interplay of neuropsychological and environmental issues that may be operating. Underlying learning problems, and the behavioral manifestations and reactions of these problems, must be dealt with in an integrated fashion through different professional modalities. Educators must coordinate their efforts with social workers, other mental health professionals, and parents to ensure that knowledge about a child's strengths, weaknesses, and style is used to the best advantage (Green, 1989).

Comprehensive biopsychosocial evaluation of children with learning disabilities yields a unique mix of each child's strengths and deficits in perceptual/cognitive, neurological, social, and emotional areas. The psychological impacts of learning disabilities can be related to the internal processing deficits, impaired cognitive maturation, and resulting impacts on ego development, or to encounters with the environment in which failure, ridicule, and humiliation are frequent outcomes, ultimately affecting self-esteem and self-concept. Or, both processes may be involved simultaneously. Maladaptive coping strategies leading to idiosyncratic self-protective solutions may add dysfunctional behavior to already-existing difficulties.

Children with learning disabilities often exhibit behavior that reflects low self-esteem, chronic anxiety, sadness, or depression. Negative interactions with peers and adults and disrupted parent-child relationships make them feel isolated and alone. Confused and frustrated by their inability to accomplish what others seem able to do easily, children with learning disabilities are frustrated and angry much of the time. What Vigilante (1983) called "the daily business of living" (p. 432) is for the child with learning disabilities a series of performance expectations that create innumerable points of friction with others. Although all adults involved with the child on a daily basis must provide both support and controls, early social work intervention provides a separate experience that is not duplicated by the supportive teacher or the empathetic parent.

The environment of the therapeutic encounter constitutes a safe place, removed from the daily stresses and expectations of home and school. Over time, as trust builds, children will risk sharing their fears, fantasies, and disappointments. For example, sometimes when these children talk about their fears of being "retards" or "weirdos" to their parents, they receive conflicting messages. On one level, the parent may empathize with the child's pain. The child experiences another, separate message through the powerful emotional overreaction that the parent may be unable to control, which may escalate rather than calm the child's concern. Discussion of the same issues with the mental health professional proceeds from a different emotional base, with the dual goal of conveying empathy and demystifying the learning disability. When individual therapy is effective, the child with learning disabilities receives self-validation from unqualified acceptance, which can lead him or her to be more open to new experiences and to reflect on past failures. New coping strategies can be tested in a private arena away from parental judgments and emotionality. New understandings can bring greater self-acceptance, which helps with development of a healthier self-concept. As Rosenberger (1988) observed, "In working preventively with children, there is opportunity to identify high risk areas and head off maladaptive defensive processes before they become entwined with the structure of the personality" (p. 277).

The child who has had a positive experience in individual therapy may be able to bank this resource for later use. One 14-year-old youngster, John, recounted memories of therapy he had had as an 8-year-old. "It was a place I could go and make model airplanes, and no one said I had to finish them. No one asked me to hurry up, or said what I was doing was wrong, or made fun of the way I talked. I began to understand my learning disability and why I was angry all the time." This youngster was able to ask his parent 6 years later if he could see a therapist during the summer vacation from school. He explained that he was thinking about things he did not want to share with his friends, teachers, or parents. It became apparent in therapy that John was very much aware of his parents' anxiety about his academic progress and uncontrollable outbursts of temper and was reluctant to fuel their anxiety with his own similar fears. By requesting therapy, he was trying to assume control and assert some independence from his parents, while finding support outside the home—an important age-appropriate step. His parents felt that, without the earlier therapeutic experience, John would not have been able to turn so easily to this resource.

Mental health professionals working with children with learning disabilities may find that the goals and objectives may be clearer than the means to achieve them. As Lippmann and Lippmann (1981) noted, "Even professionals who do have some knowledge of the various learning disabilities frequently report that their learning disabled clients are difficult to understand, seem to be resistant to interpretations, and often are difficult to engage in a productive therapeutic relationship" (p. 273). These comments were supported in responses gained in a national survey of social workers engaged with children in child welfare agencies and family service agencies (Dane, 1984).

Too often, a diagnosed learning disability leads to a subtle perception of a more globally handicapped child and the development of inappropriately lowered therapeutic, as well as academic, goals. Professional judgment and evaluation also may be channeled inappropriately by misperceptions that lead to misdiagnosis of a serious psychological disturbance. For example, serious auditory processing problems can make a child appear uncooperative and unwilling to engage. Seemingly bizarre behavior may result from misunderstood verbal communication. Young children have been misdiagnosed as schizophrenic (Ungerleider, 1986), retarded, or even autistic as a result of their inappropriate reaction or lack of response to auditory communication. Too often, the tendency is to blame the communication failure on the child and relabel the problem, rather than to create the necessary bridges to communication and understanding. Functional deficits indicating the presence of a learning disability may be buried under baffling behavioral characteristics such as short attention span, impulsivity, emotional lability, aggressiveness, passivity, or depression. At the same time, family disruption and instability may be affecting the emotional state of the child.

Clarification of the multiple sources of internal and external pressure on the child is a critical step in the establishment of an effective treatment relationship. This knowledge enables the professional to develop intervention priorities and to select the appropriate strategies to engage these children and evaluate their responses within a realistic framework. The challenge lies with the professional to establish a congenial environment and effective modes of communication, which will provide a basis for evaluating the differential stresses on the learning-disabled child, and to establish goals that meet the needs the child expresses, as well as those of parents and teachers.

Most consistently frustrating to mental health professionals working with children with learning disabilities are auditory perception and expressive language difficulties. Problems with organizational and integrative functions, such as temporal sequencing, memory, and conceptual abilities, further add to the confusion in communication efforts. The traditional reliance upon verbal and integrative skills to bring about mutually effective communication must be reconceptualized in work with children with learning disabilities. The professional may be tempted to mirror the parent's heavy investment in verification of change through changed communication content and patterns, or through tangibly changed behavior, the achievement of new goals, and a more regular maturational process.

Work with children with learning disabilities is slower than with other children, reflecting their slower and more irregular pace (Silver, 1979a). Gains may not be reflected immediately in changed behavior (Vigilante, 1985). Societal and institutional demands may outstrip newly acquired capabilities, seeming to negate actual and confirmed progress. The parent's, child's, or the mental health professional's discouragement must not be allowed to penetrate the therapeutic environment. Changes will come. But as Vigilante (1985) observed, there will be long periods in which nothing seems to be happening, and then with one final concrete example of an important concept, suddenly the links will be made and there will be a leap to a new level of maturity. The step will not come without setbacks, and possible regression, but it will have been taken. The inherent desire of children with learning disabilities to gain control of their situation and develop creative solutions to the challenges of maturational tasks creates the challenge for those professionals working with them.

Certain characteristics of specific learning disabilities may need to be addressed in the therapeutic situation. Children with auditory perception deficits will not be able to follow a discussion process very easily. They will lose track of what is being said by the therapist. Divergent thoughts may drift through their minds, particularly when they are highly anxious. They may interrupt with seemingly irrelevant topics, or daydream. These children also may have difficulty screening out irrelevant background noises, and will ask for sentences or phrases to be repeated. Further difficulties may be experienced with children who have auditory discrimination problems and who thus cannot distinguish between two similar-sounding words and may misinterpret what is being said to them. Meanings of sentences become scrambled, and the children are baffled and confused, feeling failure again.

Diverse strategies have been suggested to facilitate two-way communication under these circumstances. Lippmann and Lippmann (1981) suggested a calm, quiet environment, and, for children who tend to become distracted visually, a limited number of visual stimuli, such as toys or pictures. They also noted that some children with auditory perceptual problems are able to pay attention more effectively if they have a toy to play with or a picture to look at. This alternative focus appears to drain excess tension and energy and allow for better communication. If there is some question of whether the child is giving full attention to an important issue, a special verbal alert, or a change in speaking tone, body position, or touch can sometimes help a child to give renewed, focused attention.

Impaired short- or longer-term memory also may get in the way of a smooth process of therapy with children with learning disabilities. When this impairment is combined with temporal or sequencing problems or word-finding difficulties, the social worker may have a hard time understanding the details of the child's experience as the child tries to convey it. Children with these difficulties may have trouble recounting events that were important to them. Misunderstandings or problems with peers may be impossible for a youngster to recapture when he or she cannot convey the sequence of activities, the timing, or the names of the participants. As Lippmann and Lippmann (1981) observed, ". . . the therapist must first understand the problem for what it is, rather than automatically applying a psychological label, such as repression or blocking, when a child cannot remember an event" (p. 275). Cautioning against possible breaches of confidentiality, these authors suggested seeking important details from parents to assist in clarification. Some children will remember and store certain key words in linked pairs, such as mother-father, sister-brother, late-early. When they substitute the wrong word of the pair, they may or may not stop to correct themselves. If they do not, the listener will get a very different picture of the event being described than the one that the child is trying to convey.

Another way that a faulty memory and poor integrative capacities impede the therapeutic process is the inability of some youngsters to retain new understandings, such as cause-and-effect relationships, implications of their actions on others, or new coping strategies to deal with anxiety or impulsivity. Once this problem is recognized, units of learning can be broken down, linked with concrete actions, and repetitively rehearsed. Sessions may be tape recorded for replay between sessions for those children who are unable to use this strategy (R. A. Gardner, 1975). Repeated playbacks may be necessary.

Dealing with abstract concepts may be particularly difficult for some children. Conceptual links that are clear to the mental health professional may remain a mystery to the child with learning disabilities. Lippmann and Lippmann (1981) suggested using short, clear sentences, and very simple analogies, if any. Concrete examples and opportunities to use and reuse new terms and concepts as ways to overcome a difficulty in dealing with higher conceptual cognitive processes will be important. For many children, developing some cognitive fluency in identifying and naming their feelings is especially important. An important step toward self-understanding, the evolving comfort with the recognition of feelings is also a first step toward understanding the feelings of others, often a critical gap for children with learning disabilities. A beginning working vocabulary for feelings builds an interior bridge to the turmoil the child is experiencing.

Children with learning disabilities vary in their abilities to deal with the sophisticated levels of abstraction that accompany definitions of feelings. Use of concrete visual representations (such as puppets) may help to anchor these complex concepts for young children, particularly for those who have verbal or cognitive deficits (Burka, 1983; Bauer & Modarressi, 1976). Words that describe a range of feelings—sad, happy, hurt, mad, jealous, afraid—or characteristics of the self—smart, stupid, successful, failure—are the building blocks for the beginnings of self-advocacy. A heightened awareness of self, feelings, and needs brings the child with learning disabilities closer to being able to present himself or herself to parents, siblings, teachers, and others with greater control. When a child can say, "This is something that is hard for me, I need more time to practice" or "Can I write that down? My memory is not very good," rather than just letting the words go by and nodding as if he or she is processing what is being said, then some achievements in the realm of self-advocacy truly have been made.

Although no child has all the problems in communication that were mentioned above, because of the interdependence of many of these areas deficits in one area often will inhibit functioning in another. Children with problems of social perception and social interaction with peers frequently have some of the difficulties in auditory processing described here, and display behavior in individual sessions that mirrors their actions in social groups. For some children, visual-perceptual deficits and cognitive problems combine to make them hypersensitive to any and all group encounters. Their misinterpretations of tone of voice, facial expressions, or body movements tend to alienate others. For example, they may react to a smile as though it were a grimace, or to being nudged by others as to a push. Sometimes these children seek out adults or younger children because they know both of these groups will be more tolerant of divergent behavior. The competitiveness and lack of toleration of difference by the peer group makes this the most highly charged setting for these youngsters. Although adult approval is important to these children, it is peer rejection that is the most devastating experience and often leads to further withdrawal, isolation, and depression as these children grow older (Osman, 1982). Opportunities for these children to work individually with a mental health professional allow a focus on the development of social skills in a protected arena and some exploration of feelings associated with the social problems they have been encountering, totally removed from the pressures of parents, teachers, and classmates. Through observation, creative use of role play, mutual story telling, videotapes, and game playing, the child gains new understanding and practices more effective patterns of interaction. Ultimately, the goal may be to join a structured group services program.

Group Intervention

For some children with learning disabilities, group services offer important experiences for which they would never volunteer. For others, the group experience is seen as more supportive than individual therapy. As Gitterman (1979) noted, "In individual service, children and parents tend to feel singled out, as if their problems are unique, unusual, and perhaps serious. Group services, by their very nature, tend to generalize problems and lessen the anxiety of feeling one is alone with one's problems" (p. 220). The development of group programs for children with learning disabilities requires that social workers be familiar with the ways that learning disabilities affect children at different ages, and with the concomitant social and emotional maturational issues. The development of the ego, the use of defenses, and their impact on a child's ability to engage in appropriate social interactions with peers are important factors to consider in evaluating the readiness of a child to participate in a structured group experience.

Most children with learning disabilities have some difficulty or discomfort in their interactions with peers in group settings. The classroom and the sports field are identified most frequently as particularly devastating. Participation in structured, collective activities tends to highlight problematic areas of functioning and promote negative comparisons for the already vulnerable child. However, any place in which children congregate informally in groups, such as the lunchroom or playground, may prove equally distressing. If children do not understand verbal instruction quickly, cannot follow directions, play games, or understand jokes, or if they get confused or distracted by peripheral noises or are clumsy or awkward, they will shun group activities to protect themselves from almost certain ridicule and humiliation. Through their self-protective avoidance of group activities, these children lose the opportunity to interact with peers, model appropriate behavior, and learn from the feedback of peers. On the other hand, the pace of learning, level of skill, style of interaction, and ability to gain acceptance through adoption of behaviors and codes that dominate group life may be compromised by their perceptual and learning deficits. Loosely formed play groups, or the more traditionally structured Little League, Girl Scouts, or 4-H classes may not be viable entry points for children with learning disabilities unless specific adaptations are made to program activities and specific attention is given to the social process within the group. Vigilante (1985) noted that

> Social group work, as an intervention modality, based on ego psychology, can enhance the social experiences of children with learning disabilities. Group work goals for the individual as part of group, and for the group as an entity, are ideally suited for these children since their needs straddle two areas: their own development and their special dependence on group experiences for that development. (p. 178)

The choice of the appropriate group setting for a child with learning disabilities must be based on an analysis of age, social, and emotional needs; social skills; interests; and abilities. For example, for some children with motor ability difficulties, new opportunities to interact with peers in a play setting where skills of helping, sharing, and cooperating are stressed over competition and comparison may promote feelings of acceptance and self-esteem. For other children with impulsivity or perceptual and spatial deficits, feedback should be focused on making friends and the impact of certain behaviors, such as overreactions to situations, taking turns, talking too loudly, standing too close, interrupting, interpreting facial expressions, and body language. Greenblatt (1988) found that "Participation in a group can provide children with a major source of feedback about behaviors that are annoying or pleasing to others. . . . Peers provide reinforcement by helping others, members practice strategies for helping themselves, thus giving them a sense of competence" (p. 7).

Other aspects of group activities involve the chance to share frustrations and feelings. All children with learning disabilities can benefit from the opportunity to talk about their frustration with and confusion about their learning disability, as it affects life at home, at school, and with classmates. Opportunities to identify children's strengths, interests, and things that make them feel good about themselves must be part of this discussion. For these children, opportunities to be praised by peers are all too infrequent, and may never occur outside the protection of a structured group.

Homogeneous Groups

Therapy groups for children with learning disabilities may take many forms and serve a variety of purposes. Groups may be homogeneous, with an overall diagnosis of learning disability, despite members' different specific deficits. One group leader described the target population for the development of a new homogeneous group as youngsters "whose learning problems are primarily due to neurophysiologic factors, not secondary to emotional problems . . . hyperactivity, attention deficit disorder, dysgraphia, speech and language problems (receptive, integrative, and expressive), visual-motor and visual-perceptual deficits as well as auditory-perceptual deficits as well as auditory perceptual problems" (Greenblatt, 1984, p. 5). In this "homogeneous" population, there must be careful attention to the levels of functioning, as well as to other interactive dynamics. Composition has been found to be a critical variable in the effectiveness of social group work services. Groups consisting of children with learning disabilities are no exception. Gitterman (1979) cited the following selection criteria:

- children experiencing difficulties in similar areas, such as school work and peer relations
- exclusion of children who were seen as too hyperactive or distractible
- selection of children not in conflict with each other outside the group
- limited total membership of four to six children, spanning no more than two grades
- individual interviews with potential group members to screen, to introduce the idea of participating in the group, and to form the basis for a relationship with the group leader.

For elementary-school–age children with learning disabilities, the benefits of the establishment of a homogeneous group are significant. These children frequently have not experienced school group life as "safe." Their classmates quickly may have identified them as different, their teachers may have shown their frustration and disappointment, and ostracism on the playground may have added to their sense of isolation. The opportunity to be with other children who are experiencing the same difficulties and to hear their frustrations and embarrassments makes them realize that they are not unique, and they feel less alone. After they have achieved a degree of comfort, they may even voice fears of being retarded or crazy. They begin to develop a new vocabulary to explain how they are feeling and what they see as their problems. New options for dealing with difficult situations at home and at school may emerge. A process of recognition of self-value, and control of situations previously out of their control, may lead to the beginning steps toward regular friendships. This process is less likely to happen in a heterogeneous group in which the child with learning disabilities is one, or one of a few, children with school and social problems.

111

The planning, design, and implementation of structured group experiences for children is familiar to social workers, particularly to social group workers, whose training is focused on meeting the developmental needs of children through group programming (Roberts & Northen, 1976). Groups for children with learning disabilities, from early elementary age through adolescence, have been found to be most successful when there is a specific program structure related to the developmental needs of the children composing the group. Groups that attempt to achieve therapeutic goals solely through talk and discussion tend to escalate anxiety and discomfort in ways that younger children find very difficult to handle. Often, these children are less adept at putting their thoughts into words, and have difficulty when there are direct expectations of performance in this area. They are highly anxious about the way they present themselves to peers. Several social group workers have discussed "program" as an essential part of the structure of groups for these children (Gitterman, 1979; Greenblatt, 1988; Guerney, 1983). Small (1986) described the uses of program:

> Program is a tool that can be used in groups to facilitate interaction between the members, provide opportunities for gratification through mastery, and thereby increase self-esteem, foster sublimation of aggression, and provide opportunities for mutual aid. Program, or the use of activities, can be effective in the reduction of anxiety, particularly with nonverbal group members, and enables the members to share a common experience. This reduces the feelings of isolation. (p. 167)

Based on that definition, it should be evident that program is essential for children with learning disabilities, to ground free-floating chronic anxiety. However, attention must be given to the selection of program activities, so that they do not escalate anxiety and tension. Program activities that require working together allow children who have often experienced themselves as helpless to be in a position to help others. The mutual trust that develops has implications for a sense of mastery and improved self-image.

Greenblatt (1984) described experiences with two groups, one of four children between the ages of 6 and 8, and the other of six children between the ages of 9 and 11. With the younger group, she described the extensive use of animal and jungle play and its value in the release of energy and aggression. The introduction of hand puppets in creative play allowed the children to explore their feelings about home and family life safely, reversing roles and trying out alternative responses to situations. Stories read aloud in which children talk about the characters and their feelings also allowed the children to enter safely into the realm of feelings without making themselves overly vulnerable. Snack time and clean-up became opportunities to focus on cooperation with others, sharing responsibility, and planning. Greenblatt (1984) noted that an episode of spilled juice can become an opening for a discussion about feeling embarrassed at being clumsy by a child with spatial and motor problems.

In contrast, Greenblatt (1984) found that the group process of the older group (9- to 11-year-olds) focused more quickly on discussion of home and school pressures, of feeling different, and of being teased at school. Projects undertaken by the older group also required specific leadership intervention. The children tended to choose large, complicated projects, in this case the development and videotaping of a puppet show. As is typical with children with learning disabilities, they were frustrated quickly by the time it took to do the planning and by several false starts, and were ready to abandon the idea by the third session. In situations like this, the group leader must provide an example of coping strategies and ego strength necessary to continue in the face of frustration and setbacks. Above all, these children need the message that they can accomplish what they have set out to do, and they must see the tangible evidence. As mentioned earlier in this section, children with learning disabilities do not always equate effort and perseverance with success. They need examples in which effort and hard work do pay off.

Greenblatt (1988) observed in social groups a tendency for the group members to mirror the way they were treated by their classmates within the group itself. They are quick to find a scapegoat and engage in ridicule, focusing on the very areas in which they themselves are most vulnerable. Thus, the group becomes a microcosm of the outside environment, immediately available for discussion, reflection, and learning. Skillful leadership is necessary to ensure that the group environment remains a safe one, and that the atmosphere becomes one of tolerance, acceptance of differences, and support. The mutual aid function of the group must be encouraged through leadership and example.

Structured group experiences that combine program and therapeutic interventions serve overlapping purposes with individual intervention. A group approach offers opportunities for observation and intervention specifically focused on the dynamics of interaction with peers. As social interactions occur, discussion of alternative solutions can capitalize on the immediacy of the experience.

Heterogeneous Groups

Heterogeneous groups include children with more divergent kinds of problems, or with no identified problems at all. Issues regarding composition and the goals of the group still are important to consider when introducing children with learning disabilities into heterogeneous groups. Although the goals of each type of group may vary, there are common objectives for children with learning disabilities that hold for all groups. The provision of a safe and supportive environment offers these children new opportunities to interact with peers and develop friendships, enhance communication skills, expand general coping skills, and, above all, experience themselves as competent.

For example, some children with learning disabilities may be in special classes throughout the school day but still participate in regular after-school programs and activity groups. When this combination appears to be an option, professionals and parents must make every effort to ensure that it is a truly viable one. The right choices must be made in terms of group composition, activity, focus, and style of leadership. Some children with learning disabilities will be able to function very effectively in one heterogeneous group but have a devastating experience in another. For the child who can function effectively in these settings, being in a "regular" group can be a critical indicator to the child that he or she is essentially "okay." For other children, when the wrong group selection is made, or the group leader cannot successfully adapt the group experience to encompass the child, the discomfort experienced and the decision to leave the group become a negative reinforcement of continued failure. If there is any chance that the opportunities will not emerge, then the group leader should consider not including children with learning disabilities. Some variables that have been found to promote inclusion of children with learning disabilities are small size of the group (to allow the leader to give individualized attention); selection of collaborative group projects of a noncompetitive nature, or individual projects in which different levels of success are recognized; encouragement of mutual assistance among the group members; and a flexible, warm leadership style.

The importance of belonging to a group and being accepted by peers cannot be overestimated. Throughout childhood, groups form naturally, and their essence frequently is their exclusivity. The experience of belonging diminishes the sense of isolation. Acceptance validates self-worth. Learning is reinforced through peer and leader modeling and approval. For the child with learning disabilities, inclusion in a group does not happen by chance. Children with learning disabilities are left out almost uniformly (Osman, 1982). The inclusion in group activities must be orchestrated. The critical learning that can come only through group social experience during the early years provides a basis for the emotional and social adjustment of the adolescent and, eventually, the social comfort of the adult.

More professional involvement is needed to ensure that children with learning disabilities have opportunities to develop social skills and ego strengths and to repair self-esteem through engaging successfully in interactions with their peers. As professionals skilled in both group and individual modalities, social workers can play unique bridging roles to promote the integration of learning from the group therapeutic setting to the regular school- and home-based groups with which the child is engaged. By sharing the knowledge gained about strengths and new skills, as well as special vulnerabilities, with classroom teachers, parents, and other professionals working with these children, the social worker can help these adults to modify and adapt their expectations, and even change their group structure to make it more supportive.

Social workers are involved as catalysts, designers, organizers, supervisors, and leaders of programs for children with learning disabilities. Serving in administrative, supervisory, and direct service capacities, social workers have both an understanding of the diverse needs of children with learning disabilities and the skills to implement needed programs. The best group opportunities for children with learning disabilities have developed through collaborative work with parents, teachers, psychologists, recreation workers, physical education instructors, and others working together. Social workers engaged with children with learning disabilities must attempt to identify the components of the optimal group experience, and then set about determining its availability.

Availability and access are often critical issues. Professionals and parents must work together to create resources that often do not exist. In the past, families of children with learning disabilities have had to take the leadership role in developing group experiences for their children with special needs, and persuade advocacy organizations, churches and synagogues, YMCAs and YWCAs, 4-H centers, schools, mental health agencies, and independent professionals to sponsor special programs. No matter how groups are formed to accommodate the needs of these children during specific developmental stages, the life span of any particular group is limited. Unless there is an ongoing organizational commitment to the provision of group services, parents and professionals must begin their efforts anew each time a need arises.

Environmental Context

From the time they wake up until they fall asleep, children with learning disabilities confront the expectations of others. Too often, they fail to meet the challenges. Dressing, getting ready for school, remembering lunch money, meeting peers on the bus or at the school door, being called on in class, lining up, recess, lunch, afternoon play, homework, dinner, and bed—each of these activities involves multiple, complex expectations, timetables, and consequences for nonconformity. Conceptualizing learning disabilities as a life space problem (Silver, 1979a) ensures that a broad perspective that encompasses interactions in the home, at school, on the playground, and in the community will identify appropriate targets for change.

Social workers maintaining a biopsychosocial perspective toward intervention must consider all facets of the environment as potential targets for intervention and change. The establishment of ongoing communication and links with social agencies, recreational facilities, religious and civic organizations, and summer camps to support flexible group programming to include children with learning disabilities is imperative. Particular emphasis should be placed on linking school with community after-school resources and on developing interorganizational relationships to facilitate a smooth transition for children from the demands of the school day to an entirely different social group experience (Dane &- Vigilante, 1984).

Social workers must advocate and mediate with institutional bureaucracies to ensure that planning for children with special needs is included routinely. Parents must be supported and encouraged to develop consistent intervention strategies to gain access to and monitor their children's participation in community program activities. If the local Boy Scout troop is not aware that special routines for gaining badges are approved for children with learning disabilities, then parents or social workers must educate the local leaders. Multiple avenues outside school and home must be sought. The influences, expectations, and norms of family culture and neighborhood are important in determining the direction for the child's activities. The fit between child, family, culture, group experience, and school experience will determine the extent to which the environment is supportive of the child's social and emotional needs. Exploration of new options that may be outside the family vision may be necessary to ensure that the child with learning disabilities gets the best chance for a healthy maturational process.

Social workers have the potential to play broad preventive and interpretive roles, as well as therapeutic and remediative ones. They intercede directly with children, individually and in groups, and indirectly, through systems and institutions. Social workers promote the exploration of latent talents and skills and offer opportunities to work on vulnerable areas. They are in a position to prevent maladaptive and restrictive defenses from becoming entrenched and to promote healthier adaptations to new risks and challenges.

In an environment that supports learning, exploration, and risk-taking, children learn who they are and how to accept their unique mixture of talents and deficits. Imagination and creativity stem from differing perceptions of the world and from individually selected modes of expression. The artist may be unable to explain her work. The dancer may not be able to do basic arithmetic. The chef may be unsure of his spelling. The photographer may not be comfortable putting pen to paper. The recluse may provide us with a poetic vision that encompasses a far-reaching reality. Highly personal and selective vision becomes a gift to the varied human experience of the world.

REFERENCES

Bauer, R., & Modarressi, T. (1976). Ego disturbance model of minimal brain dysfunction: Experiential implications. *Journal of Clinical Child Psychology, 5,* 32–34.

Burka, A. (1983). Emotional reality of a learning disability. *Annals of Dyslexia, 33,* 281–301.

Cohen, J. (1984, March 23). *Learning disabilities and childhood: Psychological and developmental implications.* Paper presented at the Orton Dyslexia Society Meeting, New York.

Cohen, J. (1985). Learning disabilities and adolescence: Developmental considerations. In S. C. Feinstein (Ed.), *Adolescent psychiatry: Developmental and clinical studies* (Vol. 12, pp. 177–196). Chicago, IL: University of Chicago Press.

Cohen, J. (1986). Learning disabilities and psychological development in childhood and adolescence. *Annals of Dyslexia, 36,* 287–300.

Dane, E. (1984). [The child welfare and family service systems: A national survey of social work involvement with learning disabled children]. Unpublished raw data.

Dane, E. (1986). About creativity. *Their world* (pp. 17–18). New York: Foundation for Children with Learning Disabilities.

Dane, E., & Vigilante, F. W. (1984, November). *Pairing neighborhood schools and settlement houses to design comprehensive group work programs for learning disabled children.* Paper presented at the Advancement of Social Work with Groups annual symposium, Chicago, IL.

deHirsch, K., & Jansky, J. (1980). Patterning and organizational deficits in children with language and learning disabilities. *Bulletin of the Orton Society, 30,* 227–239.

Education for All Handicapped Children Act, Pub. L. No. 94–142, § 5, 6, 89 Stat. 773–796 (1975).

Erikson, E. (1963). *Childhood and society.* New York: W. W. Norton.

Gardner, S. (1983, April 3). Suicides by the young on increase. *New York Times,* pp. 1, 8.

Gardner, R. A. (1975). *Psychotherapeutic approaches to the resistant child.* New York: Jason Aronson.

Gitterman, N. P. (1979). Group services for learning disabled children and their parents. *Social Casework, 60,* 217–226.

Green, R. J. (1989). "Learning to learn" and the family system: New perspectives on underachievement and learning disorders. *Journal of Marital and Family Therapy, 15,* 187–203.

Greenblatt, N. (1984, March). *A new role for the community mental health center: Treatment of learning disabled children and their families.* Paper presented at the International Conference of the Association for Learning Disabled Children, New Orleans, LA.

Greenblatt, N. (1988, February). *After school groups: The social worker as collaborator with the educator.* Paper presented at the International Conference of the Association for Children with Learning Disabilities, Las Vegas, NV.

Guerney, L. F. (1983). Play therapy with learning disabled children. In C. E. Schaefer & K. J. O'Connor (Eds.), *Handbook of play therapy* (pp. 419–434). New York: John Wiley & Sons.

Kagan, J. (1984). *The nature of the child.* New York: Basic Books.

Kinsbourne, M. (1973). Diagnosis and treatment: School problems. *Pediatrics, 52,* 697–710.

Kohn, M., & Rosman, B. L. (1974). Social-emotional, cognitive and demographic determinants of poor school achievement: Implications for a strategy of interventions. *Journal of Educational Psychology, 66,* 267–276.

Levine, M. D. (1982). The low severity-high prevalence disabilities of childhood. In L. Barness (Ed.), *Advances in pediatrics* (pp. 529–554). Chicago, IL: Yearbook Publishers.

Levine, M. D. (1987). *Developmental variation and learning disorders.* Cambridge, MA: Educators Publishing Service.

Levine, M. D., & Zallen, B. G. (1984). The learning disorders of adolescence: Organic and non-organic failure to strive. *Pediatric Clinics of North America, 31,* 345–370.

Licht, B. G., & Kistner, J. A. (1986). Motivational problems of learning disabled children: Individual differences and their implications for treatment. In J. K. Torgesen & B. W. L. Wong (Eds.), *Learning disabilities: Some new perspectives* (pp. 225–255). New York: Academic Press.

Lippmann, S. B., & Lippmann, D. B. (1981). Treating children with learning disabilities. *Social Casework, 62,* 273–283.

Osman, B. B. (1982). *No one to play with: The social side of learning disabilities.* New York: Random House.

Palombo, J. (1979). Perceptual deficits and self-esteem in adolescence. *Clinical Social Work Journal, 7,* 34–60.

Palombo, J., & Feigon, J. (1984). Borderline personality development in childhood and its relationships to neurocognitive deficits. *Child and Adolescent Social Work Journal, 1,* 18–33.

Puig-Antich, J., & Rabinovich, H. M. (1983). Child and adolescent psychiatric disorders. In M. D. Levine, W. B. Carey, A. C. Crocker, & R. T. Gross (Eds.), *Developmental behavioral pediatrics* (pp. 865–890). Philadelphia: W. B. Saunders.

Roberts, R., & Northen, H. (Eds.). (1976). *Theories of social work with groups.* New York: Columbia University Press.

Rome, H. D. (1971). The psychiatric aspects of dyslexia. *Bulletin of the Orton Society, 21,* 64–70.

Rosenberger, J. (1988). Self-psychology as a theoretical base for understanding the impact of learning disabilities. *The Journal of Child and Adolescent Social Work, 5,* 269–280.

Rosenthal, H. (1971). Maturational lag as cause for emotional disorders. *Treatment Monographs in Analytic Psychotherapy, 3,* 11–15.

Ross, A. O. (1976). *Psychological aspects of learning disabilities and reading disorders.* New York: McGraw-Hill.

Rothstein, A., Benjamin, L., Crosby, M., & Eisenstadt, K. (1988). *Learning disorders: An integration of neuropsychological and psychoanalytic considerations.* Madison, CT: International Universities Press.

Shapiro, T., & Perry, R. (1976). Latency revisited: The age 7 plus or minus 1. *Psychoanalytic Study of the Child, 31,* 79–105.

Silver, L. B. (1974). Emotional and social problems of children with developmental disabilities. In R. E. Weber (Ed.), *Handbook on learning disabilities* (pp. 97–120). Englewood Cliffs, NJ: Prentice-Hall.

Silver, L. B. (1979a). Children with perceptual and other learning problems. In J. Noshpitz & S. Harris (Eds.), *Basic handbook of child psychiatry* (Vol. 3, pp. 605–614). New York: Basic Books.

Silver, L. B. (1979b). The minimal brain dysfunction syndrome. In J. Noshpitz & S. Harris (Eds.), *Basic handbook of child psychiatry* (Vol. 3, pp. 416–439). New York: Basic Books.

Silverman, R., & Zigmond, N. (1983). Self-concept in learning disabled adolescents. *Journal of Learning Disabilities, 16,* 8–14.

Small, S. (1986). Learning to get along: Learning disabled adolescents. In A. Gitterman & L. Shulman (Eds.), *Mutual aid groups and the life cycle* (pp. 161–176). Itasca, IL: F.E. Peacock.

Spacone, C., & Hansen, J. E. (1984). Therapy with a family with a learning disabled child. In J. Hansen (Ed.), *Family therapy with school related problems* (pp. 46–54). Rockville, MD: Aspen.

Steinberg, Z. (1986). Comments. *Churchill Forum, 8,* 2.

Stevenson, D. T., & Romney, D. M. (1984). Depression in learning disabled children. *Journal of Learning Disabilities, 17,* 579–582.

Ungerleider, D. (1985). *Reading, writing and rage.* Rolling Hills Estates, CA: Jalmar Press.

Ungerleider, D. (1986). Developing a third ear. *The Educational Therapist, 7,* 9–10.

Vigilante, F. W. (1983). Working with families with learning disabled children. *Child Welfare, 62,* 429–436.

Vigilante, F. W. (1985). Reassessing the developmental needs of children with learning disabilities: Programmatic implications. *Child and Adolescent Social Work Journal, 2,* 167–180.

Vigilante, F. W., & Dane, E. (1989). Multiple strategies in response to the identification of learning disabilities. *Churchill Forum, 11,* 5–6.

Weil, A. P. (1978). Maturational variations and genetic dynamic issues. *Journal of the American Psychoanalytic Association, 26,* 461–492.

Chapter 5
Families of Children with Learning Disabilities

There is increasing professional recognition of the complex interplay between organic influences and the modifying effects of the environment in the development of specific learning disabilities. The family plays the most crucial role in determining the child's environment. The families of children with learning disabilities play particularly critical roles in the successful movement of their children through childhood and adolescence. When the expectations and needs of the child interact and conflict with the expectations and the developmental stage of the family, adjustments are needed.

Kagan (1984) noted that "the effects of most experience are not fixed but depend on the child's interpretation. And the interpretation will vary with the child's cognitive maturity, expectations, beliefs and momentary feeling state" (p. 240). This concept has a parallel in the family interpretation of experience. The ways that parents interpret and respond to the needs of their children with cognitive and behavioral problems affect all members of the family. Both child and adult interpretations are embedded in the values and myths of the family as they have been communicated to family members. Variables such as family structure, culture, class, race, and status in society also will affect parental theories of behavior, standards for acceptable progress, and sources of learning and behavior problems.

Professional knowledge is increasing about the ways that families respond to the needs of children with developmental dysfunctions and the interactive effects of these children on their parents, siblings, and the family as a system (Rosenberger, 1990). Families report an increase in stress, a tendency toward social isolation, and a reduction in personal and family autonomy (Slater & Wikler, 1986). Research on variables contributing to family adjustment to stressful events has isolated three critical resource areas: (1) personal resources such as financial assets, education, health, and psychological well-being; (2) the family system's internal resources, such as the flexibility of family roles, shared power, the promotion of personal growth, and the support for individual autonomy; and (3) the existence of, and ability to develop, extended family resources among relatives, friends, and neighbors (McCubbin et al., 1980). Parents of learning-disabled children vary in their abilities to develop and utilize these essential supportive resources to promote effective family functioning. The biopsychosocial perspective of the social worker provides a multifaceted approach to the assessment of predictable stresses and to finding sources of support for families with children with learning disabilities.

Erikson (1959) identified four early developmental stages of childhood, each of which encompasses a set of parental expectations for growth and development. In infancy, the expectations revolve around the emergence of a mutually satisfying relationship between child and parents, particularly between the primary caretaker and the child. This period corresponds to Erikson's first psychosocial stage of trust versus mistrust. During the preschool years, parental expectations begin to relate to the child's ability to be with other children and to his or her ability to begin to conform to some small group limits that would be encountered in day care or preschool activities. This period corresponds to Erikson's second and third stages: autonomy versus doubt and initiative versus guilt. During the elementary school phase, the parental expectations generally are that the child will adjust to school and enjoy the new challenges of planned learning activities, corresponding to Erikson's psychosocial stage of industry versus inferiority. These stages are related to important transitions for the child in relation to the primary caretaker, traditionally the mother; the relationship between the child and different members of the family or the extended family; and the child's increasing interaction with the community. The reactions of parents and siblings to a child who does not develop at the expected pace create a family environment that can range from supportive to destructive.

IMPACT OF DEVELOPMENTAL STAGES ON FAMILY LIFE

Infant Development

The birth of any child brings changes to family life and stress to the parental relationship (Olson et al., 1983). The usual stresses often are exacerbated when a child's developmental pace differs from the culturally expected norm and upsets the regularity of developmental milestones of both child and family (Rhodes, 1977). The possible imbalance between what the child needs for successful development and what the parents can offer can be detrimental to the family as a unit, as well as to all its members as individuals.

An infant depends completely on his or her mother or other primary caregiver. Care must be given in a way that engenders trust in a safe environment and security that wants will be met. According to Erikson's (1959) developmental perspective, the building of basic trust is one of the crucial early tasks. When this is accomplished, the child has a foundation of security that later supports a sense of hope and optimism and the ability to give to others. When trust is lacking, the child will develop with a growing sense of mistrust that his or her needs will be met and will require constant reassurance that may lead to insecurity in personal relationships.

121

Although many children with learning disabilities do not show any developmental differences in their early years, others show evidence of special needs from a very early age (Als, 1985). For example, in some studies children later identified as learning disabled always had been perceived as "different" by their parents, even though the parents might not have been able to articulate why they made a distinction between this child and others (Faerstein, 1986). These parents might have presented the issues in terms of their own perceived inadequacies as parents, such as that they were unable to comfort their child, they needed more experience, or they were too tired after work. Usually, these comments are taken at face value. Unless the child's discomfort appeared extreme, and the family was severely disrupted, many parents assumed their infant's idiosyncrasies represented normal temperament and behavior and did not seek out experts for further consultation. Only in retrospect were early clues identified.

Some infants are finicky and irritable. They may not establish adequate sleeping and feeding patterns, which deHirsch and Jansky (1980) identified as early difficulties in "pattern management." Some infants have an extreme tactile sensitivity that makes them reject being touched or held—the normal method of parental comforting. Other babies may be easily overstimulated because of poor early processing abilities. Still other infants may not be able to recognize a parental voice or smile, possibly indicating early organizational deficits. This unstable perception of the mother may contribute to a lack of "object constancy" (deHirsch & Jansky, 1980). These children present a seeming indifference, even an aversion, to their parents' overtures. The neurologically intact infant slowly learns to organize and control external stimulation by refining perceptual and motor skills. However, some children with inefficient perceptual and motor controls cannot organize their perceptions, remember signs of positive reinforcement, or learn readily from daily experiences.

When a mother cannot comfort her child, feelings of impotence, incompetence, and even anger at the child may interfere with the bonding that takes place between mother and child. The mother may withdraw and become more perfunctory in providing care. The infant's needs to practice and develop skills in social responses, such as cooing or smiling, or perceiving touch as comforting, are not met, and a series of negative or distancing patterns of interaction may evolve, leaving unmet the underlying mutual needs of both parent and child. Thus, although this developmental phase traditionally is characterized as that of the infant's complete dependence on the environment, the infant actually contributes to his or her own environment in very important ways. Children with certain kinds of early developmental delays and dysfunctions may play a critical, although unconscious, role in shaping a less than optimal environment for themselves.

The disturbances that emerge in relationships when the fit is poor between parents and children may be long-lasting. Parents may shift affection toward their other children and not push to overcome the barriers to building a nurturing relationship with the child who does not appear to benefit from, or reciprocate, their overtures. Early secure attachment can be jeopardized. In turn, this may affect the child's later receptivity to trying to please the parent and the ongoing socialization process in which both child and parent are engaged. If the young child continues to be a disappointment and there is not careful evaluation of the situation or support for parents, a negative cycle is established and the strength of the attachment is at continued risk. Research has shown that children with mild disabilities are more vulnerable to abuse (Martin & Beezley, 1974), which may be related to parental difficulties in developing appropriately adapted expectations of behavior (Friedrich & Boriskin, 1976).

For a host of reasons, parents vary in their abilities to meet their distressed child's needs. Many parents have rigid expectations of the way infants should behave and the "right way" to raise their children. Depending on the maturity and flexibility of the parents, and on their ability to create ways to nurture the child who appears to be rejecting, an adequate trusting relationship may be developed despite the difficulties posed by the lack of fully positive feedback. Some parents are able to interpret their infant's negative responses as part of an early language of self-protection, as described in recent research on observation of premature infants. Small body movements—turning the head away, hand gestures indicating pushing away, and denial of eye contact—may signify overstimulation and the infant's need to rest from interaction (Dixon et al., 1981). Although not all premature infants have learning disabilities, a significant number have immature sensory systems or have developmental delays that may present similar problems for them during early infancy. Enhancing parents' ability to interpret these small signs can give parents an increased sense of competence and understanding of their overly sensitive infants and increase the potential for positive bonding, despite initial barriers.

Professional intervention with this age group is hampered by the lack of visibility of the infant-parent relationship. Early professional intervention in the form of counseling, role modeling, and support groups or training films (such as those by Dorner, 1984a, 1984b) also may be useful in assisting mothers who are less verbal to develop appropriate strategies for positive communication with their infants who require a special introduction to the world. The pediatrician, clinic worker, visiting nurse, or social worker must find interventions that are congenial to the parent's style of communication and that support the development of a positive mother-child relationship.

Many mothers of children at risk for developmental problems do not seek help with parenting. Assumptions that parenting skills are automatic and not taught, or the fear that if the mother is found wanting the child will be moved into foster care, interfere with movement of some mothers to get help. Some mothers are young and estranged from formal institutional systems. Others are current or former drug users and may be reluctant to form relationships with social workers or other professionals that might impinge on their life-style. Still other parent-infant or family-infant difficulties may fester until they come to public attention as abuse or neglect identified in the hospital emergency room.

Preschool Development

During the preschool period, children begin to develop some autonomy, self-awareness, control, and verbal skills. By age 2, they develop an awareness of standards for behavior. They are vulnerable to stress and anxiety if they cannot perform at the levels they believe their parents expect (Kagan, 1984). Children of this age have a fear of their own unmanageable impulses, as well as a fear of external forces. They still need the constant support of parental protection and encouragement to test new skills and strengths.

During this period, some parents begin to develop rigid expectations of what their children should and should not do, often based on strong cultural and class influences. Children are increasingly visible outside the home. Social behavior in public places begins to acquire new definition. Neighbors may comment on noisy or unruly behavior. This disapproval may impel parents to be more demanding in their expectations and to engage in more punitive responses, setting the stage for a negative and distanced relationship.

From ages 2 to 4, children have increasing initiative and independence, and aggressive drives to pursue goals begin. Development of a sense of self-control and a sense that they can learn what they need to learn and gain parental approval is necessary for children to move on with enough security to take the risks needed for future learning and growth. If the issues of dependence versus independence are not successfully resolved at some level of comfort, a loss of self-esteem ensues, with consequent inhibition of flexibility and initiative. Children with learning disabilities may be poorly equipped to handle these developmental transitions alone. They may have increasing difficulty with their own burgeoning wants and their desire for autonomy, as well as with parental demands for conformity in such areas as eating, cleanliness, toilet skills, and social behavior. Poor coordination may interfere with more acceptable table manners and cause difficulty in dressing. A limited ability to control anger and aggressive impulses may be aggravated by frustration at not being able to accomplish expected tasks easily. Overactive, distractible, or impulsive behavior may emerge full force, blending with the active exploration of the environment that is characteristic of this age group. Some children may not acquire the cognitive skills needed to begin to perceive their role in the family structure and modify their behavior accordingly. Thus, they may alienate siblings, relatives, and visitors.

Increasingly, parents expect that they will be able to use language to enhance their child's understanding of expected behavior. For example, the warnings "don't touch" or "hot" usually are soon learned. Constant reminders often are necessary for behavior that has less automatically painful consequences. However, children with receptive language, memory, or attentional difficulties may not be able to understand, remember, or attend to the verbal warning. Explanations or even punishments may not help because these children may not be able to understand the cause-and-effect implications of more abstract negative actions. Parents may continue to find these children unrewarding. Thwarted in their attempts at child rearing and teaching, rejected in their efforts to give encouragement, and exhausted by the energy level of children of this age, in their disappointment parents become overly impatient, angry, and rejecting.

Kagan (1984) proposed that parents use five basic approaches to teach and socialize their children: (1) observation, (2) punishment, (3) praise, (4) withdrawal of support signs of value, and (5) acting as a role model. Children with learning difficulties may not be responsive to one or another of these approaches. For example, children with receptive language and auditory problems will not respond well to verbal explanations or admonitions. They may get increasingly angry or frustrated, or just keep doing the undesired behavior. Other children will have trouble extracting learning from parental modeling or observation. Parents sometimes impute willful disobedience to their children's actions when this is not the case. It is important for parents to experiment with a broad range of methods and approaches to find the form that their child is most able to use. Additional time, encouragement, minimization of distractions, and clear rewards for small successes and gains are important. However, it is most important for parents to be able to gain greater understanding of their child's deficits and the difficulties they pose for the child. Parents may need encouragement themselves in their attempts to maintain support for the positive efforts of their child, particularly when there are not always clear indicators of success.

As children with learning disabilities move outside the home to the playground or day care center, parents become increasingly concerned about conforming social behavior. Vulnerability to community judgments about parenting skills is heightened when children enter preschool and kindergarten. Some people fear their children will be too shy, too aggressive, destructive, or disobedient. Some parents may feel that their children's behavior reflects badly on the whole family. Other parents may avoid the family with a child with learning disabilities because the child makes an unpredictable playmate and may be hard to control. Parents of children with learning disabilities who are concerned about the development of social skills of their children must risk overtures to reluctant playmates, offer tempting opportunities like excursions to amusement parks or movies, and intervene more frequently to ensure playmates for their child.

Thus, during the years when social networks are most likely to be built around child care and mutual support, the parents of children with learning disabilities may be excluded. Or, parents may exclude themselves, because they are reluctant to let others see what their children are "really like," or fearful that no one else could handle them. They may even avoid regular baby-sitters owing to their embarrassment. Of all parents, they are the ones who most need relief from child care responsibilities. This situation adds considerable stress to the family, and increases

125

the demands on all family members. Continuing patterns of social isolation are deleterious for all members of the family (Slater & Wikler, 1986). The pattern of social isolation usually begins at the point of the child's formal diagnosis. However, it can begin earlier if a child is particularly difficult to manage and develops a "reputation" in the tight community of the playground or day care center.

Parents' perception of the acceptability and normalcy of their children's development guides the degree of concern and kinds of intervention the parent chooses. Even during the preschool years, parents' values regarding the qualities they want their child to have as an adult guide their actions. For all young children, this may be a difficult scale of parental judgments, but it can be particularly difficult for children with developmental differences. For example, conformity, not showing anger, and being obedient were the values by which one working-class father evaluated his children—qualities that would ensure acceptance in the work world. His children chafed at his constant reminders, but none more so than his learning-disabled, and very active, son. Although still in nursery school, this child was excessively exuberant, curious, messy, and overly talkative. The more the father tried to curb his son's behavior, the angrier and more frustrated both became. Several years later, a learning disability was identified with the major features of auditory problems, information processing, memory difficulties, and impulsivity. It became clear that this was a child who was desperately trying to make sense out of a world he perceived as chaotic. The social worker was able to help the parents redefine their son's activities. The drive and persistence he used to try to satisfy his need to understand were reframed as valuable qualities that could serve him well in adult life. This helped the parents reevaluate the behavior in terms that were appropriate to a 5-year-old. Each parent was helped to look carefully at the situation, establish more appropriate expectations, and set limits on behavior without superimposing adult values.

Parents may have very different expectations, wishes, and goals for their children, which often stem from their cultural and class backgrounds. One of the parents in the case described above was from a working-class background and placed great weight on conformity and controlled behavior. The other parent, from a more middle-class background, stressed curiosity and risk-taking as a foundation for adult success. When there is a child with a learning disability, the characteristics admired or denied by each parent may be read into the behavior of the child. Inappropriate parental overreactions may cloud the actual problem behavior and may not be appropriate to the child's underlying needs for structure, guidance, or encouragement.

In such situations, there is potential for divergent value systems to clash, with the child becoming the focal point for more deep-seated marital differences. Complicating the situation is the recent proposition that men and women tend to have different values. Gilligan (1982) has called attention to the "two voices"— one of independence and autonomy, and the other of empathy, caring, and affective bonds—that exist in varying degrees in each parent (p. 62). Most parents try to balance these qualities in a manner that fits into their culture and class expectations. Women often are expected to carry the major empathetic, nurturing value in their relationship with their children. Men are expected to focus more on independence and autonomy. Thus, in the family described above, the husband was acting in a manner congruent with his expectations of his child's future independent status, and his wife was seeing long years of nurturance, protection, and teaching ahead before her child had to compete and be judged in the adult world. Parental conflict and contradictory, confusing messages to children can result when parents are guided by different sets of values without some satisfactory resolution representing a family ethic. It may be too difficult for children, particularly those with learning disabilities, to integrate divergent messages and accomplish this resolution on their own. There is added tension for parents with children with learning disabilities. With these children, there are more active decisions necessary on an hourly basis than there are with children who have no disabilities. The potential consequences appear to be more momentous, the options starker, and the choices more compromised because of the particular difficulties inherent in the growth of independence and autonomous behavior. Most children with learning disabilities need ongoing intervention, support, monitoring, and advocacy from their parents, for years beyond traditional expectations. Nevertheless, these children have a tremendous need to learn self-advocacy strategies at early ages. On the other hand, the risk of too much failure has the negative consequence of diminishing the child's self-esteem. Behavior too far outside the norm may reduce choices for after-school programs or weekend activities for months. There are a limited number of community resources available for the child who does not conform. If the child is asked to leave the last available program, parents then must turn to the more expensive solution of a sitter, just when their child is most desperately in need of socialization opportunities. These are some of the issues with which parents are faced on a daily basis. These issues become more urgent as children grow older, the stakes get higher, and the outside world becomes less forgiving of behavior that is different.

Elementary School

The elementary-school–age child has major tasks bound up with his or her school life. Conforming to expected performance levels of reading, writing, arithmetic, spelling, and social play, the child is constantly competing with others for attention. Erikson (1959) described the tasks of this period as being learning and industry versus inferiority. Children who cannot attain the expected competencies come under considerable stress. They may seek to deny the importance of the areas in which they fail. "School is boring" is translated easily into "I can't seem to make it in this situation, so I'll opt out." In American society, school is a child's major work and major proving ground. In other cultures in which children are important economic members of the household, children have a variety of opportunities to prove their worth through their daily contributions to the family security (Kagan, 1984). In the United States, failure in school, whether academic or social, even at an early age, is a severe blow to the child's self-image, and by extension, to the family's sense of competency.

Particularly perplexing for families are the behavioral manifestations of delays in the development of the ego functions that cause uneven maturational processes in children. The impact of deficits and delays in ego functioning on the developmental tasks of the child frequently becomes apparent when the child has to negotiate the environment outside the home. The impersonal demands of school, more objective relationships with teachers, unavoidable interactions with peers, and organizational demands of the classroom require an increasing mastery of independent functioning and the assumption of new roles (Pine, 1985). The tremendous increase in stimulation in the school environment brings a corresponding increase in stress to all children. This stress is magnified for children with learning disabilities. Greater physical control over body movement and increased control of impulsive verbal and physical reactions to internal emotions and external events are expected. For children who have not had prior school experience, the competition for adult attention plus the expectations of their performance add to the already heightened anxiety of the elementary-school–age child with learning disabilities.

The academic, social, and behavioral manifestations of learning disabilities require parents to intervene at home, in the school, and on the playground to ensure that their child has a learning environment that facilitates inclusion and acceptance and promotes learning appropriate to the child's capacities. Although children may want desperately to participate, they also want to protect themselves from teasing and possible humiliation. These feelings are heightened by a growing sensitivity to others in their age group.

During this period, defensive coping mechanisms and rigid self-protective defenses are developed. Parents are called to the school to deal with temper tantrums, clowning, or aggressive behavior that may be masking frustration, confusion, and failure. For example, one mother was called to school by her son's first grade teacher because the child had thrown the carrot-peeling knife at the other children, instead of peeling the carrots. The mother expressed a fear that her child's apparent violence was a precursor to juvenile delinquency. The unexpected ways in which the learning-disabled child expresses frustration and helplessness may touch chords of fear and fantasy in parents, causing overreactions that are not helpful to either parent or child. The social worker met with the teacher and the mother. She helped the mother to understand that the child's lack of fine motor coordination and the high visibility of his failed efforts in the group cooking project had led to overwhelming frustration and humiliation and that he was not a future juvenile delinquent. The teacher was helped to see that group projects that exposed this child to the possibility of ridicule by his classmates affected his still fragile internal emotional control system.

128

Most children with learning disabilities sense that they are not measuring up to others' expectations. This feeling tends to increase their frustration level, undermine their self-image, and frequently add an overlay of self-protective behavior. This emotional fragility can impede their maturational progress further. The responsibility for helping the learning-disabled child negotiate the often perilous worlds of school, neighborhood, and home devolves primarily on the family. For both child and parents, the elementary school years are critical entry points of a long, collaborative effort.

During the late elementary school period, children need to feel increasingly responsible for their actions. Academic achievement now looms as a more important goal in preparation for high school. The need to be accepted by friends brings intensive conformity to peer expectations regarding behavior, dress, and interests. Children need to feel that the goals they set for themselves, and those set for them by the community, are attainable. Ideally, parents perform as mediators of the environment, ensuring that opportunities for success are available, providing reassurance and feedback of faith in their children's competence, and monitoring the overload of stress. However, this role becomes increasingly difficult in the pre-adolescent years. Children are no longer as receptive to positive feedback from their parents. Increasingly aware of their differences and history of failures, children sometimes feel betrayed by parental efforts and hopeless about their ability to succeed in arenas that have become more complex and demanding over the years.

For the family with the learning-disabled child, this developmental period is particularly baffling. How much independence should be encouraged and how much dependence should be allowed? How much monitoring of homework is needed? How much feedback and interpretation of behavior is appropriate? How much support should be given to unrealistic dreams? Parents of learning-disabled children must continue to have a much closer involvement with all aspects of their children's lives during this period, despite a child's apparent rejection of parental concern. The vulnerability of these children to poor role models in the school playground, their poor judgment at the street corner, and their readiness to join risky ventures that promise peer acceptance may place these youngsters in particular jeopardy. At the same time, these years are critical for testing independence, trying out self-advocacy skills, learning when to ask for help, and beginning to use independent judgment.

During each phase of development, there are numerous opportunities for "enlarging the basis for congruence and continuity of experience at every stage" (Rosenberger, 1988, p. 276). Rosenberger emphasized the importance of parental intervention to ensure that the child has the opportunities needed to "keep in contact with his abilities as he discovers his disabilities" (p. 276). But time, space, ingenuity, and access to resources greatly affect the parent's ability to fulfill this mandate. The demands of other children in the family, a full work day, poor health, or inadequate community resources may be formidable barriers to parents' achievement of this crucial task.

129

FAMILY ISSUES: SAILING AN UNCHARTED SEA

Families with children with learning disabilities range from resilient to vulnerable. There are many families who never seek outside help, as well as many who do. Families who come to the attention of mental health and social agencies often are in severe distress. They have provided the basis for the growing body of literature describing clinical intervention with learning-disabled children and their families. As one might anticipate, the emphasis in the literature is on dealing with family dysfunction and pathology. For example, there has been much research devoted to unbalanced relationships between mother and learning-disabled child (Amerikaner & Omizo, 1984; Berger & Kennedy, 1975; Humphries & Bauman, 1980; Miller & Westman, 1964; and Staver, 1953), to the distanced or absent father (Grunebaum, Hurwitz, Prentice, & Sperry, 1962; Perosa, 1980), and to the at-risk sibling (Osman, 1979; Osman & Blinder, 1982; Trevino, 1979). There also have been comparisons of the functioning of families with learning-disabled children to that of the psychosomatic families (Perosa, 1980) exhibiting patterns of "enmeshment, overprotectiveness, rigidity and lack of conflict resolution" (Spacone & Hansen, 1984, p. 53). Children with learning disorders do add to the stresses in families and do change the balance in some family systems. Most families regain a healthy balance, but some do not.

The highly individualized patterns of biopsychosocial growth and development of children with learning disabilities place parents in an uncharted sea regarding the establishment of appropriate expectations in the family. The identification of family strengths and the variable impacts of the external environment that contribute to families' ability to promote a nurturing environment and positive "fit" for children have been neglected in research. Creative and highly individual solutions to seemingly intractable problems grow from family ingenuity and careful observation of children's talents as well as weaknesses (Vigilante, 1985). Many families develop negotiating, advocating, and political skills to cope with the lack of community resources, poor coordination of existing services, and institutional rigidities. Other families develop teaching and training skills in response to the lack of skilled professionals in educational and recreational helping services.

At other times, the choices that are made impinge on the quality of life of the entire family. Parents may cut back on planned family trips, spontaneous outings, or family parties because of the anxiety and stress of dealing with their child's reaction to changes in routine. These adaptations may persist longer than necessary, becoming integrated into the family's style of operation, and causing increasing family isolation. "Parent burnout" is not an empty phrase. By the time their learning-disabled children reach their teenage years, many parents are in a state of chronic exhaustion due to their constant struggles to maintain a balance at home, and to interpret the needs of their child to playmates, relatives, neighbors, schools, professionals, and institutions. Many families do not realize the amount of time, energy, and financial resources they devote to dealing with the needs of their children with learning disabilities, or the accompanying accumulation of different levels of stress (Gallagher, Beckman, & Cross, 1983). Chronic stress becomes a fact of life. Bracing for transition-related stress, such as change of teachers, the move from spring to summer schedules, or introduction of a pet to the household, becomes automatic. The threat of acute stress in the form of impulsive gestures or self-destructive behavior is always pending. By the time most families seek or are referred to help, some of the initially adaptive patterns of coping have developed some negative outcomes for one or more members of the family. At some level, a crisis has been reached that requires new coping strategies, skills, and often a realignment of family relationships and expectations.

The Mourning Process

For parents with a child with learning disabilities, the mourning process has some characteristics different from processes of mourning for more visibly or obviously severely disabled children. The stages of mourning—denial, anger, open grief, and finally, resolution—have been amply described in the literature (Kübler-Ross, 1969; Kaslow & Cooper, 1978; Solnit & Stark, 1961). For parents with a child with learning disabilities, denial can persist for a long time, fanned by limited knowledge about learning disabilities and by legitimate questions about the validity of evaluation and testing processes. The irregularity and subtlety with which learning disabilities may be manifested and the refinement of the compensatory strategies used by some children allow parents to make allowances for variations in learning style and behavior long after such tolerance may be warranted. Signals of distress may be ignored until much time has been lost and maladaptive defense mechanisms have become part of the child's character.

In other instances, one parent, sometimes the father, may distance himself from the situation, denying evidence of learning disability that may emerge at home or at school. Such statements as "He's all boy" or "I never could stand being told what to do myself" are heard frequently. Outbursts of asocial clowning or antisocial behavior may be endorsed (Spacone & Hansen, 1984). In one example, the father of one 10-year-old boy with learning disabilities encouraged his son to beat up the boys who were teasing him about his poor performance in school. The father, afraid that his son was a "sissy," refused to see his son's behavior as symptomatic of his distress and an unsupportive classroom atmosphere where ridicule for failure was the norm. Denial also may appear mingled with family and cultural expectations, as exemplified by the statement, "I've never seen a girl yet who could do math. Why do we bother with the expense of all this special tutoring?" Parental denial may continue through a child's adolescence, with the active collusion of the child who fights to maintain the facade that everything is "okay." Sometimes this surface is broken only by a crisis, precipitated by demands that break through the compensatory strategies and permit visibility of the underlying fragility of the adolescent's hold on age-appropriate competencies.

Parental anger, assumed to be a second stage in the mourning process, may also continue in a seemingly irrational pattern long after it would have been assumed that there should be acceptance of the situation. Vigilante (1983) clarified why acceptance is not a single event:

> The assumption is that mourning is time-limited; going on with life implies a once-and-for-all resolution. Once-and-for-all solutions seem quite super-ficial when applied to the complex tasks of parents of handicapped children. Parents often need continuing help to understand their own idiosyncratic responses to their child's needs while they are helped to meet the needs of the child. For example, each stage of the child's life requires parents to reconsider expectations of performance and adjust to them (Rappaport, 1965). As families move through the normal experiences of life, parents have to reassess and reintegrate continually the meaning of the handicap, for themselves and for the child. This, in turn, suggests that mourning may be an indefinite process that consumes considerable quantities of psychic energy. . . . The quixotic persistence of a learning disability reinforces the chronic state of mourning, partly because of repeated hopes that arise with spurts of accomplishment or creativity in scattered areas of the child's functioning. Each hope is battered by subsequent failure in academic and social spheres. (p. 431)

The emotional toll on parents may be large, and parents may alternate in using distancing behavior to regain emotional strength. If there is open recognition of a parent's need for "time out," parental responsibilities can be reassigned. Too often, one parent may find himself or herself left with all of the work and decision making, then blamed when things do not improve. In extreme, but not rare situations, one spouse abandons the family (Featherstone, 1980). When a single parent is the sole provider of the emotional and financial needs, the family is particularly vulnerable to the development of poor coping patterns and disorganization (Rhodes, 1977).

For the past 30 years, researchers have noted the high representation of adopted children with learning and behavior problems (Brodzinsky, Schecter, Braff, & Singer, 1984; Dalby, Fox, & Haslam, 1982; Deutsch et al., 1982; Kenny, Baldwin, & Mackie, 1967; Taichert & Harwin, 1975; Zill, 1985). For example, Silver (1970, 1989a) determined that the frequency of adoption with children with learning disabilities was about 4 percent higher than the adoption frequency rate of a nondisabled control group. First, out-of-wedlock pregnancies, which are overrepresented in adoption cases, have also been found to be correlated with factors predisposing to learning disabilities, whether prenatal, perinatal, or demographic (Hoopes, 1982; Kadushin, 1980). Adoptive parents are also likely to seek help more readily than other parents, having been conditioned to use social agencies through initial infertility and adoption processes (Melina,

1986). Therefore, it is important for social workers to be familiar with some of the differences in the process of mourning that may affect the adoptive family.

A wide range of conflicting feelings may surface in adoptive families who did not state explicitly at the time of the adoption process that they would be able to accept a child with disabilities into their family. These parents also may retain lingering unresolved anger and resentment that the extra risk of adoption was not positively rewarded on some magical balance sheet of life events with the arrival of a perfect child. Unanticipated expenses that change family circumstances and opportunities also may bring parental resentment. Adoptive parents may have to reengage in the original mourning process related to not bearing a biological child before they can effectively work through the process of recommitment and rebonding with their adoptive child.

Parental distancing may take place as parents create space between themselves and the problems in learning and behavior of their adopted children. Statements like "In our family, anyone with an IQ below 120 is considered retarded," or "she can't have inherited that from me" have been heard, reflecting a distancing and removal of the adoptive parents from the presumed poor genetic heritage of their adopted child. After diagnosis, adoptive parents may need help with the process of reintegrating the child with learning disabilities into the family.

Family Expectations

Parents react to their children with learning disabilities in diverse ways that are in part dependent on their own life experiences, their expectations of parenthood, and their sense of their children as definers of self-worth (Kozloff, 1979). All parents have expectations and dreams for their children. Although few children follow a life course that actually coincides with these expectations, parents retain active fantasies of achievement and a sense of open possibilities. On some level, most parents do acknowledge their children's limits and vulnerabilities. However, the implications of finite boundaries to ability or performance that are associated with the diagnosis of a learning disability can be overwhelming.

Cultural differences bring other variables regarding expectations for children (Caplan, Whitemore, Bui, & Traukmann, 1985; McGoldrick & Rohrbaugh, 1987; O'Conner & Spreen, 1988). Among some groups, the behavior of the child with learning disabilities may be incorporated into the family ethic. The extent to which the behavior and performance of the child conform to other patterns of behavior in the family or the extended family affects perceptions of the need for outside intervention or change. Cultural or idiosyncratic familial values may be visible through analysis of the kinds of behavior that are rewarded and punished, and the intensity of the parental response. For example, in some families a child must not appear to need too much, want too much, or demand too much. The child who violates the unspoken limit receives a negative response (Vigilante &

133

Rosenberger, 1988). For the child with learning disabilities who needs constant reassurance of being "okay," the rebuff contained in a negative reaction is confirmation that he or she is not okay. Anxiety may overwhelm the child, and a resurgence of demands, acting-out behavior, or withdrawal may result, beginning a new cycle of misunderstanding between parent and child.

Families for whom the experience of children as late talkers is a familiar one may not view a daughter who does not talk clearly at age 4 as having a problem. However, if she enters preschool and her speech is unclear, teachers may suggest a language or psychological evaluation. Other families may place little value on school performance or behavior conformity. Family-school conflict may result if the family resists viewing the situation as problematic (Klein, Altman, Dreisen, Friedman, & Powers, 1981a, 1981b). As children reach adolescence, parental concerns about career choices and options begin to gain more importance. One middle-class teenager entering high school became very interested in auto mechanics. His parents were taken aback, but supportive when he took a summer vocational course in auto repair. They watched with amazement as the summer progressed, and their nonverbal, shy son became talkative at the dinner table, had a group of friends for the first time, and was able to engage in lengthy telephone conversations with junk dealers about spare parts. Initially, the parents begrudged the expenses associated with the purchase of an old car to be refurbished for drag racing. However, as they thought about the changes in self-confidence, esteem, competence, and general happiness of their son, they realized that the educational and psychological benefits of this new area of interest far outweighed their reservations about expense or appropriateness. Able to put off their original goals of a college education, they are waiting and following their son's lead.

Impacts on Siblings

Siblings learn, compete, and naturally influence each other through their close and intense relationships (Dunn, 1983). Much of the literature on siblings of children with disabilities has focused on sibling relationships in the family when there is a child with mental retardation or other severe or chronic conditions (Crnic, Friedrich, & Greenberg, 1983; Garguilo, 1984; Powell & Ogle, 1985; Seligman & Darling, 1989). According to a recent review of the psychoanalytic literature, there has been little attention to the therapeutic issues for siblings of children with learning disabilities (Rothstein, Benjamin, Crosby, & Eisenstadt, 1988). However, the psychosocial issues for siblings are emerging in the context of work with families of learning-disabled children by members of the medical (Levine, 1987), social work (Trevino, 1979; Vigilante, 1983), and special education (Osman, 1979) professions.

The recently formed Sibling Information Network promises to shed more light on a broader range of these elusive sibling relationships. Extrapolating from work with siblings of children with other kinds of disabilities reveals both similarities and differences. Lupi (1987), reporting on research of the past 15 years on siblings of individuals with more severe handicapping conditions, noted that there is a recognition that nonhandicapped siblings are at risk for behavioral problems. A number of variables have been identified as influential, including the number of "normal" siblings in the family, their ages and genders, and parental responses, attitude, and degree of acceptance of the disability. The difficulty in sibling adjustment increases when there are only two children in the family, when the normal sibling is younger than or close to the same age as the child with a disability, and when there is lack of parental acceptance of the disability.

Learning disabilities present some particular stresses for siblings. The invisibility of learning disabilities makes it difficult for other children in the family to "see" what is different. The range of a learning-disabled child's behavior, from absolutely normal to dysfunctional, may appear to parallel the behavior of other children in the family except for its intensity and frequency. The difference in parental responses make the non–learning-disabled siblings wonder why their brother or sister is getting such special treatment. For example, different expectations for standards of behavior and accomplishments may appear when school report cards are brought home. One child may appear to be rewarded for effort while another is rewarded for results. The non–learning-disabled sibling may be very puzzled by what seems like favoritism, and may conclude erroneously that he or she is less loved and appreciated.

Other children in the family may fear that learning disabilities are catching, as their hidden fears of failure become manifest in the actions of their sister or brother. The experience of growing up for the child with learning disabilities may be so tumultuous that other siblings are left with many unreasonable fantasies. Having seen only one maturational pattern, they assume that they will have the same difficulties (Osman, 1979), and that they also will have similar, if less intense, problems with school, sports, or social life. Parents must be alert to these unspoken concerns of their other children and provide safe, individual opportunities for discussion. Embarrassment, shame, and guilt in relation to a sister or brother who may have a neighborhood reputation as a "retard" or "weirdo" can produce unspoken wounds and conflicts of allegiance for siblings (Bloch & Margolis, 1986). The subject may be forbidden in the household, and siblings may receive the message that they are not at liberty to explore their ambivalent feelings with parents. These stifled feelings become increasingly "unsafe" for the child.

The physical and psychological drain of learning-disabled children on parental energy reserves may leave little room for spontaneous response to the needs of other children. Daily life with a child with learning disabilities requires attention and emotional energies far greater than the energy expended with other children in the family. Numerous aspects of family functioning and decision making, such as financial expenditures, space allocation, meal schedules, family recreation, and special events, all may revolve around accommodating the special needs of the child with learning disabilities (Vigilante, 1983). Family tensions, exacerbated by the stress of the special requirements of the learning-disabled child, are felt by all of the children. As Osman (1979) remarked, "Children's learning differences are, indeed, a family affair! Whether or not a family discusses the problems openly or keeps them a secret, everyone in the family responds in some way to the child's difficulties" (p. 29).

The needs of siblings may be overshadowed. There may be an unspoken expectation that other children in the family perform well in school, be responsible at home, and not add to the pressures on family life. If the child with learning disabilities has a tendency to become disruptive, parents may provide a tight structure for family activities. This may adversely affect other children in the family, who need greater flexibility, independence, and spontaneity. The mixture of love, guilt, anger, jealousy, embarrassment, and fear must be addressed again at different developmental stages for both the child with learning disabilities and his or her siblings.

In a family, competition for parental attention among children is common. In some instances, the child with learning disabilities always may appear to win, whether he or she is "good" or "bad." In other instances, the child who is foundering wins only negative attention. If the child with learning disabilities is always in trouble and always getting punished, or is even the victim of abuse, the other children in the family may feel intolerable feelings of guilt and relief. The pressure is off of them, but at the same time, they know it is not fair. They also know that to intervene would be perilous. Competition also exists between children, particularly in terms of what is valued by parents—academic work, sports, or social skills. The sibling may decide to excel or not to compete at all.

Changing needs of other children in the family may bring competition as siblings try to gain parental attention (Powell & Ogle, 1985). A variety of attention-seeking strategies may be used, depending upon the age of the children. For example, younger children may mimic the "successful" negative school or home behavior of the learning-disabled sibling. The parents may overreact with panic, anger, or depression, fearful that a second child in the family also has a learning disability. Older children may seek other ways to attract attention, such as drifting toward less desirable peer groups, or using drugs or alcohol. Increasingly, parents are forced into reactive behavior unless they become aware of the uneven pattern of their attentions that may be triggering the situation.

Younger children frequently look up to and admire their older brothers or sisters. However, when the older child has a developmental impairment or delay that interferes with the development of age-appropriate competencies, a much younger child may surpass the older child's academic skills or general conceptual abilities. The younger child may feel a pervasive sense of discomfort with this situation and refuse to use the skills. Or, the child may lord it over the learning-disabled sibling, using the superior skills to taunt and belittle.

Unknowingly, parents may exacerbate the unbalanced situation through their responses to the poor ego functioning of their learning-disabled son or daughter.

Such actions as leaving a younger child covertly or overtly in charge when parents go out or referring the older child to the younger one when help is needed with schoolwork can be viewed as assaults on an already shaky self-concept. For the younger sibling, who really does not want to exceed the capacities of the older one, these gestures just heighten the sense of the disparity of skills and create a dilemma. This child has to weigh the pride of being thought competent by the parents against the cost of bringing humiliation to the less able, but older, sibling. The upset to the prerogatives of birth order is distressing to both children.

Ultimately, the family value system has great significance for the way in which parents interpret and resolve the stresses of raising children with learning disabilities. The ways that all the children in a family are taught to experience difference, the degree of competitiveness, the definition of success in the family, and the recognition of intrinsic worth of the individual all have bearing on the ways that siblings deal with their learning-disabled brother or sister. Siblings can play active and positive roles through encouraging and supporting efforts, or they can be destructive in their use of their own superior or more easily won successes. A great deal depends on the way that parents interpret the special needs of their child with learning disabilities, and individualize, nurture, and respect the unique talents of each child. Optimally, all family members support and encourage the less able child, as well as each other.

As adults, many siblings of handicapped persons report that they were enriched by the experience of helping, and that through watching positive parental role models they became more flexible and compassionate. Some siblings have sought careers in helping professions. This has not been reported in the area of learning disabilities. The author's conversations with parents of learning-disabled adults have revealed a more complicated mixture of sibling emotions, with strong residues of resentment, anger, and guilt long after childhood.

SOCIAL WORK INTERVENTION WITH FAMILIES

Some families with children with learning disabilities never seek or need professional help beyond the remediation necessary for their children to maintain an adequate academic performance. Many more families can benefit from short-term or intermittent help to cope with stressful transitions during their child's growing years. Still others require more long-term assistance to deal with major family relationship or system issues that the child with a disability has activated. Some of these families will actively engage help, but others view seeking professional help as a profound admission of failure. Issues of class, race, culture, and gender of the child affect the family's response, their interpretation of special needs, and their perceptions of the value of professional help.

To work effectively with parents with learning-disabled children, social workers must have some understanding of what this disability means to a family. Behavior identified as deviant in one family context may be ignored in another. Only by understanding the specific limitations of the individual child and the child's behavior within the context of its fit within the family and cultural group can the social worker begin to design appropriate strategies for intervention. The extent to which a family may be experiencing other difficulties—whether financial, social, medical, or emotional—also may have an impact on the priority assigned to the needs of the child with learning disabilities. Finally, if the child is in a foster or substitute family, this also may affect family perceptions of their role in aggressively seeking assistance for the child with learning disabilities. In this instance, parents may alert the child care worker and expect the sponsoring social agency to assume more active planning and arrange intervention with appropriate specialists. The agency, operating under the pressure of having too few trained social workers on staff, may assume that the child care worker is aware of and sensitive to the family issues in the raising of a child with learning disabilities. This may be the case, but often it is not. Frequently, the stresses of raising a learning-disabled child are exacerbated when the child is placed temporarily with a foster family. Prior moves—and threatened future moves—undermine family and child bonding and commitment (Dane, 1988).

Early Intervention

The findings of a recent national survey suggested that the majority of learning-disabled children encountered in child welfare and family service agencies were identified between the ages of 6 and 11 (Dane, 1985b). This period coincides with their formal entry into school and the application of expectations of development and academic performance that do not fit the maturational and achievement level of the child. Social work with children with learning disabilities and their families usually is initiated when the behavioral performance of the child in school does not conform to an expected norm. (This may change as federally mandated early intervention programs become effective.) Expectation levels are widely variable, dependent on peer group behavior and professional norms and values biases, as well as on resource availability in the school system and community. These variables also may affect the age at which problems are recognized and whether learning disabilities are identified correctly.

The fact that a child has a learning disability often is not known at the onset of many school difficulties. However, once identified, learning disabilities frequently are isolated as a "school problem." Parents assume that the problem will be handled by the school, through special programs or classes. Home behavior is not always seen as being linked with the manifestations of the learning disability at school. Rather, these children may be seen by school personnel as having emotional problems, and the parents may be identified as major contributors to the difficulties (Silver, 1989b). Parallel problem-solving approaches can result in the search for separate cause-and-effect relationships. Evaluation, tutoring, and placement in a special class or school rarely resolve the interdependent cognitive, social, emotional, and behavioral issues affecting the development of a child with learning disabilities. Therapeutic interventions, foster care, or residential placements that focus only on curbing behavior and neglect underlying cognitive deficits that impede ego development cannot fully address the complex maturational needs of children with learning disabilities or effectively assist their families.

The firm link that has been established between cognitive and emotional growth and stimulation and variety of experience emphasizes the importance of early intervention when developmental lags and delays are seen. Though neurological or psychological evaluation may not be the first recourse, working with the child and family to ensure that stimulation and appropriate challenges are available becomes an important preventive measure. Early intervention has been found to be particularly important in work with learning-disabled children and their families. However, early screening in health centers and early childhood centers is not uniformly available. Social workers in hospital settings, family life education programs, foster care services, community centers, and preschool groups may play important early intervention roles. Informed by knowledge of infants and toddlers who may be at high risk for developmental difficulties, social workers have a basis for reaching out to parents. Awareness of cultural, racial, and class issues is critical. For example, although studies have emphasized a correlation among multiple risk factors such as prematurity, low birth weight, and low socioeconomic status with learning disorders, this does not mean that all children with these characteristics will have learning problems. Social workers who become familiar with cultural patterns, help-seeking behavior, and acceptable ways of giving help will be most effective at developing intervention strategies.

Establishment of individual and group programs to educate parents to signs of special developmental needs among their children serves a multitude of purposes supportive to new and young parents. Simple guidelines for parental observation of common milestones in the areas of motor skills and language acquisition are particularly relevant to future developmental difficulties. For example, the child who does not make sounds at 3 months, does not smile or laugh at 6 months, or cannot sit alone at 10 months should be a focus of concern (Bloch, 1987). Parents can be helped to adapt their parenting style to include more stimulation and attention to areas in which their child may need extra practice. Social workers can model new parental behavior and provide positive feedback and encouragement. If they have ongoing involvement with the parents, social workers can provide recognition and support that can fuel parents' energies.

In other situations, parents may not realize the degree to which they have adapted their own behavior to their child's extraordinary demands because they may be unaware of the extent to which their child's behavior deviates from the norm. Sharing principles of child development and growth allows parents to begin their own assessment of the stresses this "minor" disability exerts on all members of the family. Social workers can model ways that the usual milestones of development may be partialized, to capture and highlight the gains of the child with learning disabilities. For example, in one family the child was always asking his father to help him build model airplanes. The father was very task-oriented and uncomfortable with the amount of time he spent working on models that his son never finished. The father's frustration turned to anger and sarcasm. The social worker helped the father partialize the goal of completing a model by identifying the milestone of a goal related to increasing task persistence and time spent working autonomously. The father was helped to recognize that his son was able to spend increasing amounts of time alone attending to the process of building a model. Although it was difficult for him, the father began to praise his son for the actual work accomplished and the effort and time spent, and not to focus on the fact that the models were not finished. Later, the father revealed that he was not very good at model building, and felt inadequate in helping his son. It took a long time before the father was able to accept the fact that the time spent with his son was more important than either person's level of skill in model building. Thus, the father's own expectations and fears of inadequacy, combined with his loss of perspective that the child's general distractibility and short attention span were related to the learning disability, contributed to a situation in which neither was able to get what he needed from the other.

Social workers can assist parents to anticipate the critical stages in their learning-disabled child's maturational process. When children with learning disabilities are of elementary school age, the functions of parents as caretakers are extended. They assume the roles of interpreter and advocate to help their children negotiate the school, classroom, and playground. Without such intervention, children with learning disabilities rarely have the opportunity and protected time to develop their academic skills, practice social interaction, and have available models of peer behavior. Too often labeled as troublemakers, these children are isolated from an appropriate range of experience. Each new teacher or playground supervisor, each new grade, and each new group requires a period of adjustment for both the adults in charge and the children.

Social workers can assist parents and their children in developing criteria and boundaries for parental intervention. The unpredictable behavior of the child with learning disabilities, who shows good judgment one day and poor judgment the next, makes the decision exceedingly hard for parents. Appropriate protective behavior at one developmental stage may, if carried forward to a later stage, accentuate the child's dysfunction and stifle growth and appropriate risk taking, leading at times to regression (Solan, 1981) and a situation of learned helplessness. Difficulties emerge when the child's waning need for extended protection merges with the parental need to maintain the status quo. A child's possible negative experiences with peers affects his or her ability to separate from the parents. Identification of when parental advocacy becomes overprotective or is founded in parental self-esteem, anger at institutions, or overidentification with the child is important. A structural approach toward assessing the family system provides a perspective that helps the social worker determine the kinds of realignments that may be helpful in improving the functioning of individuals in the family unit (Rosenberger, 1990).

As children mature, they need to develop their own skills in order to advocate for themselves. If they have not had the opportunity to develop the appropriate vocabulary, timing, and tone for self-advocacy, they may choose an inappropriate time to negotiate changes in situations causing them unnecessary stress. For example, the teenager in school who blurts out in class that he needs to take an untimed test may make it very difficult for the teacher to respond differentially to the student's needs. A visit to the teacher's office to explain the situation may bring a greater likelihood of a positive response.

Family Types

A framework for assessing and planning strategic intervention with families with children with learning disabilities has been developed by Ziegler and Holden (1988). Their focus is on the development of professional interventions that will aid parents in promoting their child's self-esteem, frustration tolerance, and self-control. Ziegler and Holden identified five types of family systems that influence the child's psychological adjustment and management of his or her dysfunctions. The following discussion is an adaptation and expansion of Ziegler and Holden's typology of family organization and its implications for children with learning disabilities.

Most discussions of family systems are based on a two-parent family as a model, as are the family types presented by Ziegler and Holden (1988). However, half of the nation's children are living in single-parent homes. Although the difficulties associated with raising a child with learning disabilities are not always intensified when there is only one parent in the home, there are a number of situations in which this is the case. There are definite strains when one parent is carrying out the functions that under other circumstances would be carried out by two parents (Carlson, 1985). Sufficient financial resources and time, parental health and resilience, the number of other children in the family, and available community supports all contribute to a single-parent family's ability to manage effectively. A significant number of single-parent homes comprise young, black, single mothers from low economic and social backgrounds (Cordes, 1984). There are many factors associated with these young mothers' life-styles, pregnancy care, birth, and early parenting experiences that constitute high-risk conditions for their children. Often, these are families in need of a wide range of services, which include attention to cognitive and behavioral delays that may be present in their children.

All parents have a need for individuation, nourishment, and refueling (Mahler, Pine, & Bergman, 1975). Feelings of self-efficacy can be strengthened when social workers can reflect back to the parents the importance of maintaining a balance between their children's needs and their own individual needs. A goal for work with all families with a child with learning disabilities is the development of effective coping strategies. Resources contributing to a healthy family system have been identified as health, energy, morale, problem-solving skills, social networks, basic utilitarian resources, and specific beliefs (Folkman, Schaefer, & Lazarus, 1979). Gaining an understanding of individual family resources is important in working with all types of families.

Healthy Families. In the *healthy family,* the learning disability is the only problem affecting a basically emotionally stable family. Parents are not overwhelmed with grief and there do not appear to be any secondary gains, scapegoating, or avoidance of marital relationship issues. Parents individualize all of their children. They are able to conceptualize and plan for anticipated stressful periods. Generally, these families can call on adequate resources to support both individual child and family member needs (Ziegler & Holden, 1988).

Work with the basically healthy family may focus on supporting parental skills for problem solving with their child with learning disabilities, and helping to define appropriate behavioral and educational goals (Ziegler & Holden, 1988). Although these families may have read about learning disabilities and be well informed about them, there may be a need to provide educational resources to further familiarize parents and other family members with issues of particular concern for the developmental stages of their child. Even with the healthy family, it is important to support parents in keeping a balance between commitment to providing the best environment for the child with special needs and maintenance of some detachment to ensure that their own and their other children's needs also are met.

Recent work has shown that children with learning disabilities do their best when they are expected to function as normal members of the family. Although this may require significant effort on the part of parents, it also reinforces the child's efforts to be part of the family and accept the limits associated with family membership. Such tasks as sharing dinner table conversation, containing impulsivity, or being responsible for chores or self-care require constant supervision, but also provide multiple opportunities for role modeling and parental support. Siblings also benefit from knowledge that there are clear expectations of their brother or sister with learning disabilities that to some extent parallel what is expected of them. However, even in these families parental anger, frustration and depression, or marital arguments emerge, aggravated by the intense pressure associated with raising a child with learning disabilities. For example, the child's loss of self-control may trigger hidden control issues for the parent. These fluctuations in family functioning should not be viewed necessarily as evidence of family pathology (Vigilante, 1983). Even in the most healthy and balanced family, children with developmental dysfunctions add an unpredictability to daily life that produces temporary family imbalance. However, the basically healthy family has both internal resources and external support systems to help it through particularly trying stages. The healthy family, as distinguished from some others, is able to communicate and conceptualize issues and usually reaches out for short-term professional assistance on an as-needed basis.

Healthy parents' psychic and physical energies are not totally depleted by managing their children and homes. They may be involved or want to become involved with promoting the development of more adequate community resources, engaging in advocacy on behalf of other parents, or providing legislative monitoring. It may be appropriate, depending on the interest and inclination of the parents, to refer them to local or national organizations to support their interests. For the healthy family, sharing of knowledge and skills can be a very rewarding confirmation of their competency and can provide important broader networks of support for issues that may emerge later with their children.

The healthy single-parent family may be more burdened by the costs of the periodic need for evaluation; medication, if needed; and supportive services, such as counseling, tutoring, speech therapy, or after-school social groups. These services may be available through the local school system. If not, linking the family with low-cost, high-quality services may be an important role of the social worker.

One of the greatest difficulties of the single parent in a functionally healthy family may be the parent's denial of his or her own needs in favor of the more insistent needs of the child with learning disabilities and other children in the household. These parents may benefit from encouragement to attend to their own needs. Time off for recreation, interests apart from child-rearing, or socializing with friends offers the parent some sense of regaining lost autonomy, and protects against a drift toward social isolation based on the pressure of parental responsibilities.

Fragile Families. The *fragile family* can be characterized as one in which child-rearing skills were at a marginal level before the learning disability was identified as a problem. Parents often have poor coping skills and may tend to let things slide until they boil over, rather than deal with them directly. There may be limited ability to conceptualize problems and translate new knowledge into changes in behavior. However, these families do not show a system imbalance or have extreme psychopathology (Ziegler & Holden, 1988). Often, these parents have limited repertoires of coping strategies both within and outside of the home. Suffering from low self-esteem themselves, they have difficulty reaching out for assistance.

Frequently, adults who feel incompetent in important spheres of their lives have spent years compensating for and hiding their deficits. Challenges to their competence in any area may cause intense emotional stress and often result in negative or defensive behavior. If the parent's self-esteem is fragile, the parent may have a defensive response to the child's attempts to nourish his or her own sense

143

of self-esteem. Parental use of sarcasm and belittling of accomplishments can be a pattern of response to a child's overtures and attempts to win approval or praise. This negativity can be crushing to the struggling self-concept of the child. At times, the limited skills of these parents may reflect undiagnosed learning deficits in one or another of the parents. Great sensitivity is required in working with parents who may manifest adult symptoms of learning disabilities.

In work with the fragile family, it is important to provide a basic education about the characteristics and symptoms of learning disabilities with very concrete examples, based on school or home expectations (Ziegler & Holden, 1988). This approach provides a base for understanding and empathy. Offering knowledge to the parent in a nonjudgmental manner demonstrates the social worker's ability to individualize and respect the parent. If the parent has learning disabilities, this may encourage a parent to share that he or she encountered the same problems as a child, and still may feel inadequate in the adult world because of gaps in education or difficulties with self-advocacy. If this kind of openness is achieved, the social worker can respond to the parent's feelings of powerlessness and low self-esteem directly. This recognition of the parental needs as independent of the children's needs may be an important way of showing respect and recognition for all members of the family.

Concrete parenting guidelines and rules become very practical ways of helping the parents in the fragile family overcome their own sense of powerlessness in the home. Ziegler and Holden (1988) suggested that if the children are in the room during meetings with the parents, a social worker can provide a role model by stating in words that all can understand what parents should expect in terms of the behavior of their children. The thrust of social work intervention with this type of family is to provide parental support and a basic vocabulary to allow them to better understand their children's problems.

The fragile single-parent family presents similar challenges. Without a spouse or companion present, there are fewer in-home supports available. Fears that the child may be taken away and that the parent may be declared incompetent may inhibit the parent from sharing vital concerns. The active social worker should look to the community institutions in which the child is already engaged. For example, the social worker may want to explore whether additional monitoring and advocacy in the school may be necessary to ensure that the child is receiving appropriate help. The parent in a fragile family may not have been able to engage effectively with school personnel. Development of strategies and routines for the single parent to effectively monitor school activities without losing time on the job would give the parent an added sense of control. The social worker also should look to community support systems to relieve the pressure on these parents, who may not seek out these resources for themselves. Exploration of after-school programs and weekend activity groups for both the children with learning disabilities and other siblings in these families would assist overburdened parents.

The fragile family poses a serious challenge for the social work practitioner. Realistic goals must be established to ensure that professional expectations for change do not overwhelm this frail family system. The social worker should propose structured opportunities for change that present the lowest level of threat and appear to support the positive inclinations of the parents to do the best for their children. The social worker must identify ways that particular elements of the parenting style and responses of the parents can be interpreted as strengths (Ziegler & Holden, 1988). For example, the parent who becomes emotionally overwrought may be demonstrating frustration and anger. Underlying this is a deep concern and fear for what the future holds for the child with special needs. If a common ground of concern for the child can be established, the basis for a therapeutic relationship may emerge.

Disorganized Families. The *disorganized* or *multiproblem family* typically misses appointments and has difficulty following through on ideas and new approaches worked out with involved professionals. If the child is on medication, directions may be followed sporadically (Ziegler & Holden, 1988). Disorganized or multiproblem families often alienate those who work with them because of the lack of follow-through or consistency and a passive resistance to outside intervention. Often, these families are socially isolated. They do not manage to build support networks, and may have alienated relatives and friends by their undependable behavior. Families that have been further fragmented by illicit drug use, acquired immune deficiency syndrome, and other major health problems are included in this group.

Even in early infancy, children with central nervous system dysfunctions react negatively to chaotic early surroundings. Due to their difficulties in organizing perceptual stimuli, these children require a stable, predictable, and nurturing environment for the optimum opportunity for healthy development (deHirsch & Jansky, 1980). For the child with learning disabilities, life in the disorganized family has a lack of such crucial daily structure. At times, there is a possibility of violence or neglect. There is little consistency in parenting routines, and the variability and unpredictability of emotional, and often physical, response to behavior underlines the child's sense of being out of control. The child's environment constantly devalues his or her efforts to influence the behavior of the adults on whom he or she is dependent. If children in disorganized families have difficulty with organization and planning, they will be overwhelmed internally by their own impulses and impressions as they are being buffeted by the external environment (deHirsch & Jansky, 1980). Because of the child's own vulnerabilities and deficits, it is predictable that he or she will identify with the part of the parent that is out of control. As these children grow older, this identification makes intervention focused on underlying problems of low self-esteem and anxiety about the home or school situation more difficult (Ziegler & Holden, 1988).

Work with disorganized families requires the social worker to become involved on many levels. Parenting skills are often few. Barriers to family stability are often both internal to the family, and present in the external environment. Low income, lack of job opportunities, and situational problems such as poor housing and deteriorated neighborhood services may undermine parental morale and energies. When there are other children in the family, problems may be compounded. The social worker's efforts to develop a support network outside the home for the child with learning disabilities can provide a temporary respite. Relatives may be able to provide more stable nurturing and role models on a part-time basis. This help may provide a temporary or, in extreme cases, permanent refuge. Use of various types of recreational programs that can provide opportunities for experiencing relationships with other adults, as well as offering stability and predictability, may be helpful to learning-disabled children with such limited role models at home.

Social workers in other agencies involved with the child need support in focusing on the child with learning disabilities as a priority (Ziegler & Holden, 1988). Interagency team meetings might help to coordinate services for the family and child with learning disabilities and avoid fragmented professional intervention that mirrors the disorganization of the family. For example, if school personnel are aware that professionals in other agencies are involved, the school personnel are more likely to attend to the child's special needs. Targeted involvement with specific school personnel involved with the child, such as special education or resource room teachers, the school nurse, or other staff members, may be needed to encourage collaborative strategies for providing some out-of-home parenting. Once school staff members feel that the total burden of intervention does not rest with them, they often are able to work more effectively with children with special needs.

The disorganized family may be the most difficult type of family to work with. Engagement is frequently tenuous. All members of the family may have many individual needs as well as family needs. Change may be very slow or nonexistent. Work with these families involves finding ways to be a resource for the family on its own terms, and striving to maintain its functioning as a social system of support (Ziegler & Holden, 1988).

When there is only one parent in the home, the emotional and physical resources are likely to be fewer, and the need for increases in concrete interventions is greater. In some communities, the use of homemakers who can come daily to teach and model basic organizational and parenting skills may be an option, as it might be for the fragile family. However, this help is less likely to be accepted by the disorganized family.

The social worker may be faced with critical judgments regarding the support of the child's best interests. The goal of maintaining the child in the home may become impossible if parental neglect or abuse is evident. The behavioral attributes of children with learning disabilities often are very trying to parents. If the parent has any tendency to lose control, this can be aggravated. As has been noted before, significant numbers of children being removed from their homes have shown behavioral and/or learning problems before the abuse or neglect took place (Helfer, 1979). Once these children reach their teens, they frequently act out

146

in destructive ways, such as running away or turning to drugs or violence. Because of their impulsivity and poor judgment they are at greater risk than other children in these situations and may require more aggressive protective intervention.

Blaming Families. The *blaming family* tends to find ways to make the child feel responsible for the strong negative emotions felt by the family, such as pain, anger, and deprivation (Ziegler & Holden, 1988). In such families, a mythology develops in which a fantasized better life would have been possible if the child did not have the learning disability. For example, the parental tensions would not have led to divorce if the child had not required expensive therapy, schooling, or remedial work. Opportunities for travel, new appliances, and benefits for other children would not have had to be forfeited. If the child had not behaved so badly, parents would not have lost the support of relatives. Emotional fragility and even poor health status of parents may be blamed subtly on the stress produced by the child with learning disabilities. The impacts of these messages on children's self-esteem and self-worth are significant. Some children accept the posture of their parents and assume the guilt for causing their families pain. Many children just bury their anger, hurt, and resentment, and relate only to the guilt that they are made to feel, because of their fears of being abandoned in their struggle toward maturity. They then carry these contradictory and submerged feelings into their adulthood. Others fight against the blaming, and may reflect back an anger laden with the sadness of rejection. In extreme situations, children may verbalize hostility and a desire to inflict pain on the parents. These children choose many avenues. They may leave school, cease trying to conform to their parents' expectations, turn to substance abuse, or retreat into permanent dependent behavior.

Complicating social work with these families is the fact that within these myths may be kernels of truth. The special needs and type of dysfunction a child presents may alter radically the course and choices available for all family members for many years. Just as learning disabilities constitute a life space problem for the child, so may they affect all major elements of family life.

It is important for social workers involved with these families to partialize the issues presented, or risk being overwhelmed themselves. Some parents actively use the child as a scapegoat for all the dysfunctional areas of family relationships. The child may be punished verbally or physically by constant parental overreactions to his or her failures. The low self-esteem of the parents and the basic dysfunction of the family, as well as the parental interaction with the child, need to be addressed (Ziegler & Holden, 1988). For some parents, there may·never have been a resolution to the mourning process associated with the original diagnosis of learning disability. A persistence in denial and lack of acceptance of changes necessary to encompass the child with special needs in the family may be evident. Changes may be viewed as forced on the parents by the child, circuitously justifying the parent's display of anger at the child. At times, this may show itself in excessively punitive or abusive behavior. Every time the child comes to a developmental transition and dysfunctions reappear, the parental anger may reemerge, and the child is once again punished for upsetting the family balance.

Blaming parents need help in returning to their original sense of sadness and loss upon first learning of their child's deficits. The goal of this exercise is to help them to regain their feelings of loving and caring and develop a level of acceptance that allows them to develop some emotional reserves. The child with learning disabilities and special needs may become a vehicle for long-standing historical feelings of loss or deprivation on the part of one or both parents. It may be useful for parents to have the opportunity to trace some of these sources, to disengage the inappropriate burden of their own unmet needs from their child's needs. These parents also need recognition for what they are doing well. Ultimately, the goal is to reestablish the child's place in the family as an individual who has strengths as well as deficits and makes positive contributions to family life. The informal use of the parents' version of the ANSER questionnaire (Levine, 1980) may help to stimulate the discussion of the child's positive attributes and contributions. The social worker can help the parents separate their own needs from those of their child, and recognize that their child may be doing his or her own mourning (Cohen, 1986). An underlying issue for blaming parents may be a sense of being out of control, and a loss of boundaries between parent and child needs. When this type of family focuses on the deprivations the child is causing, it may be reacting to the loss of personal and family autonomy identified by Slater and Wikler (1986), a critical issue for parents of children with disabilities.

Social work intervention may help to reestablish some of these boundaries. For example, clear expectations of behavior encourage parents to focus on their own needs and interests for entertainment, hobbies, and time away from the family. These issues become particularly salient for the single parent who has a child with learning disabilities. Intervention may involve the search for specific resources to broaden parent options and clarify the boundaries between parent and child.

Split Families. In the *split family*, there are profound differences between parents in point of view and parenting approach. This split can stem from cultural or class-based differences between parents as to their roles, expectations, and goals for their children; their styles of intervention; or their manner of showing affection, recognition, and acceptance of their child as a separate human being.

Social work intervention may focus on the need for a consistent parental approach to promote a home learning environment that is predictable and stable. The learning-disabled child is less able than others to make sense out of conflicting messages from parents. Ziegler and Holden (1988) suggested dealing with these tensions between parents by providing concrete tasks of behavior management that require parental collaboration. The difficulties of the split family tend to surface quickly in joint sessions with parents. These problems must be dealt with from two perspectives—the integrity and balance of the family system, and the specific needs of the child for constancy. One of the parents may attempt to manipulate a shift of emphasis to gain support for a particular point of view in a battle for control. If friction between the parents continues to be intrusive, it may represent underlying rifts and tensions that will continue to deflect from the primary focus on family balance and support for the child with specific behavior and cognitive deficits. Couple therapy may be necessary for parents unable to develop a mutually satisfactory common stance.

Traditionally, fathers have been seen as denying their children's disability, and mothers have been viewed as overreactive (Ziegler & Holden, 1988). However, the evidence is controversial. In most families, mothers spend more time with their children during the day and must deal directly with the different institutional systems with which their child is involved, monitor their progress, and make critical on-the-spot judgments about their child's emotional, social, and physical needs and general well-being. It is difficult for a parent engaged to this extent to maintain appropriate distance. At times, a more objective view is lost, leading the engaged parent to be more optimistic or pessimistic than is warranted. Efforts to encourage the family to reallocate some responsibilities with regard to the child may be helpful. Fathers need more first-hand knowledge of the child's vulnerabilities and strengths, and a chance to talk directly with the involved professionals.

As noted by Ziegler and Holden (1988) and Vigilante (1983), most families are honestly trying to do their best with the baffling problems and difficulties with which their children are struggling. When given recognition for the exceedingly difficult choices they are faced with on a daily basis, families are more open to collaboration with helping professionals. An overall task for the social worker engaged with these families is helping both parents and children to distinguish the specific symptoms of the learning disorder from the emotional reactions related to the additional pressures on the family and from their emotional reactions to school failures.

Class, racial, or cultural stereotypes must be avoided carefully in assessing the characteristics of different family types. The articulate middle-class or upper-class family with many resources that initially may be presumed to be a base for healthy family development may in fact be fragile, disorganized, neglectful, or abusive. Despite plentiful financial resources, a family may be excessively blaming. The reverse may hold true as well. The family with limited means may nevertheless be able to encompass a child with marked developmental deviation and provide appropriate support, encouragement, and advocacy. However, disability of any kind threatens family equilibrium and intensifies existing strains and tensions. All families can benefit from support on an intermittent or regular basis.

Parent Empowerment and Resource Development

Social workers should recognize that all parents of children with learning disabilities may feel a reduction of personal and family autonomy (Slater & Wikler,

149

1986). Choices regarding work, career, financial risks, recreational activities, types of friends, or availability of appropriate schooling generally are made based on the needs of their child with learning disabilities. For example, a move to a community with poor schools may require special tutoring or residential schooling. States have enacted different provisions regarding resources for children with disabilities. The availability of resources may affect other financial options severely. Whether or not parents would make decisions differently may not be as much the issue as the sense of loss of individual autonomy (Boggs, 1984).

Parents are not always fully aware of the reserves of strength and creativity they bring to bear on their work raising a handicapped child, or of the toll this work may take. This additional time, energy, worry, and care have been termed *psychic* or *indirect costs* (Boggs, 1984). Helping all members of the family to identify what they actually do provides a framework for a joint evaluation of the strengths and vulnerabilities of the operational family system. Each family member's contributions should be recognized formally. While encouraging the development of supports in the extended family and the community, social workers must carefully assess the extent to which different community resources support the family or provide a substitute for the family. The wrong balance of interventions can undermine family strengths and contribute to family dependence (Moroney, 1983; Slater & Wikler, 1986).

Families of children with learning disabilities must play more active roles with their children for a longer period of time. Their strengths must be enlarged, and their capacity to continue positive support buttressed. Informal support networks must be enlarged, which means that families must be helped to explain the problems of their children in ways that help extended families and friends deal with the child. This effort should begin as soon as the learning disability is discovered. Through their formal and informal understanding of resources, family members can assist in creating the necessary linkages to minimize social isolation and broaden the base of support for all families caring for children with disabilities.

An overall objective of social work with families of children with learning disabilities is to empower parents to make independent decisions in asserting control over their family situation, and to ensure an active sense of chosen goals in work, recreation, and family direction. Additionally, empowerment can mean using one's individual ability to influence the external environment. Sensitizing professionals to the needs of children with learning disabilities and developing new services are two important avenues for parental action. Social workers can work with parents to support negotiations for appropriate services for their children. Some parents choose to become quite expert in understanding the exact nature of their child's disabilities and have educated those professionals working with their children. These parents frequently take the initiative in advocating for new resources, as well as for upgrading existing services to benefit all children with learning disabilities. Families in this group usually have skills in negotiating many different kinds of systems, and the time and resources to ensure that their children receive every support possible. For example, social workers and parents have worked with local schools to introduce a creative relaxation program in the classroom, after-school programs for children who tend to be overly active or anxious in school, telephone hot lines, and special lobbying groups.

Social workers must be aware, however, that parents from different ethnic, racial, and socioeconomic groups have different degrees of comfort in assuming advocacy roles and challenging educational and other institutions. Many of these families may be isolated and wary of contact with community organizations, fearing a loss of their privacy, or feeling inadequate to deal with professionals of a different background. These parents may need help in gaining access and advocating to ensure that their child's needs will be met.

Social workers have special skills in developing institutional linkages and recognizing the potential for building new patterns of services. For example, many learning-disabled children need a protected experience in socializing with their peers. Supportive and controlled group experiences beginning in school could be extended to after-school activities. Social workers, who are aware of the ways that services are developed and supported in their community, can work cooperatively with these families to develop new services, or expand existing ones. For example, schools, local community centers, civic organizations, or churches could sponsor a Boy Scout program with the modified approved program for children with learning and socialization problems. The concept of institutional pairing (Dane & Vigilante, 1984) offers an approach toward program design for children with learning disabilities, drawing on the combined strengths of the neighborhood school and the community center. Bridging these institutions through coordinated programming creates a new, safe environment for children with learning disabilities.

Social workers can encourage parents to develop or join existing self-help and support groups. The opportunity to share common problems, laugh about mistakes, and find solace in common dilemmas relieves the isolation of each family. Although all children differ in the manifestations of their difficulties, parents face remarkably similar stresses in raising these children as part of a family. The attitudes and approaches toward problem solving can provide support and behavior modeling (Eaton, Lippman, & Riley, 1980). Groups perform multiple functions, including normalizing family situations, providing additional friendships and support networks, educating and supporting family strengths, and offering opportunities for leadership. Historically, almost all of the major legal gains, increased access to resources, and changes in service provision for learning-disabled children have come about through collaboration of parents and professionals.

Parents are the lifelong advocates for their children. Social workers must envision their role as one that provides support and insight to assist parents in meeting this challenge. Like any other disability, learning disabilities place an added responsibility on parents and on all helping professionals. The social work profession emphasizes responding to an individual in the context of his or her surrounding family and society. Social workers and parents become increasingly adept at seeing the world through the eyes of the child with a learning disability. Both social workers and parents are brought a new awareness of societal neglect, institutional rigidities, unnecessary procedures, and subtle discrimination:

> The strength and unswerving commitment of families to seek the best for their children revitalizes the professional social worker, who often is too closely bound by institutional reality. The answer, "It can't be done," must be countered by the question, "Why not?" For those who are listening, it is clear that families of children with disabilities are reinvesting the social work profession with its commitment to innovative service. (Dane, 1985a, p. 509)

REFERENCES

Als, H. (1985). Patterns of infant behavior: Analogs of later organizational difficulties? In F. H. Duffy & N. Geschwind (Eds.), *Dyslexia: A neuroscientific approach to clinical evaluation* (pp. 67–92). Boston: Little, Brown.

Amerikaner, M. J., & Omizo, M. (1984). Family interaction and learning disabilities. *Journal of Learning Disabilities, 17,* 540–544.

Berger, M., & Kennedy, H. (1975). Pseudobackwardness in children: Maternal attitudes as an etiological factor. *Psychoanalytic Study of the Child, 30,* 279–306.

Bloch, J. S. (1987). *The five Ps manual for children with special needs.* Syosset, NY: Variety Pre-Schooler's Workshop.

Bloch, J., & Margolis, J. (1986). Feelings of shame: Siblings of handicapped children. In A. Gitterman & L. Shulman (Eds.), *Mutual aid groups and the life cycle* (pp. 91–108). Itasca, IL: F. E. Peacock.

Boggs, E. (1984). Feds and families: Some observations on the impact of federal economic policies on families with children who have disabilities. In M. A. Slater & P. Mitchell (Eds.), *Family support services: A parent/professional partnership.* Stillwater, OK: National Clearinghouse of Rehabilitation Training Materials.

Brodzinsky, D. H., Schecter, D. E., Braff, A.M., & Singer, L. M. (1984). Psychological and academic adjustment in adopted children. *Journal of Consulting and Clinical Psychology, 52,* 582–590.

Caplan, N., Whitemore, J., Bui, Q., & Traukmann, M. (1985). *Scholastic achievement among the children of Southeast Asian refugees.* Ann Arbor: University of Michigan, Institute of Social Research.

Carlson, C. (1985). Best practices in working with single-parent and step families. In A. Thomas & J. Grimes (Eds.), *Best practices in school psychology* (pp. 43–60). Kent, OH: National Association of School Psychologists.

Cohen, J. (1986). Learning disabilities and childhood: Psychological and developmental implications. *Annals of Dyslexia, 36,* 287–300.

Cordes, C. (1984, August). The rise of one parent black families. *APA Monitor,* pp. 16–18.

Crnic, K. A., Friedrich, W. N., & Greenberg, H. T. (1983). Adaptation of families with mentally retarded children: A model of stress, coping and family ecology. *American Journal of Mental Deficiency, 88,* 125–139.

Dalby, J. T., Fox, S. L., & Haslam, R.H.A. (1982). Adoption and foster care rates in pediatric disorders. *Developmental and Behavioral Pediatrics, 3,* 61–64.

Dane, E. (1985a). Professional and lay advocacy in the education of handicapped children. *Social Work, 30,* 505–510.

Dane, E. (1985b). *National survey of family and child welfare agencies.* Unpublished manuscript.

Dane, E. (1988, November). *Interdisciplinary intervention for a life space problem: Children with learning disabilities in the child welfare system.* Paper presented at the 11th Provincial Conference of the Learning Disabilities Association of Alberta, Calgary, Canada.

Dane, E., & Vigilante, F. W. (1984, November). *Pairing neighborhood schools and settlement houses to design comprehensive group work programs for learning disabled children.* Paper presented at the Advancement of Social Work with Groups Annual Symposium, Chicago, IL.

deHirsch, K., & Jansky, J. J. (1980). Patterning and organizational deficits in children with language and learning disabilities. *Bulletin of the Orton Society, 30,* 227–238.

Deutsch, C. K., Swanson, J. M., Bruell, J. H., Cantwell, D. P., Weinberg, F., & Baren, N. (1982). Overrepresentation of adoptees in children with attention deficit disorder. *Behavior Genetics, 12,* 231–238.

Dixon, S. E., Yogman, M. W., Tronick, E., Adamson, L., Als, H., & Brazelton, T. B. (1981). Early infant social interaction with parents and strangers. *Journal of the American Academy of Child Psychiatry, 20,* 32–52.

Dorner, A. (Producer). (1984a). *Prematurely yours* [Videotape or Slide tape]. Boston: Polymorph Films.

Dorner, A. (Producer). (1984b). *To have and not to hold* [Videotape or Slide tape]. Boston: Polymorph Films.

Dunn, J. (1983). Sibling relationships in early childhood. *Child Development, 54,* 787–811.

Eaton, J. T., Lippmann, D. B., & Riley, D. P. (1980). *Growing with your learning disabled child.* Boston: Family Services Association of America and Resource Communications.

Erikson, E. (1959). *Identity and the life cycle* (Psychological Monographs 1). New York: International Universities Press.

Faerstein, L. M. (1986). Coping and defense mechanisms of mothers of learning disabled children. *Journal of Learning Disabilities, 19,* 8–11.

Featherstone, H. (1980). *A difference in the family: Life with a disabled child.* New York: Basic Books.

Folkman, S., Schaefer, C., & Lazarus, R. S. (1979). Cognitive processes as mediators of stress and coping. In V. Hamilton & P. W. Warburton (Eds.), *Human stress and cognition* (pp. 265–300). New York: John Wiley & Sons.

Friedrich, W. N., & Boriskin, B. A. (1976). The role of the child in abuse: A review of the literature. *American Journal of Orthopsychiatry, 46,* 580–590.

Gallagher, J. H., Beckman, P., & Cross, A. H. (1983). Families of handicapped children: Sources of stress and amelioration. *Exceptional Children, 50,* 10–19.

Garguilo, R. M. (1984). Understanding family dynamics. In R. M. Garguilo (Ed.), *Working with parents of exceptional children* (pp. 41–64). Boston: Houghton Mifflin.

Gilligan, C. (1982). *In a different voice.* Cambridge, MA: Harvard University Press.

Grunebaum, H. G., Hurwitz, I., Prentice, N. M., & Sperry, B. M. (1962). Fathers of sons with primary neurotic learning inhibitions. *American Journal of Orthopsychiatry, 32,* 462–472.

Helfer, R. (1979). The etiology of child abuse. *Pediatrics, 51,* 777–779.

Hoopes, J. L. (1982). *Prediction in child development: A longitudinal study of adopted and non-adoptive families; The Delaware family study.* New York: Child Welfare League of America.

Humphries, T. W., & Bauman, E. (1980). Maternal child rearing attitudes associated with learning disabilities. *Journal of Learning Disabilities, 13,* 54–57.

Kadushin, A. (1980). *Adoption in child welfare services.* New York: Macmillan.

Kagan, J. (1984). *The nature of the child.* New York: Basic Books.

Kaslow, F., & Cooper, B. (1978). Family therapy with a learning disabled child and his/her family. *Journal of Marriage and Family Counseling, 4,* 41–49.

Kenny, T., Baldwin, R., & Mackie, J. B. (1967). Incidence of minimal brain injury in adopted children. *Child Welfare, 46,* 24–29.

Klein, R. S., Altman, S. D., Dreisen, K., Friedman, R., & Powers, L. (1981a). Restructuring dysfunctional parental attitudes toward children's learning and behavior in school: Family oriented psychoeducational therapy (Part 1). *Journal of Learning Disabilities, 14,* 14–19.

Klein, R. S., Altman, S. D., Dreisen, K., Friedman, R., & Powers, L. (1981b). Restructuring dysfunctional parental attitudes toward children's learning and behavior in school: Family oriented psychoeducational therapy (Part 2). *Journal of Learning Disabilities, 14,* 99–100.

Kozloff, M. A. (1979). *A program for families of children with learning and behavior problems.* New York: John Wiley & Sons.

Kübler-Ross, E. (1969). *On death and dying.* New York: Macmillan.

Levine, M. D. (1980). *The ANSER system.* Cambridge, MA: Educators Publishing Service.

Levine, M. D. (1987). *Developmental variation and learning disorders.* Cambridge, MA: Educators Publishing Service.

Lupi, M. (1987). Siblings of the handicapped. In C. R. Reynolds & M. L. Mann (Eds.), *Encyclopedia of special education* (pp. 1431–1432). New York: John Wiley & Sons.

Mahler, M., Pine, F., & Bergman, A. (1975). *The psychological birth of the human infant.* New York: Basic Books.

Martin, H., & Beezley, P. (1974). Prevention and the consequences of child abuse. *Journal of Operational Psychology, 6*(68), 19–74.

McCubbin, H. H., Joy, C. B., Cauble, E. A., Comeau, J. K., Patterson, R. M., & Needle, R. H. (1980). Family stress and coping: A decade review. *Journal of Marriage and the Family, 42,* 855–870.

McGoldrick, M., & Rohrbaugh, M. (1987). Researching ethnic family stereotypes. *Family Process, 26,* 89–99.

Melina, L. R. (1986). *Raising adopted children.* New York: Harrow.

Miller, D. R., & Westman, J. C. (1964). Reading disability as a condition of family stability. *Family Process, 3,* 66–76.

Moroney, R. M. (1983). Families: Care of the handicapped and public policy. In R. Perlman (Ed.), *Home health care services quarterly* (Vol. 3, pp. 188–212). New York: Haworth Press.

O'Conner, S. C., & Spreen, O. (1988). The relationship between parents' socioeconomic status and education level, and adult occupational and educational achievement of children with learning disabilities. *Journal of Learning Disabilities, 21,* 148–153.

Olson, D. H., McCubbin, H. I., Barnes, H., Larsen, A., Muxen, M., & Wilson, M. (1983). *Families: What makes them work.* Beverly Hills, CA: Sage Publications.

Osman, B. (1979). *Learning disability: A family affair.* New York: Warner Books.

Osman, B., & Blinder, H. (1982). *No one to play with: The social side of learning disabilities.* New York: Random House.

Perosa, L. (1980). *The development of a questionnaire to measure Minuchin's structural family concepts and the application of his psychosomatic family model to learning disabled families.* Unpublished doctoral dissertation, State University of New York, Buffalo.

Pine, F. (1985). *Developmental theory and clinical process.* New Haven, CT: Yale University Press.

Powell, T. H., & Ogle, P. A. (1985). *Brothers and sisters: A special part of exceptional families.* Baltimore: Paul H. Brookes.

Rappaport, L. (1965). The state of crisis: Theoretical considerations. In H. J. Parad (Ed.), *Crisis intervention: Selected readings* (pp. 22–31). New York: Family Service Association of America.

Rhodes, S. (1977). A developmental approach to the life cycle of the family. *Social Casework, 58,* 301–311.

Rosenberger, J. (1988). Self-psychology as a theoretical base for understanding the impact of learning disabilities. *Journal of Child and Adolescent Social Work, 5,* 269–280.

Rosenberger, J. (1990). Social work in the field of learning disabilities: A systems framework for assessment and intervention. *Learning Disabilities: A Multidisciplinary Journal, 1,* 24–29.

Rothstein, A., Benjamin, L., Crosby, M., & Eisenstadt, K. (1988). *Learning disorders: An integration of neuropsychological and psychoanalytic considerations.* Madison, CT: International Universities Press.

Seligman, M., & Darling, R. B. (1989). *Ordinary families, special children: A systems approach to childhood disability.* New York: The Guilford Press.

Silver, L. B. (1970). Frequency of adoption in children with the neurological learning disability syndrome. *Journal of Learning Disabilities, 3,* 11–14.

Silver, L. B. (1989a). Frequency of adoption of children and adolescents with learning disabilities. *Journal of Learning Disabilities, 22,* 325–327.

Silver, L. B. (1989b). Psychological and family problems associated with learning disabilities: Assessment and intervention. *Journal of the American Academy of Child and Adolescent Psychiatry, 28,* 319–325.

Slater, M. A., & Wikler, L. (1986). "Normalized" family resources for families with a developmentally disabled child. *Social Work, 31,* 385–390.

Solan, H. A. (1981). Rationale for the optometric treatment and management of children with learning disabilities. *Journal of Learning Disabilities, 14,* 568–572.

Solnit, A., & Stark, M. H. (1961). Mourning and the birth of a defective child. *Psychoanalytic Study of the Child, 16,* 523–537.

Spacone, C., & Hansen, J. C. (1984). Therapy with a family with a learning disabled child. In J. C. Hansen (Ed.), *Family therapy with school related problems* (pp. 46–58). Rockville, MD: Aspen Systems Corporation.

Staver, N. (1953). The child's learning difficulty as related to the emotional problem of the mother. *American Journal of Orthopsychiatry, 23,* 131–140.

Taichert, L. C., & Harwin, D. D. (1975). Adoption and children with learning and behavior problems. *Western Journal of Medicine, 122,* 464–470.

Trevino, F. (1979). Siblings of handicapped children: Identifying those at risk. *Social Casework, 60,* 488–493.

Vigilante, F. W. (1983). Working with families of learning disabled children. *Child Welfare, 62,* 429–436.

Vigilante, F. W. (1985). Reassessing the developmental needs of children with learning disabilities: Programmatic implications. *Journal of Child and Adolescent Social Work, 2,* 167–180.

Vigilante, F. W., & Rosenberger, J. (1988, February). *Evaluating family characteristics in relation to their impact on learning disabled children.* Paper presented at the International Conference of the Association for Children and Adults with Learning Disabilities, Las Vegas, NV.

Ziegler, R., & Holden, L. (1988). Family therapy for learning disabled and attention-deficit disordered children. *American Journal of Orthopsychiatry, 58,* 196–210.

Zill, N. (1985). *Behavior and learning problems among adopted children: Findings from a U.S. national survey of child health.* Paper presented at the meeting of the Society for Research in Child Development, Toronto, Canada.

Chapter 6

Federal Legislation: Intent, Implementation, and Impacts

Social workers need a basic understanding of the major pieces of legislation that directly affect the access of children with learning disabilities to resources and services. Much of the emphasis of this legislation is placed on meeting the educational and social needs of children with learning disabilities from birth to age 21. However, the existence of enabling legislation has not guaranteed adequate, appropriate, or timely intervention. Schools and communities frequently are overburdened in responding to complex, learning-related difficulties of children. Resources may be limited, or administrative, political, and staffing issues may take precedence over planning for individual students' needs. Parents often are poorly informed and unfamiliar with institutional requirements and legal mandates.

To work effectively with families in negotiating appropriate services, social workers must become familiar with the federal, state, and local municipality regulations and guidelines. The legislation discussed in this chapter does not represent all of the legislation that may affect children with learning disabilities. The focus here is on laws that are aimed specifically at protecting the rights of children with learning disabilities, the social and emotional impact of those laws, and the problematic issues involved in implementing them. Excellent manuals have been published by national and local advocacy groups that present the general procedural and due process rights of parents and children (Bogin & Goodman, 1985; Children's Defense Fund, 1989; Lapham, 1980).

Social workers are familiar with complex institutional systems, and have expert skills in the dynamics of working with families who have children with different handicapping conditions. Individualizing family needs is imperative when integrating the requirements of the legislation with the particular strengths and vulnerabilities of a family. A good resolution for one family may not be a good plan for another. For example, certain groups of children and parents under constant environmental stress are more vulnerable to institutional neglect (Schorr, 1983; Snyder, Hampton, & Newberger, 1983). Teenage parents, whose own past interactions with school systems have been unsuccessful; single parents whose work schedules prohibit frequent school visits; families in public shelters; families for whom English is not a primary language; and recent immigrants to the United States all may have difficulty communicating with school personnel.

Children with learning disabilities who are in foster, group, or institutional care represent an especially vulnerable population, whose learning disabilities can make it difficult for them to comprehend and deal with the complexities and instabilities of their transient lives. Their biological parents usually have surrendered—temporarily or permanently—their rights to the state or a social agency. A number of these children first receive care because they have been abused and neglected (Snyder et al., 1983). The emotional and possible physical impacts of these childhood experiences may have particularly negative consequences for children who also have learning disabilities. These children are particularly in need of surrogate parents who can perform ongoing educational advocacy, but because such children may attract educators' attention by their disruptive behavior or their depressed emotional state, full attention may not be given to their underlying developmental problems and current learning needs. The failure of these children to gather supporters and advocates at home may be mirrored in their alternative care arrangements, as well as in the school system. These children are at high risk of being mislabeled and of falling through the cracks in the educational system. Legislative access to services and resources are only a beginning for this group. However, all children with learning disabilities require individualized attention and continuing advocacy throughout their school careers. The social worker's responsibility begins with understanding the complexity of the legislation establishing educational policy and ensuring its implementation in a manner that responds to the special needs of each child.

HISTORICAL BACKGROUND

The separation of children with disabilities from those in regular public education in the United States dates from the mid-1800s. When public schools were established, children with disabilities either sat in classes until they were old enough to drop out, were discouraged from going to school at all, were hidden at home, or were living in institutions with no educational services. There were no immediate legal protections, because the U.S. Constitution did not directly ensure citizens' rights to education. However, a conceptual framework for federal involvement did exist through the equal protection and due process clauses of the Constitution. These clauses were interpreted to mean that if a state took the responsibility to educate some of its citizens, then an equal education for all citizens must be provided.

Following the groundbreaking path of 1950s civil rights legislation, in the 1960s parent and professional advocates lobbied successfully for protective and enabling legislation for children with disabilities in individual states. Two critical lawsuits (*Pennsylvania Association for Retarded Citizens v. Pennsylvania*, 1972; *Mills v. Board of Education in the District of Columbia*, 1972) successfully contested the exclusion of children with handicaps from schools. The federal role in addressing the needs of children with disabilities began in the late 1960s and culminated in the 1970s with the passage of the first federal Education of the Handicapped Act of 1971 (P.L. 91–230). It was not until a complete revision of Part B of this legislation was undertaken in 1975 that learning disabilities were identified and defined as part of the federal law.

The Education for All Handicapped Children Act of 1975 (P.L. 94–142) (EHA) has been called the most significant child welfare legislation of the 1970s (Weatherly, 1979). With the addition of the amendments of 1983 (P.L. 98–199) and the amendments of 1986 (P.L. 99–457), EHA rights and protections were extended to children from ages 3 through 5 years old, and grants to states to provide programs for eligible children from birth through age 2 were established. By law, all states should have developed programs for learning-disabled children aged 3 to 5 by 1991. The programs mandated by EHA are administered by the U.S. Department of Education Office of Special Programs. Each state education agency must develop regulations and guidelines that conform to the federal regulations before the state can receive federal funding for the programs.

EHA established how federal money was to be allocated and spent in the program. The percentage of children who can be classified as handicapped in each state was set at 12 percent of the total school-age population between ages 5 to 17 and the number of children who can be classified as learning disabled was set at 2 percent of the total school-age population in the state. Procedures were established to guide provision of services. Some states have expanded the rights mandated by the federal law and funded the additional costs. Other states have used the most restrictive language possible. Interpretation of the legislation varies widely between states, and change is occurring constantly in state regulations, either due to the pressure of legal challenges or to lobbying groups (Bogin & Goodman, 1985; Lapham, 1980).

EDUCATION FOR ALL HANDICAPPED CHILDREN ACT

EHA implementation has been fraught with controversy. Some children have benefitted from its programs. Many other children have not. Difficulties and tensions have revolved around six basic principles that had not been applied nationwide in school systems before the enactment of the law: (1) the right of access to public education programs, (2) the individualization of services, (3) the principle of least-restrictive environment, (4) the scope of broadened services to be provided by the schools and a set of procedures for determining these, (5) the general guidelines for identification of disability, and (6) the principles of primary state and local responsibilities (Walker, 1987).

The use of a medical model of disability in EHA has led to the categorization of handicapped versus nonhandicapped students and a resulting segregation of students into regular and special education classes. The number of referrals to special education classes has grown exponentially since the implementation of EHA. The quality of special education has been questioned. However, there also have been increasing questions about the quality of education received by students in regular education classes. Some groups have pressed for a unified educational system that would be "special" for all students (Gartner & Lipsky, 1987). Other groups have suggested streamlining and refining special educational approaches. Few groups are satisfied with the way that services now are being provided in either regular or special education.

Service to Children with Learning Disabilities Mandated

The EHA mandate that underlies all other requirements, procedures, rights, and safeguards of the legislation is found in this statement (Ballard, Ramirez, & Zantal-Wiener, 1987):

A free appropriate public education which emphasizes special education and related services designed to meet their [handicapped children's] unique needs to assure that the rights of handicapped children and their parents or guardians are protected . . . [and] to assess and assure the effectiveness of efforts to educate handicapped children. . . . Special education is defined as specially designed instruction, at no cost to parents or guardians, to meet the unique needs of a handicapped child, including classroom instruction, instruction in physical education and instruction in hospitals and institutions. (Education for All Handicapped Children Act, 1975)

Children with handicapping conditions who are covered by the legislation include those who are mentally retarded, hard of hearing, deaf, speech-impaired, visually handicapped, or seriously emotionally disturbed. Also, children with orthopedic or other health impairments, deafness-blindness, multiple handicaps, or specific learning disabilities are covered. Throughout the Congressional deliberations on EHA, there was great controversy about the inclusion of learning disabilities as a separate category. The clarification of diagnosis and placement of children with learning disabilities were among the most complex tasks required by the legislation. For this reason, a special definition of learning disabilities was included in EHA:

Those children who have a disorder in one or more of the basic psychological processes involved in understanding or in using language, spoken or written, which disorder may manifest itself in imperfect ability to listen, think, speak, read, write, spell or do mathematical calculations. Such disorders include such conditions as perceptual handicaps, brain injury, minimal brain dysfunction, dyslexia, and developmental aphasia. Such term does not include children who have learning problems which are primarily the result of visual, hearing, or motor handicaps, of mental retardation, of emotional disturbance or environmental, cultural or economic disadvantage. (Education for All Handicapped Children Act, 1975)

Although handicapping conditions included under the EHA mandate are federally defined, each state must set eligibility standards for each condition. For example, there has been considerable controversy among professionals regarding the definition of a learning disability. Usually, the basis for determining whether a learning disability exists rests on a predetermined degree of discrepancy between ability and performance based on age, grade, or intelligence quotient score. The amount of discrepancy allowed by a state determines how many children will be classified as learning disabled. For example, a New York court (*Riley v. Ambach*, 1981) ruled that the state 50 percent rule of discrepancy between ability and achievement could not be applied rigidly, but that each child had to be viewed individually. Even with a 50 percent discrepancy between ability and achievement, a child who falls into that category may or may not be learning disabled. In other states, efforts continue to try to resolve the eligibility issue in different ways. However, there is great concern about the steady expansion in numbers of children designated as learning disabled. Social workers in and outside of the school system must become familiar with the eligibility standards for learning disabilities that have been applied in their state.

Legislative Mandate for Social Work Intervention

EHA provided the first national recognition of the social work role in the educational setting and encouragement for states to develop more specific guidelines (Allen–Meares, Washington, & Welsh, 1986). Social workers are heavily involved in three areas: (1) the provision of related services, in which psychological and counseling services are specifically mentioned in the federal law; (2) the development of the social history at the time of an initial evaluation, and later at annual and triennial reviews; and (3) serving as multidisciplinary team leader, case manager, or participant in the multidisciplinary team meetings and performing educational liaison and advocacy functions for parents. The extent that social workers actually are used in these capacities depends on state codes, availability of trained social workers, local custom, and individual initiative. State and local school district officials generally develop their own guidelines for social service personnel. The overlap of social workers' professional domains with those of psychologists and guidance counselors has forced social workers to develop negotiation skills to work out cooperative relationships. The use of social workers and the importance of their role varies across the United States, depending upon the relative strength of the state and local social work associations, relationships with educational administrators, and legislative linkages.

EHA requirements are mainly procedural. This allows social workers latitude for creativity in developing roles that are supportive to children with learning disabilities and their families. There is a rich tradition of school-based social work counseling and psychosocial history development in the professional literature. For this reason, these areas are not highlighted here. It is important to recognize that community-based, as well as school-based, social workers may become involved in working with families and advocating for their educational rights. The following examples illustrate the kinds of formal and informal roles social workers may play under EHA mandates.

161

Child Find. According to Allen-Meares et al. (1986), "All handicapped children who have been excluded in the past and are within state compulsory school age limits must be located and provided with appropriate educational services. All states are required to implement child-find procedures to locate unserved children and to inform parents of available programs" (p. 138). EHA requires that services be available for children from ages 3 to 21. With the addition of the amendments of 1986, children from birth through age 2 also are covered. For early intervention and prevention of the cumulative negative impact of a learning disability to take place, there must be a recognition of the complexities in the identification of these children. Both groups—the previously unidentified and the very young, early identified children—pose specific challenges for the social worker.

EHA was designed to redress past neglect of children with handicapping conditions and to identify children who had newly emerging functional difficulties with school. Social workers should remember that identifying children who have been neglected or overlooked may be viewed as a tacit indictment of the school system, and that they may encounter bureaucratic resistance to identification of children who have been passed over year after year (Levine, Brooks, & Shonkoff, 1980; Ungerleider, 1985). Parents of these children may become angry and accusatory. They need to be helped to work with the school to ensure appropriate future planning. Although this situation does not apply to the majority of children, those whom it does affect may have lost months or even years of valuable learning opportunities. Heightened emotions should be expected.

Social workers' knowledge about high-risk groups provides a beginning guide for outreach even before children are school-aged. Community social workers must be aware of the state Child Find regulations and be alert to signs of learning delay among the children they encounter in health and mental health clinics, preschool programs, settlement houses, community centers, and foster homes. The EHA Amendments of 1986 (P.L. 99–457) require follow-up services to be available.

Social workers must explore with parents how their children are doing in school, how they like school, and whether they are finding it unusually hard or stressful. For example, the child who has been labeled unofficially as "class dummy" or "class clown" may be hiding an inability to meet classroom expectations. Other children with learning disabilities develop school avoidance patterns, such as stomachaches or headaches, in response to the anxiety and humiliation they encounter in the classroom. Community social workers should create opportunities to develop informal relationships with local school social workers, so that they can become more familiar with the local school's early childhood programs and referral procedures. School social workers should develop and maintain communication and referral channels with community groups, social and health agencies, independent professionals, and parents. For effective early identification to take place, there must be collaboration between school social workers and professionals working in other areas.

Initiating Procedural Due Process. EHA requires

> written prior notice to the parents or guardians of the child whenever such agency or unit (i) proposes to initiate or change, or (ii) refuses to initiate or change the identification, evaluation or educational placement of the child or the provision of a free appropriate public education to the child; procedures designed to assure that the notice required fully informs the parents or guardian, in the parents' or guardians' native language unless it clearly is not feasible to do so, of all the procedures available pursuant to this section. . . . (Education for All Handicapped Children Act, 1975)

Children suspected of needing special education services may be referred for a special education evaluation by their parents or by school personnel. The referral can be made by phone, in person, or by mail, and should state why the child might need special education. As stated in EHA, no evaluation processes or procedures can be initiated before the parents have given written consent. Every effort must be made by the social worker to ensure that parents understand the evaluation procedures, the timing and sequence of testing, and the roles parents can and should play during the different steps of the process. Some states publish a small handbook or brochure outlining parents' rights to participation in the process. The social worker may wish to supplement this publication with a simpler outline of the relevant processes that is geared specifically to the local school.

School and community social workers should advise parents that, even when school officials have the best intentions and want to act in the best interests of the children, the complexity of the bureaucracy and lack of sufficient resources may impede the process. It is important for parents to maintain an accurate record of communications between themselves and school personnel, documenting these by date and return receipts. The social worker should counsel and, if necessary, assist parents in keeping a log documenting the name, date, and content of every communication, however casual. All unwritten communications should be followed by a dated letter sent by certified mail. Parents should keep a copy for their files and keep all envelopes with the date and stamp of all mail they receive from the school. Although these safeguards seem to add an unnecessarily adversarial overtone to every communication, remember that it is not because of malice that a child in need slips through the bureaucratic cracks. Often, it is because of administrative expediency or lack of professional oversight that the best plan is not made. For some parents, this may be a very difficult course to follow. In vulnerable family situations, such as the fragile or disorganized family, parents may not be able to effectively monitor the school situation. The social worker should assess the support network of the family and determine whether additional resources should be brought in to support the parents.

School and community social workers may encounter parents who do not agree with a recommendation for referral for an evaluation. Social workers must seek to understand the basis for a family's refusal or reluctance to have their child tested for special education placement. For example, parental resistance may be based on lack of information and awareness of the child's special needs, on the child's earlier bad experiences in school, or on fear of consequences of special education labeling. In some communities, once the decision to move a child into special education is made, it becomes extremely difficult for children to move back into a regular educational setting. Parents may be aware of this and may view special education not as an opportunity for individualized educational assistance, but as a permanent, stigmatizing loss of future opportunities for a regular education.

Parents' objections must be respected. There is a preponderance of research data supporting these concerns. Excessive numbers of school children have been identified as having learning disabilities. From 1985 to 1986, these children accounted for 42.8 percent of all students getting special educational services in the age 3 to 21 eligible age group (Keogh, 1987). There also is a wide divergence among states and cities in the numbers of children identified as learning disabled (Council of Great City Schools, 1986). Shepard, Smith, and Vojir (1983) pointed out the apparent ease and arbitrariness with which children are labeled learning disabled: "At least half of the learning disabled population could be more accurately described as slow learners, as children with second language backgrounds, as children who are naughty in class, as average learners in above average systems" (p. 220).

School officials are not always willing to develop the necessary diversity and flexibility of teaching methodologies to encompass the wide range of learners who could remain in regular classrooms. Appropriate assessment and interpretation by skilled professionals is necessary throughout the evaluation and placement process. Identification of specific learning disabilities is one of the most difficult of all of the handicapping conditions to evaluate. The issues are complex, and the resolution of individual student situations is neither easy nor always optimal. As advocates for the best educational interests of the child, social workers must help parents to weigh the options, which may include seeking assessments outside the school system, finding tutoring services, keeping the child in the regular classroom with appropriate monitoring, or seeking special classrooms and education services.

Parents of children with learning disabilities may attempt to blame their child's learning problems on the system—on poor teaching, not enough discipline, discrimination, or prejudice. Or, the disabilities may be categorized as the child's fault, because the child is lazy, disobedient, or bad. These parental rationales may come from reality, ignorance, avoidance, or fear. All possibilities must be fairly assessed.

Social workers must try to engage parents in productive activities in the school setting or in the community, to ensure that the child receives an appropriate evaluation. On the other hand, there are times when social workers must advocate for continuance of mainstream education and help parents seek outside supports.

EHA was designed to ensure that parents' rights would be respected through all of the implementation phases. The social worker, whether based in a school or a community agency, performs the critical functions of informing parents of their rights, mediating between parents and school personnel, and promoting nonadversarial meetings between parents and school staff. Social workers must help parents recognize that their advocacy for their child does not necessarily place them in an adversarial position with the school. The ultimate goal is a partnership aimed at ensuring an appropriate learning environment for the child.

When disagreements cannot be resolved, the social worker should support parents in retaining appropriate legal assistance. This step should be taken well before any move is made toward a due process hearing. The due process hearing, a quasi-legal procedure, was designed to resolve disagreements between parents and a local school district about four key aspects of the special education process: (1) identification, (2) evaluation, (3) placement, and (4) free appropriate education.

Through their understanding of individual and family needs, organizational issues, and legislation, social workers may play important roles in promoting a positive collaboration between families with learning-disabled children and schools. This collaboration cannot take place unless parents are aware of their rights and responsibilities. The social worker is not the only professional who discusses these topics with parents, but often is the single professional who has the mandate to serve as a systems advocate on behalf of the best interests of the child and family.

Nondiscriminatory Testing. EHA requires that

> procedures to assure that testing and evaluation materials and procedures utilized for the purposes of evaluation and placement of handicapped children will be selected and administered so as not to be racially or culturally discriminatory. Such materials or procedures shall be provided and administered in the child's native language or mode of communication, unless it clearly is not feasible to do so, and no single procedure shall be the sole criterion for determining an appropriate educational program for a child. (Education for All Handicapped Children Act, 1975)

All social workers are trained to recognize a discriminatory or incomplete assessment. Social workers are skilled in counteracting bias and discriminatory testing approaches, based on their understanding of the cultural and racial issues that need to be recognized in the evaluation process. Through home visits and the compilation of the psychosocial history, an understanding of the child and the family gives the social worker insight into how and where certain assessment processes may penalize children of diverse backgrounds.

If social workers suspect bias or discrimination in the testing or placement processes, they should work inside the school system to rectify the situation. They also should urge parents to seek an independent evaluation and help them to find low-cost resources. Parents should know that the independent expert they choose for testing can evaluate the child's current classroom as well as visit the proposed new placement if one is recommended. This professional also may be asked to serve as an expert witness if a due process hearing is held. If a professional evaluator who is called for due process hearings has known the child and the situation over a period of time, his or her credibility with the hearing officers increases (Bogin & Goodman, 1985). These precautions have been found to be particularly important in work with children with learning disabilities where the identification and assessment process is recognized to be exceedingly difficult.

If school officials can prove at a due process hearing that their own evaluation gave a fair picture of the child's functioning, then the parents must pay for their outside evaluation. If the school is found to have conducted an incomplete or discriminatory evaluation based on state and federal guidelines, and a fair picture of the child's functioning was not given, then the parents are entitled to be reimbursed for the outside evaluation and legal fees (Handicapped Children's Protection Act, 1986). Whatever the outcome of the due process hearing, the outside evaluation reports may be considered when the individualized education plan (IEP) is developed. Social work advocates and parents must be sure that any outside evaluation reports and educational recommendations are included in the IEP discussions.

There are other parts of the identification and evaluation process in which discriminatory processes may take place. For example, parents should be encouraged to observe the classroom, or ask the social worker to make a classroom visit. Teachers sometimes find children with learning disabilities to be particularly unrewarding pupils, and present a more negative picture of their behavior than necessary. Children with learning disabilities may not pick up teachers' cues of appropriate classroom behavior. They may speak out of turn, misunderstand directions, never complete the assigned work, or forget today what they learned yesterday. The teacher's frustration at not being able to help a child academically may spill over into other daily interchanges and create an atmosphere of negative expectations. Children with learning disabilities are very sensitive to a rejecting environment. They are quick to pick up impatience, hostility, and negativity, even though they are unable to control their own behavior or its effects. This does not necessarily mean that these children do not belong in the regular classroom, but it does mean that some classroom adaptations may be called for to help them (Vigilante, 1990).

Some children without learning disabilities who come from non-mainstream class, cultural, racial, or ethnic backgrounds may exhibit some of the behavioral characteristics of the child with learning disabilities. They may have difficulty following the pace, style, and expectations of the teacher and may not always conform to classroom norms. Teacher frustration may be the source of many inappropriate and unnecessary referrals for special education evaluation. Social workers must help parents to distinguish between appropriate and inappropriate referrals and to select strategies that will be helpful to the child whatever the outcome.

166

Parental Participation and Involvement. There is a strong history of parent leadership in obtaining access to public education for children with disabilities. The institution of the critical class-action suits in the early 1970s, the passage of individual state laws, and the inclusion of specific parental rights and roles in the federal legislation all were won with the strong participation and leadership of parents. However, these hard-won rights have not been extensively used and parents generally have not been encouraged to continue their leadership roles (Gartner & Lipsky, 1987).

The strong parental guidelines in EHA were included with the expectation that parents would fulfill a number of diverse roles that would promote a partnership with school officials. Parents were expected to provide historical and updated information and feedback; participate in planning and programming decisions through the IEP, multidisciplinary team meetings, and specific meetings with teachers; and to serve as parent advocates to other parents. To carry out these roles, the law granted parents specific rights, stressing that the procedural safeguards of parents' rights were not limited to those stated in the legislation.

EHA provisions mandate stated rights, and limits to these rights, for parents. Parents must become familiar with the law and be able to have quick access to its exact language. Administrators and teachers usually know about the law, but few have read it. Social workers can begin by making sure that parents are acquainted with the following parental rights granted by EHA provisions and their implications:

- Parents must receive a written prior notice when their child is identified for possible special education evaluation. Parents must give written consent before an evaluation is conducted or placement is made in a special education class. Parents can withdraw consent at any time. If parents do not give their consent, the school can proceed to have an impartial hearing to override the parents.
- Parents must receive written notice of all proposed changes or, if the school refuses to initiate a change, notice of class placement; or an explanation of why action is proposed or refused. Parents also must be notified of each assessment or report to be used in any evaluation or review process related to a proposed change.
- All communications are to be in the parents' native language. (The assumption that parents are literate in their native language should be explored. Additionally, it is likely that the language used in such school communications may be unfamiliar to some parents, no matter what language it may be written in.)
- Parents must be notified about each evaluation or report to be used in formal discussions about their child and they must have the opportunity to review all written school records about their child.
- Parents have the right to obtain an independent evaluation at no or low expense, and to be told about the procedures through which the school pays

167

for any of this expense (as discussed above in the due process hearing description).

• Parents must be informed about when and where the multidisciplinary team conference to develop the IEP and decide on a placement plan for their child will be held. The meeting should be held at a time and place that will promote parental participation. If parents are unable to attend, their participation must be solicited through other means and these efforts must be documented.

• Parents have the right to an impartial due process hearing if they do not agree with the final placement decision. If parents or others disagree with the outcome, an appeal may be made to the state education agency to have an impartial review. During the period of these proceedings, the child must remain in the current school placement or, if just starting school, be placed in a generally appropriate class.

• During any school meetings or hearings, parents have the right to have an advocate, counsel, or expert who is knowledgeable about their child present with them.

The multidisciplinary team, or Committee on Special Education (CSE), is the pivotal entity in the school linking regular education programs with special education programs. Each state develops specific guidelines for the composition of these school-district–based CSEs, based on federal requirements and local needs. Nationally, CSEs are mandated by EHA to include a school psychologist, a teacher or administrator of special education, a physician, and a parent of a handicapped child who lives in the school district (but not the child being evaluated). The current teacher of the child being evaluated also is expected to be present. School districts may include any number of related service professionals. Social workers and guidance counselors frequently are CSE members. More infrequently, psychiatrists, vocational or rehabilitation counselors, and nurses are included.

The CSE performs a number of important functions. Once a referral is made, each team member evaluates the child's strengths and weaknesses from the perspective of their professional expertise. At the IEP planning meeting, to which the child's parents must be invited, CSE members discuss the results of evaluations and the child's school history. With the parents' input, an IEP to guide in-class placement is developed. The CSE meets annually to review each child's progress. Triennially, the team reviews the appropriateness of the IEP and the child's need to remain in special education. Parents are expected to be an integral part of these processes. However, experience has shown a vast difference between EHA goals and reality.

One study of parental involvement showed that parents provided very little input into the development of the IEP for their children (Baker & Brightman, 1984). Another study noted that only half of the children's parents attended IEP meetings and that their contributions were not seen as very useful by the professionals (Goldstein, Strickland, Turnbull, & Curry, 1980). Some parents share the professional view and belief that when they do attend meetings their role is to give information, not to share in decision making (Lusthaus, Lusthaus, & Gibbs, 1981). According to a recent federal report on the implementation of EHA, in the majority of IEP conferences parents are presented with the team's decisions, demonstrating that a prior meeting had taken place (U.S. Department of Education, 1987). These findings are even more startling because of the distinct legislative charge to local public school officials to exert the maximum effort possible to ensure that at least one parent attend the IEP meeting.

The legitimate concerns that parents may have about the lack of appropriate programs, their child's lack of progress, ambiguities in reports, and vague IEP goals often are seen as obstructive by school officials. The implication is that if the parents only understood, they would not be so resistant. Other reports have described the devaluation of parental concerns and the information these concerns provide about the child's behavior and skills (Ferguson & Asch, 1989).

Parents' knowledge of their rights and legitimate roles in the process of evaluation and placement comes from several sources: hearsay from other parents who share their experience; printed information made available by the local school, the district, or the city or state education agency; discussion with professionals employed by the Board of Education (the school social worker may be one of these); and finally, through parent or professional advocacy groups and organizations.

Most parents do not talk with other parents who have been through the special education evaluation process. There often is embarrassment at having a child who is not performing acceptably in school. The subtle implication that the parents may be at fault often puts parents on the defensive and isolates them from learning from others' experiences. Some parents may be isolated in their communities and not have an information network to draw on. Other parents who are serving as foster parents may not want to share that the child they are caring for is having specific problems. The written materials developed to inform parents of their rights under EHA have been found not to be useful to a large number of parents (Roit & Pfohl, 1984). The language in these materials may be correct, but the ways in which a parent can gain access to support and advocacy in negotiating the education system are not made clear. For parents who may distrust the school system, the semilegal framing of some of the written materials may be seen as distancing rather than encouraging involvement.

There are many possible avenues for social work intervention to protect the rights of parents and their children with learning disabilities as they become involved with the special education system. Social workers can use their professional skills to educate and empower parents, and to serve as intermediaries and interpreters throughout the assessment and planning process. Social workers can interpret the importance of sequential steps, outline the roles of different school personnel, and preview the kinds of outcomes likely at different meetings, while exploring the short-term and long-term implications for the child. By validating the parents' knowledge and experience with their child, social workers can help parents to gain the confidence to press to have their views heard and incorporated in planning discussions. Social workers also can help parents bridge race, class, culture, and educational differences by interpreting their traditions and customs, clarifying the nature of environmental pressures, and sharing relevant facts and family history with the school professionals. Social workers also are aware of other variables that may affect the way that parents' actions and words are interpreted in formal and informal meetings.

Enhancing parental participation not only is in keeping with the EHA mandate, but also helps parents accept the outcome of the evaluation and IEP processes and spurs them to work collaboratively with the school system to ensure an appropriate education for their child. Although outside advocacy groups and mutual aid groups also promote parental involvement, their agendas may conflict with those of school officials.

When legal custody for a child has been transferred to a court or social agency, EHA states that a surrogate parent must be appointed to represent the child's educational interests. The social worker must determine that this actually has been accomplished, and ensure that the surrogate parent is involved in a more than perfunctory way. The social worker may have to assume a more active role than if the child were cared for by a biological parent, and work more closely with the foster or surrogate parent. For example, a social worker from a community agency, rather than the foster parent, may represent the state as legal surrogate parent at a CSE meeting. The social worker's presence may prove critical to the outcome of the meeting. When the social worker can demonstrate that a child with learning disabilities has an advocate in an outside agency who is willing to monitor and be a resource for the school, the members of CSE are more likely to consider options that build on the social worker's support and may select less restrictive placements than otherwise would have been chosen. Effective surrogate parent involvement broadens the options for the child under evaluation, through the demonstration of a comprehensive support network around the child that alters the child's learning environment.

Individual Educational Programs. According to EHA, the IEP is a written statement that must include

> a statement of the present levels of educational performance of [the] child, a statement of annual goals, including short term instructional objectives, a statement of the specific educational services to be provided to [the] child, and the extent to which [the] child will be able to participate in regular educational programs, the projected date for initiation and anticipated duration of such services, and appropriate objective criteria and evaluation procedures, and schedules for determining, on at least an annual basis, whether instructional objectives are being achieved. (EHA, 1975)

170

The IEP should be viewed as a management tool that does not necessarily include a detailed account of specific instructional plans (Ballard et al., 1987). The IEP is a mechanism through which an appropriate education is determined for the child with learning disabilities. For this reason, parents must fully understand and concur with the IEP before signing their agreement. The plan must be truly individualized and reflect appropriate goals to meet the child's educational needs and potential for learning.

The IEP is the basis for evaluation of the child's progress. If the defined goals are not reached, then a thorough review of the placement and related services (educational and psychological) is necessary. It may be particularly difficult for parents to evaluate the appropriateness of educational goals for a learning-disabled child. Parental expectations may reflect fantasies of a normal child, depression, withdrawal, or anger, depending on parents' level of acceptance and understanding of their child's deficits. Additionally, it is difficult for professional educators to make realistic, yet challenging, goals for children with learning disabilities. Multidisciplinary teams may be inclined to select goals they know can be achieved with the use of their school's resources, rather than goals that would require additional staff expenditures. Parents may benefit from the less constrained response of an outside educational evaluator to assess the multidisciplinary team's goals for their child and, if necessary, to support parents in the suggestion of additional goals.

The IEP is not required to include discussion of any regular education programming or to outline a structure for the coordination between regular and special education services. Parents and their advocates must press for inclusion of these areas. Where appropriate, there should be discussion of efforts that will be made to return a child to a regular classroom, or to gain more involvement in regular classroom activity. It is very important that timetables and guideposts for these efforts be established in the IEP.

If a child is being reviewed for possible special education services for the first time, the CSE meeting at which an IEP is developed must take place within a specified time period. Each state department of education has guidelines and parental protections if the local education agency has not acted in a timely fashion. Parents and social workers must become familiar with the sanctions that each state imposes for slow processing of the evaluation, because these sanctions may open new opportunities for the child.

There are five steps in the development of the formal educational program: (1) identification of the learning problem, (2) referral to the multidisciplinary team, (3) diagnosis or evaluation, (4) statement of the actual program to be carried out, and (5) evaluation and monitoring during the school year (Allen-Meares et al., 1986). For parents to be effective in evaluating the IEP statement, they must be fully aware of the data about their child on which the statement is based. Social workers must assist parents in gaining access to testing reports, teachers' statements, and any other information that will be used as a basis for the team's deliberation. Parents have the right to have copies of all of their child's educational

171

records (Family Educational Rights and Privacy Act, 1974). If a social worker from a community agency or a lawyer wishes to obtain records, parents may sign a release form and access will be granted. Once a child reaches age 16 or 18, local state laws may require both parent and child to sign release forms.

Educational records generally include three types of files: (1) school records (permanent or cumulative records—grades, test scores, class assignments and attendance rates; and temporary records—guidance and anecdotal information); (2) CSE records (reports of completed educational evaluations, independent evaluations submitted by parents or a nonschool agency, anecdotal information submitted to the CSE by any school personnel); and (3) the child's computer record, available at the central office of education in the district. A summary of the child's history in the school system as reflected in these various school records is presented at the CSE meeting. Each of these records may present a different perspective on the child's performance and may play a role in the direction selected for placement.

The social worker should discuss all of the records with parents to assess the extent to which the records give a fair picture of the child's academic performance, abilities, behavior, and reasons for referral. Parents should stress the need for clear, specific reasons for referral of their child to special education. As noted by Biklin and Zollers (1986), very often children with learning disabilities are referred because of the teacher's difficulty in managing their behavior in the classroom. Often, the decision to place a student in a segregated setting is not an educational one, but an administrative decision (Lehr, 1987) based on the teacher's and the school's choice to focus on pupil change rather than structural or teacher skills change. Social workers should be alert to record entries that may result in erroneous impressions of children with learning disabilities. A common type of misleading entry is a description of a single incident that may be identified as a characteristic behavior pattern because there is no statement in the record to offset the negative report. Attempts should be made to find out if there were changes in the home environment at the time of negative incident reports, such as a family becoming homeless, parental illness, divorce, or exposure to violence. The record may not include any notation of these changes in the child's environment, which may have had a direct impact on the child's emotional resiliency (Unger-leider, 1985).

The positive anecdotal information in a child's records may be downplayed by the CSE when it actually deserves elaboration. There also should be attention to deleting any irrelevant or inappropriate data that might reflect prejudicial attitudes toward the child, such as parental living arrangements or criminal involvement. If such material is found and deemed not to be relevant, parents should be encouraged to make a formal, written request to the school principal that the inappropriate material be removed. Parents should collect any important documents they have about their child that would help give a more well-rounded picture of his or her performance in and out of school, such as notes from teachers with whom the child has had a good relationship and any after-school program participation or church activities.

Although schools may undervalue the role of the parent representative on the multidisciplinary team, the representative can be extremely helpful to the anxious parent coming before the CSE committee for the first time. Unfortunately, many schools have been unable to get a parent representative to attend the CSEs consistently. Parents who do participate may not be skilled in the complex role of parent advocate when surrounded by a group of professional school staff members.

Parents or guardians must be present at the IEP meeting. When appropriate, the child with learning disabilities also may attend. The school social worker should encourage the parents and the child to ask questions or share information that may be helpful in establishing a good IEP plan. Parents can and should be a source of knowledge about their children. Drawing on an understanding of the parental level of sophistication, the social worker should intervene, interpolate, or slow the IEP process to promote parents' maximum understanding of the process and issues and to ensure that parents play an active role.

The individual instructional program that is developed in the CSE team meeting is not a binding contract, and may be changed at any time. A draft of the IEP is read to parents at the meeting. Before the IEP can be put into operation, parents must accept the goals, objectives, and placement that have been recommended. A number of areas that should be closely examined, depending on the age of child concerned, follow:

- Is there any mention of return to the regular classroom, or next least restrictive setting, as a goal?
- Is there a time frame for this?
- Is there a prevocational curriculum to expose youngsters to future areas of training in vocational education? Recent legislation (Carl D. Perkins Vocational Education Act, 1984) stresses that students should have information about the availability of vocational education options at least 1 year before these are offered, and no later than the ninth grade. This information process can begin as early as seventh grade.
- Does the educational program suggested include the requisite number of instructional hours and subjects necessary for a high school diploma?
- Are provisions made for inclusion in a sports program? (Sometimes youngsters in special education are excluded from participation on school sports teams on the basis of poor grades. If poor grades are due to a disabling condition, then it is illegal to exclude these children from the opportunity to participate.)
- What social and behavioral goals are included?

Social workers must be particularly attentive to the inclusion of goals for the development of appropriate social skills. The social worker must encourage parents to articulate academic, social, and behavioral goals that are particularly relevant to their child. In the case of children with learning disabilities, reaching these goals may require individual social work counseling or participation in socialization groups during or after school. The advantage of having social skills as a curriculum area in special education is that it can be included on IEP and integrated into the student's schedule. Care must be taken that socialization groups are not scheduled at a time when meetings will compete with academic subjects. Youngsters with learning disabilities also may need speech or language therapy or the assistance of specialists in other areas. Social workers may assist parents in the clarification of which related services are mandated by their state, and which professional groups are licensed to perform them. The local school may not offer all of the services a child may need. However, if these services are state mandated, the school must make some arrangements for them to be available when needed.

Study after study has shown that the goal of effective parental participation in CSE IEP meetings is not always achieved. One study of children with mild learning problems revealed that the most frequently discussed topics were curriculum, behavior, and performance, with little emphasis on other areas despite their relevance and importance (Goldstein, et al., 1980). In this study, the authors' observations revealed a pervasive problem for parents in IEP meetings:

> It is doubtful that parents were aware of the day to day functioning of resource rooms or of issues such as the nature of coordination between resource and classroom teachers. The reason that parents did not ask placement questions could be that they did not realize the complexity of all the issues involved in [e]nsuring that the child is, indeed, appropriately served. Further, parents made no requests for related services such as speech therapy or counseling even though these services would have been highly appropriate in several cases. The legal rights of parents were glossed over in the majority of conferences. (p. 283)

Although this study was not large and was completed some years ago, little in the current literature indicates that significant changes have taken place in subsequent years (Research Triangle Institute, 1980; Scanlon, Arick, & Phelps, 1981; U.S. Department of Education, 1987). Another study noted how rarely classroom teachers were present for children who were placed in mainstream classes, raising the question of the extent to which these teachers were utilizing the information available through the IEP, or responding to its goals and objectives (Gartner & Lipsky, 1987). The integration of an IEP into a child's total school program continues to be a critical issue.

The IEP multidisciplinary meeting is intended to provide an opportunity for professionals to meet with parents for discussion about the results of the evaluation process, placement options, curriculum goals, the introduction of special support services, rights and responsibilities of school-based staff, parental roles, future contacts, and planning. In view of the importance of IEP meetings, social work advocates involved with families have a responsibility to promote better use of CSE meetings by both parents and professionals.

Least Restrictive Placement. The goal of EHA is to ensure that youngsters with learning disabilities have access to the most normal environment for learning that is possible, given their educational difficulties. EHA requires that

> to the maximum extent appropriate, handicapped children including children in public or private institutions, or other care facilities, are educated with children who are not handicapped, and that special classes, separate schooling or other removal of handicapped children from the regular educational environment occurs only when the nature or severity of the handicap is such that education in regular classes with the use of supplementary aids and services cannot be achieved satisfactorily. . . . (Title 20, p. 1412)

A number of issues must be addressed when considering the adherence to the least restrictive placement. Federal guidelines state that the type of placement chosen must not be based on the generality of a category of handicapping condition, the configuration of the service delivery systems, availability of space, curriculum content, or on availability of methods of curriculum delivery. Parents and educational experts, both in and outside the school, should assess whether the child with learning disabilities really needs the special education services that are being offered as alternatives to the regular classroom. Some school officials move too quickly to remove the child who learns at a different pace from others from the regular classroom. Other school officials neglect the needs of mainstreamed children who languish in the regular classroom. There are different reasons why children do not thrive in regular classrooms. Embarrassment due to their different learning style, social problems, and negative teacher attentions all may contribute. When children with more severe developmental difficulties are mainstreamed, parents also may be negatively affected. Their feelings may range from shame and exacerbated sadness in coping with the daily reminders of their child's difference, to increased isolation and social withdrawal. Although the concerns and daily management issues are different for the parent of a child with more severe special needs (Turnbull & Blacher-Dixon, 1980), these issues also may exist for the family of the child with learning disabilities.

States vary significantly in the extent to which they utilize separate programming, resource room or *"pullout" programs*, or leave children with learning disabilities in regular classrooms. In 1987, 77 percent of learning-disabled students were served in regular classrooms, many with a combination of the regular classroom and resource room (U.S. Department of Education, 1988). Analysis of state funding patterns for special education has revealed that, in states where the funding formula appeared to reward the placement of students in more restrictive settings, fewer learning-disabled children remained in regular classrooms. Conversely, in states where there was no financial incentive, many fewer students were placed in separate classes (Walker, 1987).

There are many models of provision of special education services that can be offered to meet the requirements of the least restrictive environment. The decision of whether to offer a child a self-contained classroom, or pullout program, or to provide the regular classroom teacher with a learning disabilities consultant is at times made on the basis of the school's organizational style rather than on the needs of the child (Ysseldyke, Algozzine, Shinn, & McGue, 1982). Additionally, some studies have shown that no model is intrinsically better or worse than another (Gartner & Lipsky, 1987). The skills of the teachers, the atmosphere of the school and the classroom, the child, and parental reactions all must be considered.

Social workers must help parents to evaluate each program offered. Pullout programs are criticized as disrupting the school day (Reynolds & Wang, 1983), causing a child to miss classes that he or she should be attending because of timing, resulting in a lack of coordination of curriculum goals, exposing the child to contradictory teaching methodologies and learning goals, and causing a loss of accountability and coordination of a child's overall educational program.

Other issues that have been raised about pullout programs revolve around the stigma and discrimination that result from the daily reminder of a child's difference, emphasized by the act of leaving the regular classroom. Both teachers and fellow students tend to treat children in pullout programs differently. Only if specific educational goals are identified, monitored, and achieved is this type of special education a positive solution for the child. Ensuring this is the responsibility of the parent and parent advocate, and often the social worker. It is unlikely that schools will offer the close evaluation of program impact that is required. Studies have shown that for many students the removal from the regular classroom results in either loss of educational skills or no advantage (Madden & Slavin, 1983). If the parents and the social worker do not feel a proposed placement is appropriate, they may move to facilitate a change in the designation. An understanding of the funding formula incentives for a more restrictive setting is important in the selection of strategies that may be necessary to convince school officials that change is needed.

The constraints on what defines an "appropriate" free public education that are imposed by state and local education budgets require that parents and social workers serving as advocates vigilantly evaluate a child's class placement. If a self-contained classroom is recommended, parents should be encouraged to visit the classroom for an extended period of time and to obtain a class profile from the school's CSE. Although school officials are not legally required to offer other placements, as a matter of politics they often do. For example, children with learning disabilities are particularly vulnerable to the influences of physically disruptive children in the classroom. If children are placed in a class according to a determination of their functional level, those with learning disabilities may not get the maximum benefit (Trusdell, 1985). Although their peers in the classroom may be functioning in a similar academic range, these children may need different teaching strategies and methodologies (Phipps, 1982). The teacher who is responsible for a class of learning-disabled children, each of whom requires particular teaching strategies, may be unable to cope with the stress and not be able to serve any of the children effectively. Behaviorally disordered and hyperactive children can be such a distraction to pupils with learning disabilities that they are unable to concentrate on work that, even under optimum conditions, would be exceedingly difficult for them. Reports from adults with learning disabilities have indicated concern about negative impacts of multicategorical classrooms on the self-esteem and self-image of learning-disabled children (Interagency Committee on Learning Disabilities, 1987). One of the pervasive fears of the learning-disabled child is that he or she is mentally retarded. Placement in a multicategorical classroom may feed these fears, and possibly contribute to a lowering of expectations on the part of both the child and the teacher.

If parents have questions about the appropriateness of a proposed classroom placement, they must demonstrate that the child's needs will not be met. Generally, arguments must identify the particular educational needs of a child that will not be met by the class that has been selected. However, the success of the school in returning students to the regular education system may be important background information. On the basis of data from 26 cities, Gartner and Lipsky (1987) reported that, on the average, fewer than 5 percent of the students in special education return to general education. Although this finding does not refer exclusively to students classified as having learning disabilities, the learning-disabilities subgroup represents almost half of the students in special education.

If parents disagree with the proposed placement and no resolution is achieved through discussion, parents are entitled to an impartial due process hearing at the local school level. If they choose to appeal the outcome of the impartial hearing and seek an impartial overview of the hearing by the state education agency, the Handicapped Children's Protection Act of 1986 (P.L. 99–372) requires the state to pay for the parents' attorney's fees if the parents' position is accepted. The impartial hearings are fairly intimidating to most parents, so it is important for the social worker to work with parents to select the most appropriate professional advocate. School districts are almost always represented by expert legal counsel (Bogin & Goodman, 1985).

Currently, there is a heightened emphasis on keeping children with learning disabilities in the regular classroom, particularly when the child does not have major behavioral or attention difficulties. As has been noted, there are many reasons why this may be desirable. However, this course is not without its own set of pitfalls. When the recommendation is to keep the child in the regular classroom, parents must carefully assess whether the teacher has a teaching style that will accommodate the varying abilities and levels of performance of different members of the class. In an observation, parents should be encouraged to look for the consistent use of the following approaches to meet the specific learning needs of both regular students and those with learning disabilities:

The teacher must (a) wait a sufficient amount of time after asking a question; (b) provide praise that is contingent and attribute success to either ability or effort; (c) provide each student with an equal opportunity to respond to questions; (d) provide continuous corrective feedback; (e) engage the student in activities that are suited to his or her achievement level (in every area); and (f) move each student through the curriculum in small sequential steps, progressing at a high (or at least moderate) rate of success. These instructional strategies are to be implemented simultaneously for each child in the classroom. (Bryan, Bay, & Donahue, 1988, pp. 26–27)

Children with learning disabilities may have a variety of difficulties in keeping up with work in the regular education classrooms. Even if a teacher were able to meet the goals outlined above, there still could be problems, depending on the particular learning problems of the child. Children with learning disabilities often have gaps in basic skills that are prerequisites to being able to respond to even the most appropriate teaching style and strategies (Bryan et al., 1988). Discussing the pressure to move learning-disabled children back to regular classrooms, Bryan and her colleagues drew on a series of recent studies that highlighted the particular cognitive and affective needs of these children.

For example, the child who has difficulty learning complex rule systems will need extra time, repetition, and bypass strategies (Morrison & Manis, 1981). This child may be no less competent than his or her peers at conceptual thinking, may be very sophisticated socially, and may have a variety of other skills. Another child may not be able to respond to the level of verbal expectations of classroom learning but may be very advanced in math when it does not require verbal interchange (Vellutino, Bentley, & Scanlon, 1983). This child may need a different pacing of questions, and an atmosphere that lowers the anxiety of competing constantly with verbally proficient peers so that the child can test and practice shaky verbal skills. Many children with learning disabilities do not develop task-appropriate learning strategies on their own (Ryan, Short, & Weed, 1986). This requires teachers to understand each child's repertoire of learning strategies, and to be able to identify particular gaps that impede successful accomplishment of academic tasks. One of the most handicapping problems that many children with learning disabilities encounter in new learning is their difficulty in generalizing newly acquired skills to different learning situations. This slows their movement through the curriculum and requires teachers to assist these children to develop specific strategies for specific tasks at specific times, a highly individualized process (Wong & Wong, 1989). As Bryan and her coauthors (1988) pointed out, it is unrealistic to put children with learning disabilities in the regular classroom without a careful assessment of their individual learning needs, the composition of the class, and the skills and style of the teacher.

Social workers must be aware of these issues when the options for the least restrictive setting are raised. Social workers do not have to become experts in teaching. However, they must become more familiar with the challenges and realities of teaching and with the issues related to working with learning-disabled children in the classroom. Social workers must help parents to ask the right questions and sharpen their observational skills.

Most solutions to meeting the educational needs of the child with learning disabilities are controversial. In different parts of the United States, widely different solutions have been used with similar types of children (Lehr, 1987). When removal to a resource room or self-contained classroom is recommended, parents always should ask themselves and the CSE members why the targeted skills cannot be taught in a less restrictive setting. The burden is generally on parents to prove why a less restrictive setting may be more appropriate for their child.

Although parents can request a change of classroom for their child at any time, there are regularly mandated review processes. Each child must have an annual and a triennial review of his or her progress and placement status. At that time his or her psychosocial history, psychological evaluation, speech and language evaluation, and educational assessment are updated. Children with learning disabilities frequently go through periods when there is a sudden consolidation of maturational and academic gains. Close monitoring may be required to ensure that the placement and class continue to be appropriate. If possible, social workers should encourage parents to seek an outside educational evaluation to develop a framework for assessing their child's progress. This evaluation provides important data for parents to discuss at the different CSE review meetings, particularly if their goal is movement of their child into regular education classes.

In sum, EHA provides only the beginning of a process for children with learning disabilities and their parents. A broad, collaborative effort must take place among parents, social workers, and other school personnel to ensure that the optimum learning environment is created for a child.

EHA AMENDMENTS OF 1986

This set of amendments (P.L. 99–457) added federally funded programs for a new population—children from age 3 to 5—to EHA coverage. A new state-funded program covering children from birth through age 2, the Early Intervention Program (EIP), also was created. The focus on these two groups is based on the recognition that the earlier the intervention, the more likely it is that children with disabilities will be less handicapped, and that children at risk for developing handicapping conditions may be protected. Because schools usually are not set up to provide the kinds of services that would be necessary for these age groups, state and local education agencies can contract with other organizations to develop a variety of preschool programs, both in home and agency settings. This requires a strong emphasis on interagency and public voluntary coordination. This coordination must extend to finding ways for families to play active roles in planning and provision of early intervention services ("Part VII," 1987). There is increasing recognition of the critical role that the family plays in creating an environment that

179

supports maximum developmental gains among preschoolers with developmental problems. There is a need for professionals who are skilled in working with distressed families in disadvantaged environments. Parents may be overwhelmed, resistant, or preoccupied with the provision of basic needs for themselves and other family members. Social workers have a long history of work with these families in a broad array of community agencies and should be in a position to actively engage with the children eligible for services through these EHA amendments. Day care centers, hospitals, settlement houses, and clinics all may become sites for working with these children and their families. For example, in 1988 12.5 percent of the children enrolled in Head Start were identified as handicapped. A total of 6 percent of these almost 65,000 children were diagnosed as having specific learning disabilities ("Report to Health and Human Services Secretary Otis R. Bowen," 1988).

The EIP has broad eligibility criteria. Included in the EIP definition of infants and toddlers with handicaps are children who

> (A) . . . are experiencing developmental delays, as measured by appropriate diagnostic instruments and procedures in one or more of the following areas: cognitive development, physical development, language and speech development, psychosocial development, or self-help skills; or (B) have a diagnosed physical or mental condition that has a high probability of resulting in developmental delay. Such term may also include at a State's discretion, individuals from birth to age two inclusive who are at risk of having substantial developmental delays if early intervention services are not provided. (EHA Amendments of 1986, p. 3456)

The proposed regulations for this group of very young children differ from those in EHA. The child-find system requires coordination with other public and private agencies working with this age group of children. Social workers are likely to be working with the child and family. It is important to find out what additional services the family may be eligible for through this legislation. The procedural safeguards for parents' participation and involvement are similar to those in EHA, but are stated in less detail. Parental involvement is mandatory. More social work advocacy and involvement may be required to support parents' efforts if there are difficulties in obtaining appropriate services. Because each state may develop its own administrative procedures, social workers and parents must be informed of their state's guidelines and resources. The individualized family service plan (IFSP) is based on the IEP but is more comprehensive and goes beyond the scope of the IEP. All public and private services offered must meet the IFSP requirements. Finally, there are broader requirements for providing special education and related services to handicapped children than were included in EHA. For example, an infant or toddler would be able to get a related service, such as social work, without receiving special education services. Also, the provision of case management services, an important social work function, are required for eligible infants and toddlers but are not required for children eligible under EHA.

The procedures for identifying, assessing, and planning for the needs of the very young children covered by this amendment are similar to those in EHA. There must be a multidisciplinary assessment, including a psychosocial evaluation, and an IFSP that must be developed with parent involvement. Among other special areas, services may include psychological services, parent and family training, counseling services, and case management. There is a special emphasis on the need for training and provision of information to parents of disabled children who are members of underrepresented groups. All of these may be carried out by social workers as well as by other related professionals. The emphasis on "conditions that typically result in delay" and children who are "at risk of substantial developmental delay" places a responsibility on professionals performing evaluations to be alert to the many variables linked to perinatal and postnatal risks that may influence later cognitive, emotional, and physical development.

The timing for implementation of the IFSP for infants and toddlers is similar to that existing for older children under EHA and presents some of the same problems. National Association of Social Workers (NASW) testimony before the U.S. Department of Education highlighted the issues. For example, the guidelines recommend that the multidisciplinary assessment of children and families be completed within 30 days. According to NASW, this does not allow sufficient time for a thorough assessment, and a 45-day period would be more appropriate. However, implementation of the IFSP should be accomplished in a 15-day period, because the needs of very young children change rapidly.

The needs of the very young child and the assessment of family needs as they relate to the at-risk infant or toddler require a different set of approaches than the social worker would use with older children. NASW executive director Mark Battle (1988) outlined the refocusing of social work services that would be necessary to support the family's role in the home:

1. Making home visits to evaluate the child's living conditions and patterns of parent-child interaction;

2. Preparing a psychosocial developmental assessment of the handicapped infant or toddler in his/her family context;

3. Providing individual and family-group counseling with parents and other family members, and appropriate social skill-building activities with the child and parents;

4. Working with those problems in a child's and family's living situation (home, community and any center where early intervention services are to be provided) that affect the child's maximum utilization of early intervention services;

5. Identifying, mobilizing and coordinating school and community resources and services to enable the child and family to receive maximum benefit from early intervention services;

6. Facilitating and coordinating the transition of the handicapped child from early intervention services to preschool services and services provided under Part B of the [EHA] Act. (p. 12)

These suggested areas of intervention can serve as guidelines for social workers involved with this population. Specific learning disabilities may be particularly hard to identify during the infant and toddler stages of the child's development. However, attention to members of groups at risk for general developmental delay is important because these are frequently the same children who later develop learning disabilities.

FAMILY EDUCATIONAL RIGHTS AND PRIVACY ACT

The Family Educational Rights and Privacy Act of 1974 (FERPA) (P.L. 93–380) gives all parents access to their child's school records, and protects the privacy rights of parents and children. According to FERPA, any school receiving federal funds must allow parents or legal guardians of students under age 18, and all students over age 18 (and their parents with student permission) the right to see and have copies of student records, and to correct any inaccuracies or misleading or derogatory information included.

Parents must provide the local school district with a written request to see the record. They may request a copy of the entire record. However, if parents believe that there is something controversial in the record, or if it contains small pieces of paper with informal notes that might not get copied, they should take notes on the dates of entries and on any information that they want to be sure to have available. This two-step process is useful in case materials are omitted from copies of the record. These materials may have direct bearing on the decision-making process. For example, in one situation anecdotal information on scraps of paper was not viewed as part of the official record and was omitted. Because the parents had written the information down in their initial review, they were able to retrieve the information, which had been discarded by school staff members (Maxman, 1982).

If parents find anything in the record that they feel is misleading, inaccurate, or derogatory, they must request in writing that school officials change it. If their request is refused, the parents can request a hearing that will be held by the local school district. The material in question may be removed entirely or left in the record according to the hearing officers' decision. If the material is left in the record, the parents may add their own rebuttal statement, which must be shown each time the records are disclosed.

Community and school social workers often are faced with issues regarding the confidentiality and privacy of records when they work with families to secure resources for children with learning disabilities. The practice issues are complex, despite the apparent clarity of the law. For example, the courts have ruled that community clinic records are the property of the clinic. However, once the information is shared with school officials to promote effective educational planning for a child, the material becomes available to many school personnel, and legally accessible to parents. School staff members or parents may use the record information in ways that are damaging to the child. In a number of community social services and mental health agencies, the issue of what material should be included in the formal record often has been resolved in favor of excluding information that could be misinterpreted or that is difficult for social workers to interpret to parents. As a result, sometimes useful background information is not made available, and some material is misused. Social workers involved with parents who are viewing their child's records must be aware of all these issues and provide interpretation and feedback to parents regarding the material that is in the record.

In comparison with FERPA, EHA includes more stringent confidentiality requirements in four areas:

1. EHA covers children from birth to age 21 and includes children who are not yet students.
2. All agencies involved in identification of and location of children, and in their evaluation and education, are included.
3. When personally identifiable information is no longer needed to provide the child's education, parents are to be informed.
4. When the child reaches 18, the type and severity of the disability are to be considered in the transfer of privacy rights from the parent to the student.

These issues are particularly important for professionals working with children with learning disabilities and their parents. The more comprehensive the assessment process, the more information will be in the record. The uncertainties of diagnosis; the necessity for informal observations and interviews with parents, teachers, and others who have worked with the child; and the child's own interviews, if the ANSER system (Levine, 1980) or one like it is used, all provide a wealth of information. School social workers must be alert to the possible breaches of confidentiality or misuse of this information in the school setting. They must be ready to interpret material to parents and advocate for parents' rights to have access to the record when necessary. This may be difficult for some social workers, because they may have mixed feelings about the parents' right to access to their child's files. Social workers who do not support this legal right of families to have access to their files should recommend that families seek another advocate if this issue is raised.

VOCATIONAL REHABILITATION ACT AMENDMENTS

The Vocational Rehabilitation Act Amendments of 1973 (VRAA) (P.L. 93–112) contain a landmark civil rights provision that prohibits discrimination on the basis of physical or mental handicap for all Americans, regardless of their age. This provision includes children from birth to age 21, the same group that is covered by EHA. The VRAA provision reads, "No otherwise qualified handicapped individual in the United States shall, solely by reason of his handicap be excluded from the participation in, be denied the benefits of, or be subjected to discrimination under any program or activity receiving federal financial assistance."

This group includes elementary and secondary schools, colleges, hospitals, and social service agencies, among other organizations. The VRAA definition of "handicapped" goes well beyond that in EHA. Physical or mental impairments include specific learning disabilities, such as perceptual handicaps, dyslexia, minimal brain dysfunction, and developmental aphasia, if they are diagnosed as a physical or mental handicap severe enough to substantially limit one or more of the major life functions.

A child who is not eligible for special education services under EHA may be eligible under Section 504 of VRAA (the Buckley Amendment). This statute has stronger guidelines regarding the "least restrictive environment" requirement through its definition of discrimination. However, Section 504 requires only that individual needs of students be considered. An IEP may be one of the different means to accomplish this consideration. EHA specifically requires the development of an IEP.

Section 504 states that no handicapped child can be excluded from a public education because of disability; that every handicapped child is entitled to a free, appropriate education, regardless of the nature or severity of the handicap; and that students cannot be segregated from nonhandicapped students. It also adds that the placement must be nearest to the home of the individual.

One of the major differences between Section 504 and EHA is that the federal government does not provide funding to ensure that Section 504 is enforced. However, Section 504 is viewed as providing a private right to civil action for discrimination against handicapped persons in availability of resources, services, education, housing, and employment. This right includes organizational grievance procedures, with recourse to a state Office of Civil Rights, and, if necessary, to a federal district court. Thus, although federal funding is not provided for Section 504 implementation, penalties may be levied for its transgression.

If, for example, state officials decided not to participate in EHA, parents could interpret the lack of educational services as discrimination and seek redress through the Office of Civil Rights. A school system would have to provide services with similar guidelines to those in EHA, but without financial support. Some states have broader mandates under Section 504 than those included in the federal VRAA law. Therefore, it is important for social workers to be familiar with their state law to be helpful to families who are seeking wider access to resources for their children with learning disabilities.

DEVELOPMENTAL DISABILITIES AND BILL OF RIGHTS ACT

This act (P.L. 94–103), passed in 1975, focuses on severe or chronic disabilities that result in substantial functional limitations in three or more major life activities, such as self-care, receptive and expressive language, learning, mobility, self-direction, capacity for independent living, or economic self-sufficiency. The act is aimed at reducing the institutionalization of severely disabled people through the provision of specialized community services. Some people with severe disabilities who benefit from services through this act also have learning disabilities. It is important that their service package include resources to address their learning disabilities.

SOCIAL WORK PERSPECTIVE ON LEGISLATION

The legislation discussed in this chapter includes the major statutes that directly affect children and youths with learning disabilities. The legislation provides the framework for legal access to education and other supportive services. However, social workers must understand a family's strengths and capabilities to engage in their own long-term advocacy to ensure that enabling legislation truly is enabling. Many ambiguities remain in the implementation of the legislation. There are no prescribed courses of action. Individualized planning and programming always are needed.

As with all legislation, public support for these statutes waxes and wanes in response to fiscal expenditures, seemingly ever-expanding individual needs, and institutional difficulties in implementation. To realize their potential, proposals for change must be carefully scrutinized by social workers and parents working collaboratively to promote increased access and support for children with learning disabilities. Social workers should encourage parents to take a more active role in the important dialogue about the rights and educational needs of their children.

Social workers must monitor changes in the local and state regulations that may affect services to children with learning disabilities. Individual state departments of education, the *School Social Work Information Bulletin* of NASW, and local branches of such national organizations as the Learning Disabilities Association of America, the Orton Dyslexia Society, the Council for Exceptional Children, and the Children's Defense Fund provide materials for parents and current information for social workers working with families. Also, law reporters offer up-to-date summaries of court decisions concerning education and the disabled.

Social workers must have a broad perspective. They must help families with children with learning disabilities gain access to the best education that the current educational system can provide, whether it is labeled regular education or special education. Social workers also must become involved in the restructuring of the school system to ensure that students are not penalized through categorization and labeling that create stigma and unnecessary segregation through educational programs. Finally, social workers must ensure that students are able to obtain the counseling and supportive services they need to be able to use their abilities to the maximum potential and fulfill their educational requirements in any educational setting.

REFERENCES

Allen-Meares, P., Washington, R. O., & Welsh, B. (1986). *Social work services in schools.* Englewood Cliffs, NJ: Prentice-Hall.

Baker, B. L., & Brightman, R. P. (1984). Access of handicapped children to educational services. In N. D. Repucci, L. A. Withorn, E. P. Mulvey, & J. Monahan (Eds.), *Children, mental health, and the law* (pp. 289–307). Beverly Hills, CA: Sage.

Ballard, J., Ramirez, B., & Zantal-Wiener, K. (1987). *Public Law 94–142, Section 504, and Public Law 99–457: Understanding what they are and are not* (rev. ed.). Reston, VA: The Council for Exceptional Children.

Battle, M. G. (1988, February). *Comments on section 303, early intervention services.* Unpublished manuscript.

Biklin, D., & Zollers, N. (1986). The focus of advocacy in the learning disabilities field. *Journal of Learning Disabilities, 19,* 557–586.

Bogin, M. B., & Goodman, B. (1985). *Representing learning disabled children: A manual for attorneys.* Washington, DC: American Bar Foundation National Legal Resource Center for Child Advocacy and Protection.

Bryan, T., Bay, M., & Donahue, M. (1988). Implications of the learning disabilities definition for the regular education initiative. *Journal of Learning Disabilities, 21,* 2–28.

Carl D. Perkins Vocational Education Act, Pub. L. No. 98–524, 98 Stat. 2435, 20 U.S.C. 2301 (1984).

Childrens Defense Fund. (1989). 94–142 and 504: Numbers that add up to educational rights for children with disabilities. Washington, DC: Author.

Council of Great City Schools. (1986). *Special education: Views from America's cities.* Washington, DC: Author.

Developmental Disabilities and Bill of Rights Act, Pub. L. No. 94–103, 89 Stat. 486–507, 42 U.S.C. 6001, 6010 (1975).

Education for All Handicapped Children Act, Pub. L. No. 94–142, 89 Stat. 773, 20 U.S.C. 1401 (1975).

Education of the Handicapped Act, Pub. L. No. 91–320, 84 Stat. 175, 20 U.S.C. 4111(a) (1971).

Education of the Handicapped Act Amendments, Pub. L. No. 99–457, 100 Stat. 1145, 20 U.S.C. 1419 (1986).

Family Educational Rights and Privacy Act, Pub. L. No. 93–380, 88 Stat. 175, 20 U.S.C. 1232g (1974).

Ferguson, P. M., & Asch, A. (1989). What we want for our children: Perspectives of parents and adults with disabilities. In D. Biklin, P. M. Ferguson, & A. Lord (Eds.), *Lessons from life: Personal and parental perspectives on school, childhood and disability* (pp. 108–140). Chicago: National Society for the Study of Education.

Gartner, A., & Lipsky, D. K. (1987). Beyond special education: Toward a quality system for all students. *Harvard Educational Review, 57,* 367–395.

Goldstein, S., Strickland, B., Turnbull, A. P., & Curry, L. (1980). An observational analysis of the IEP conference. *Exceptional Children, 46,* 278–286.

Handicapped Children's Protection Act, Pub. L. No. 99–372, 100 Stat. 796, 20 U.S.C. 1415 (1986).

Interagency Committee on Learning Disabilities. (1987). Learning disabilities: A report to the U.S. Congress. Washington, DC: National Institute of Child Health and Human Development.

Keogh, B. K. (1987). Learning disabilities: Diversity in search of order. In M. C. Wang, M. C. Reynolds, & H. J. Walberg (Eds.), *The handbook of special education: Research and practice: Vol. 2. Mildly handicapping conditions* (pp. 225–252). New York: Pergamon.

Lapham, E. V. (1980). State regulations implementing P.L. 94–142: Implications of three issues with delivery of social services in schools. In NASW Commission on Family and Primary Associations (Ed.), *School social work and the law* (pp. 96–120). Washington, DC: National Association of Social Workers.

Lehr, S. (1987). *Purposeful integration . . . inherently equal* (Monograph). Boston: Federation for Children with Special Needs.

Levine, M.D. (1980). The ANSER system. Cambridge, MA: Educators Publishing Service.

Levine, M. D., Brooks, R., & Shonkoff, J. P. (1980). *A pediatric approach to learning disabilities.* New York: John Wiley & Sons.

Lusthaus, C. S., Lusthaus, E. W., & Gibbs, H. (1981). Parents' role in the decision process. *Exceptional Children, 48*(3), 256–257.

Madden, N., & Slavin, R. (1983). Mainstreaming students with mild handicaps: Academic and social outcomes. *Review of Educational Research, 53,* 519–569.

Maxman, B. (1982). *Parent participation in special education decisionmaking: The parent member's role on the Committee of the Handicapped.* Unpublished doctoral dissertation, Teachers College, Columbia University, New York.

Mills v. Board of Education in the District of Columbia. 348 F. Supp. 866 (D.IDC 1972).

Morrison, F. J., & Manis, F. R. (1981). Cognitive process and reading disability: A critique and proposal. In C. J. Brainerd (Ed.), *Progress in cognitive development: Verbal processes in children* (Vol. 2, pp. 59–93). New York: Springer-Verlag.

Part VII: Proposal for preschool grants for handicapped children program authorized by EHA, amended by Pub. L. 99–457. (1987, November 18). *Federal Register,* p. 44346.

Pennsylvania Association for Retarded Citizens v. Pennsylvania. 334 F. Supp. 1257 (E. D. PA). Amended settlement approved 343 F. 279 (1972).

Phipps, P. M. (1982). The merging categories: Appropriate education or administrative convenience. *Journal of Learning Disabilities, 15,* 153–154.

Report to Health and Human Services Secretary Otis R. Bowen on handicapped children in special education 1985–1986. (1988, Fall). *NASW News,* p. 3.

Research Triangle Institute. (1980). *A national survey of individualized education programs (IEPs) for handicapped children.* Triangle Park, NC: Author.

Reynolds, M., & Wang, M. (1983). Restructuring school programs: A position paper. *Policy Studies Review, 2,* 189–212.

Riley v. Ambach, 668 F.2d 635 (2nd Cir.). Rehearing denied (1981).

Roit, M. L., & Pfohl, W. (1984). The readability of P.L. 94–142 parent materials: Are parents truly informed? *Exceptional Children, 50,* 496–506.

Ryan, E. B., Short, E. J., & Weed, K. A. (1986). The role of cognitive strategy training in improving the academic performance of learning disabled children. *Journal of Learning Disabilities, 19,* 521–529.

Scanlon, C. A., Arick, J., & Phelps, N. (1981). Participation in the development of the IEP: Parents' perspective. *Exceptional Children, 47,* 373.

Schorr, L. B. (1983). Environmental deterrents: Poverty, affluence, violence and television. In M. D. Levine (Ed.), *Developmental-behavioral pediatrics* (pp. 293–362). Philadelphia: W. B. Saunders.

Shepard, L. A., Smith, L. A., & Vojir, C. P. (1983). Characteristics of pupils identified as learning disabled. *Journal of Special Education, 16,* 73–85.

Snyder, J. C., Hampton, R., & Newberger, E. H. (1983). Family dysfunction: Violence, neglect and sexual misuse. In M. D. Levine (Ed.), *Developmental-behavioral pediatrics* (pp. 256–275). Philadelphia: W. B. Saunders.

Trusdell, M. L. (1985). An analysis of services delivery models for learning disability programs in the U.S. 1984–1985 school year. *Annals of Dyslexia, 34,* 175–186.

Turnbull, A., & Blacher-Dixon, J. (1980). Pre-school mainstreaming: Impact on parents. In J. Gallagher (Ed.), *New directions for exceptional children (No. 1)* (pp. 25–46). San Francisco: Jossey-Bass.

Ungerleider, D. F. (1985). *Reading, writing and rage.* Rolling Hills Estates, CA: Jalmar Press.

U.S. Department of Education, Office of Special Education and Rehabilitative Services. (1987). *Ninth annual report to the Congress on the implementation of the Education for All Handicapped Children Act.* Washington, DC: Author.

U.S. Department of Education, Office of Special Education and Rehabilitative Services. (1988). *Tenth annual report to the Congress on the implementation of the Education for All Handicapped Children Act.* Washington, DC: Author.

Vellutino, F. R., Bentley, W. L., & Scanlon, D. M. (1983). Interhemispheric learning and speed of hemispheric transmission in dyslexic and normal readers: A replication of previous results and additional findings. *Applied Psycholinguistics, 4,* 209–229.

Vigilante, F. W. (1990). Family and school responses to learning disabilities. *Social Work in Education, 12,* pp. 151–165.

Vocational Rehabilitation Act Amendments, Pub. L. No. 93–112, 87 Stat. 355, 20 U.S.C. 2310(a) (1973).

Walker, L. H. (1987). Procedural rights in the wrong system: Special education is not enough. In A. Gartner & T. Joe (Eds.), *Images of the disabled/disabling images* (pp. 97–115). New York: Praeger Publishers.

Weatherly, R. A. (1979). *Reforming special education.* Cambridge, MA: MIT Press.

Wong, B.Y.L., & Wong, R. (1989). Cognitive intervention. In K. Kavale (Ed.), *Learning disabilities: State of the art and practice* (pp. 141–160). San Diego: College Hill.

Ysseldyke, J., Algozzine, B., Shinn, M., & McGue, M. (1982). Similarities and differences between low achievers and students classified learning disabled. *The Journal of Special Education, 16,* 73–85.

Chapter 7

Future Directions

Recent innovations in assessment, curriculum design, teaching strategies, skills training, and behavior modification do not address the range of needs of children with learning disabilities and their families. Frustration and concern have mounted as many children identified as learning disabled by the Education for All Handicapped Children Act (P.L. 94–142) (EHA) have reached adolescence and young adulthood unable to function successfully in the adult world. Poor social skills, low self-esteem, depression, and anxiety exacerbate their difficulties in negotiating the complex demands of work and family life. Many professional groups are reassessing their roles at critical transition periods.

Additionally, there is renewed interest in addressing early interdisciplinary intervention. However, social work contributions to these interdisciplinary efforts have received limited attention. Although professionals still defend their different territorial imperatives, as Vigilante (1985) noted, this protectionism is not the only reason there is no clear identification of the contributions social workers could provide. Differing perspectives on service priorities and the lack of a commonly accepted definition of learning disabilities leave room for idiosyncratic professional responses. The social work profession has been slow to communicate its special functions and roles with this population. As a result, the needs of learning-disabled persons that could be met most effectively by social work intervention may go unidentified and unmet.

SOCIAL WORK DOMAIN AND FUNCTION

The social work domain lies in the interface between individuals and their situation. Problems may occur in the fit between the learning-disabled child and parents, siblings, extended family, cultural or neighborhood groups, teachers, classmates, or school. These problems lead to a conceptualization of needs that departs from a traditional disease model, in which the source of problems and the focus for change lie within the individual. The person-in-situation framework (Hollis & Woods, 1981) provides a conceptual basis for social work intervention in dysfunctional individual and system relationships that is particularly useful with this population.

From early childhood through the school years, higher education, career training, transition to work, independence, and adult relationships, children with learning disabilities and their families create interdependencies that span life changes. Although many interactions are necessary and adaptive, the risk of maladaptive solutions at critical developmental transitions is great. The distinctive interface function of social work lies in assisting children and their families in making more effective use of personal, familial, and community resources in managing regularly anticipated and special developmental stage requirements (H. Lewis, Dean, Hunter College School of Social Work, personal communication, May 20, 1989). Intervention that attends to a broad spectrum of individual and family tensions facilitates the maintenance of healthy relationships, and eventual independence and autonomy for both the child and his or her family.

Professionals' current understanding of the ways that the biologically determined aspects of a learning disability interact with environmental conditions makes the facilitative function of social work particularly important. The negative impacts of environmental risk factors such as low socioeconomic status, family instability, institutional and professional insensitivity, and resource and service deprivation have been identified as significantly influencing the opportunities available to children with developmental dysfunctions (Levine, 1987). These factors, although not related to the individual's mental or physical ability, provide the broader context for the learning-disabled person's early growth and mastery of developmental tasks as well as his or her eventual social and economic independence. The professional focus is at the interface of relationships, resources, and institutional contingencies. The complexity of the social and environmental milieus of each child and family requires social workers to play diverse roles.

SOCIAL WORK ROLES

In the past decade, considerable attention has been devoted to the identification of social work roles in work with the learning disabled. Recent research literature has shown that social workers are gaining a greater understanding of the distinctive function of the profession with this population. Vigilante (1983, 1985) highlighted social work educational and advocacy roles with parents and teachers, offering a role model for a different set of responses to a child with irregularly developing ego functions. Protecting the child by interpreting the actions of others promotes a safe environment for taking risks and learning.

Vigilante and Dane (1989) focused on teaching children to develop their own self-advocacy strategies as they become aware of situations that trigger stress. Expanding their repertoire of coping skills helps learning-disabled children gain more control over potentially perilous encounters with peers, teachers, and others. Rosenberger (1988, 1989) used the person-in-situation perspective to create a psychodynamic model integrating concepts drawn from self-psychology and

190

object-relations theories. Highlighting the interactive social matrix in which children develop, Rosenberger suggested that social workers consider system advocacy and problem-solving consultation to complement individual interventions and to create situations in which a child can perceive him- or herself as successful. The social worker or parent reflects back the child's experience and serves as an interpreter, promoting positive growth of the child's emerging sense of self.

A social worker's understanding of the family as a system provides additional opportunities for intervention that do not focus on the child as a problem. A team approach to family therapy with parents and their children with learning disabilities provides opportunities for enabling all family members to identify adaptive and maladaptive patterns of behavior (Ziegler & Holden, 1988). Incentives for the substitution of more effective patterns of interaction can be created through role play and practice in a protected setting. Interventions can include counseling, support, teaching, modeling, and consultation with other professionals on behalf of family members.

Using the structure of the peer group in work with children, N. P. Gitterman (1979) and Small (1986) emphasized the importance of mutual aid in a structured setting, to encourage the development of skills in interaction and communication. The group setting offers opportunities for feedback and reality testing with other children who struggle with similar fears and difficulties. Indelicato and Goldberg (1986) highlighted the needs of parents who are isolated and burdened by the unanticipated stresses of raising a child with learning disabilities. Indelicato and Goldberg described a traditional social work role as enabler—helping parents to find their own strengths and develop their own problem-solving capacities in response to critical life transitions exacerbated by the special needs of their children. The therapeutic functions of a guided self-help group process and a mutual aid structure (A. Gitterman & Shulman, 1986) offered a useful model for social work intervention. Here again, the social worker performs the traditional role of enabler, helping parents to find their own strengths and develop their problem-solving capacities. Kuzell and Brassington (1986) and Eaton, Lippman, and Riley (1980) offered examples of social work educational roles in a group forum, based on models of family life education and theories of adult learning. These two approaches of mutual aid and adult learning emphasize education and collaboration. Social workers and parents base their actions on nonpathological interpretation of child and family behavior.

Increasingly, social workers are taking on professional case management roles to coordinate resources for children with learning disabilities. Many professions may be involved with case management. However, social work training gives practitioners an understanding of the uses of community resources and the impact of race, class, and culture on institutional structures. These variables must be considered when developing appropriate service plans and monitoring their use. A holistic perspective encompassing both the person and environment helps to identify gaps in service provision, lapses in communication, and interdisciplinary misunderstandings.

In many situations—sometimes by default and sometimes by design—parents become the "case managers" of their children's network of supports through their adolescence and young adulthood. However, even the most competent and sophisticated parents have identified the case manager role as particularly stressful during initial assessment and program planning (Rosenberger, 1989). There is often a need for an objective intervention to assist families in setting priorities, interpreting conflicting evaluations, and designing a course of action congruent with family culture, living patterns, and financial constraints.

The EHA amendments of 1986 (P.L. 99–457) mandated special services to children with developmental disabilities from birth to age 3. The expansion of service to the very young child not yet in school requires professionals and parents to assume different roles. Case management is legislatively mandated, but not linked to any particular professional group. However, social workers are among those professionals who can offer case management services under the legislation.

In their roles as mediators, social workers interpret family needs and wishes to representatives of organizations, and organizational constraints to families, to promote mutual adjustments that support the special needs of children. Mediation is a critical way to respond to special education disputes, in which participants can move quickly into adversarial stances that preclude the possibility of a unified approach to problem solving (Gallant, 1982). At other times, social workers must assume the less comfortable stances of advocacy and confrontation necessary to challenge organizational systems, norms, and biases to obtain appropriate resources (Dane, 1985b; Mailick & Ashley, 1981), serving as child and family advocates in agencies. When new resources are needed, advocacy may be necessary on behalf of children with special needs (Dane, 1984).

Historically, the social work profession has promoted more and better resources for clients. Thus, case and class advocacy has become the basis for building effective coalitions with parents (Caires & Weil, 1985). Professional and parent organizations must work together for advances and additions in services for learning-disabled people. In their roles as community organizers, social workers have been able to contribute to the mobilization of community support for changes in policy and program opportunities.

ORGANIZATION OF SERVICES

Interdisciplinary collaboration, in addition to the introduction of practice and administrative structures, is needed to create program innovations that ensure organizational responsiveness to the needs of learning-disabled youths. For social workers to assume a broader function, the critical features of service to this population must be recognized. Bridging and integrating multi-institutional involvements, interdisciplinary evaluations, and programming to respond to swiftly changing developmental needs require extensive commitments of time, energy, and expertise. Social agencies must develop supportive internal structures that recognize these commitments. New statistical recording and weighting of the value of worker activities must include linkage, bridging, and monitoring of family and institutional inputs. Employee reward systems must be redesigned to give recognition to case management activities.

The strategic location of social work services in organizational settings also must be addressed. Optimum access to social work intervention will vary with the practice setting and with the institutional definition of the continuum of service. A proactive approach will make prevention and early intervention high priorities, regardless of setting. Social workers must be in positions that promote initiative in early identification of special developmental needs. Comprehensive identification of service needs, design of a plan for collaborative interdisciplinary intervention, development of a structure for coordination, and designation of responsibility for ongoing monitoring and evaluation can be effective only if the interdisciplinary team members fully understand the developmental issues that may be adding a hidden dimension to the child's situation. For truly coordinated service, placement of the social work resource must be consistent with the level of planned social work responsibility for all or some of these functions.

In multidisciplinary agencies, social workers must exercise their professional mandate and initiate a dialogue to develop a service structure that links the organizational mission with social work values as they apply to the needs of learning-disabled persons. The identification of a child's environmental influences, intrapsychic variables, and biological vulnerabilities must go hand in hand with the development of comprehensive intervention plans. Positive professional planning outcomes may vary widely, from a redesign of the social assessment process to the introduction of new interdisciplinary team and interagency collaborative strategies, to new consultative roles, or to the assumption of case management functions. Parents can be introduced to new roles and supported in assuming stronger stances against institutional or legislative barriers. Prevailing institutional mandates; professional belief systems; organizational culture, politics, and history; and agency resources, existing interagency networks, and community expectations all may play a role in determining the choice of appropriate intervention and the location of social work activities in the structure of the host agency service system.

If social workers are to play multiple roles in providing services for children with learning disabilities and their families, attention must be paid to filling the gaps in the child's current continuum of services and to demonstrating the ways that unserved needs further drain, rather than protect, agency resources. Interpretations of goals, objectives, timetables, resource expenditures, and benefits to the agency must be clarified. The social worker also must develop reasonable practice goals that will demonstrate success and recognizable achievement to agency administration.

The complex needs of learning-disabled children, and the finely tuned institutional responses necessary for effective work with these children and their families, do not draw system advocates naturally. Social workers must demonstrate continually the effectiveness of their strategic interventions and the positive benefits that accrue from this resource-consuming client group. For example, the development of a friendship for a lonely child may build his or her self-esteem and make school a more tolerable place. A pleasurable social environment in school may help make a child more receptive to learning, if the educational options the child needs are available. This receptiveness may lead to more constructive risk taking outside of school, such as the development of new hobbies (Dane, 1986). The child's new community linkages may help his or her parent feel less isolated and more receptive to joining a support group. Parental frustration and anger may be reduced as adult needs are met. The social worker's interpretation of an opportunity that is ripe for intervention may provide role modeling for future advocacy efforts. Thus strengthened, parents may engage in their own advocacy for program and legislative change. The social worker may have intervened in the classroom, with the parents of both the learning-disabled child and his or her "friend," and on the playground or in the after-school program to promote the building of these fragile alliances. The process may seem excessively time-consuming and the outcome small, but the benefits are significant. The social worker then must use these pivotal situations, which may require counseling, educating, modeling, interagency networking, mediation between parents, and consultation with teachers, to educate other professionals and the agency administration about the multidimensional social work role they played with these families. As with any other new service component, the effectiveness and security of the social work role and function in the overall organizational setting depend on demonstrations of success. Success must be framed in ways that support the overall mission and goals of the agency, its smooth internal functioning, and better relationships with the agencies in the service network (Hasenfeld, 1983; Weil, 1985).

EXPANDING SOCIAL WORK INVOLVEMENT

What are the next steps needed to expand social work involvement with children with learning disabilities and their families? First, the distinctive social work function of helping children and their families to make optimum use of their own resources and those of the community must be articulated. Social workers must utilize their knowledge of individual, family, group, and organizational dynamics to identify functional and dysfunctional patterns of response to the unique developmental needs of children with learning disabilities. Social workers must be committed to a broad assessment process that includes an evaluation of the interaction between the individual and the environment. Intervention strategies must safeguard the individual's integrity, autonomy, and ability to develop to his or her maximum potential. The influence of social work in the array of related disciplines can be expanded through service plans that call attention to a social worker's specific professional roles of therapist, social broker, enabler, and advocate. The articulation of anticipated outcomes related to the defined needs of the child and his or her family legitimizes social work intervention and demonstrates the active social work domain.

Second, social workers must be aware of the complex division of professional alignments in the field of learning disabilities. Aggressive moves toward building collaborative relationships to enhance communication and coordination among related disciplines can significantly improve the service package for families whose children require the expertise of pediatric neurologists, psychologists, special educators, physical therapists, and family counselors. Reports from both professionals and parents document the current fragmentation and confusion in the planning and delivery of services. Social workers are uniquely situated to perform the roles of social broker and case manager. There is a critical need for professionals who can link services, monitor the flow of activity and communication, and identify service gaps and slippage. The assumption of these roles requires social workers to be familiar with the knowledge base and contributions of individual professions, their areas of professional expertise, and any overlapping turf. Ultimately, the social worker has a legal mandate to enable family members to assume many aspects of the social brokering and case management roles.

Third, coalitions that bring together professionals and families to develop an expanded community of interest must be established. These coalitions must promote social actions that protect existing legislative programs and expand opportunities for learning-disabled children. Federal and state legislation must be designed to safeguard the rights of persons less able to compete for society's resources and to operationalize social work values in promoting equal access to services. The legal mandates that require access to preventive, diagnostic, remediative, and supportive services for the disabled also include persons with learning disabilities. However, as Caires and Weil (1985) observed, "these rights are not self-enforcing" (p. 266), which leads to the necessity for professional advocacy with, and on behalf of, clients and their families. In conservative times, when governmental funds for human services are severely constrained, formerly acceptable concepts consistent with professional practice may be reinterpreted by government officials in restrictive ways. For example, trends toward minimizing labeling and its negative effects may contribute to a denial of differences that legitimizes differential treatment. Rights and entitlements may revert to the status of embattled claims (Rein & Peattie, 1980). The area of learning disabilities is particularly vulnerable to attack.

Through educational preparation and agency program innovations, the social work profession must take the lead in developing a cadre of practitioners able to implement the defined functions and roles of the social worker in work with learning-disabled people. Social work education must place greater emphasis on the impact of developmental variation on learning patterns. Clinical and political issues pertaining to learning disabilities as a term with multiple uses must be highlighted. Specific contributions and issues of concern to diverse professional groups must be identified. The professional social worker must incorporate this new knowledge base into well-honed skills in early assessment; individual, family, and institutional intervention; interdisciplinary collaboration; and coalition building. This education must take place at undergraduate, graduate, and postgraduate levels. Continuing education programs should respond to new knowledge needs of emerging service populations (Dane, 1983, 1985a). Innovative programs must be developed to model new service approaches and train new professionals in the network of professional school and field agencies. There must be discussion and documentation in public forums and professional journals to highlight this new practice arena and the models of education and practice that have been developed in different settings.

Social workers have important roles to play in the unfolding drama of the shaping of services for children with learning disabilities and their families. This book has explored the history and the current controversial issues of definition, demography, and identification surrounding the field. Each chapter suggested functions and roles for social workers. However, these suggestions are only a beginning. The needs of children with learning disabilities far outstrip available resources. The social work profession has a unique opportunity to make a vital contribution to the design and implementation of services for this diverse population. This book is intended to serve as a stepping stone for social workers interested in forging new practice approaches, theoretical constructs, and organizational structures that meet the needs of children with learning disabilities and their families.

REFERENCES

Caires, K. B., & Weil, M. (1985). Developmentally disabled persons and their families. In M. Weil & J. M. Karls and Associates (Eds.), *Case management in human service practice* (pp. 233–275). San Francisco, CA: Jossey-Bass.

Dane, E. (1983). Continuing education in administration: The job-related principle. *Administration in Social Work, 7,* 79–89.

Dane, E. (1984). [The child welfare and family service systems: A national survey of social work involvement with learning disabled children]. Unpublished raw data.

Dane, E. (1985a). Managing organizational relationships in continuing educational programs: Is loose coupling the answer? *Administration in Social Work, 9,* 83–92.

Dane, E. (1985b). Professional and lay advocacy in the education of handicapped children. *Social Work, 30,* 505–510.

Dane, E. (1986). About creativity. *Their world* (pp. 17–18). New York: Foundation for Children with Learning Disabilities.

Eaton, J. T., Lippmann, D. B., & Riley, D. P. (1980). *Growing with your learning disabled child.* Boston: Family Service Association of Greater Boston.

Education for All Handicapped Children Act, Pub. L. 94–142, 89 Stat. 773, 20, USC 1401. (1975).

Education of the Handicapped Act. Pub. L. 99–457, 100 Stat. 1145 & 100 Stat. 1155, 3456, 3465 (1986).

Gallant, C. B. (1982). *Mediation in special education disputes.* Silver Spring, MD: National Association of Social Workers.

Gitterman, A., & Shulman, L. (Eds.) (1986). *Mutual aid groups and the life cycle.* Itasca, IL: F. E. Peacock.

Gitterman, N. P. (1979). Group services for learning disabled children and their parents. *Social Casework, 60,* 8.

Hasenfeld, Y. (1983). *Human service organizations.* Englewood Cliffs, NJ: Prentice-Hall.

Hollis, F., & Woods, M. E. (1981). *Casework: A psychosocial therapy* (3rd ed.). New York: Random House.

Indelicato, S., & Goldberg, P. (1986). Harassed and alone: Parents of learning disabled children. In A. Gitterman & L. Shulman (Eds.), *Mutual aid groups and the life cycle* (pp. 195–209). Itasca, IL: F. E. Peacock.

Kuzell, N., & Brassington, J. (Eds.). (1986). *Parenting the learning disabled child.* Ottawa, Ontario, Canada: Bradda Printing Services.

Levine, M. D. (1987). *Developmental variation and learning disorders.* Cambridge, MA: Educators Publishing Service.

Mailick, M. D., & Ashley, A. A. (1981). Politics of interprofessional collaboration: Challenge to advocacy. *Social Casework, 20,* 131–137.

Rein, M., & Peattie, L. (1980). Problem frames in poverty research. In V.T. Covello (Ed.), *Poverty and public policy: An evaluation of social science research* (pp. 234–256). Cambridge, MA: Schenckman.

Rosenberger, J. (1988). Self-psychology as a theoretical base for understanding the impact of learning disabilities. *Child and Adolescent Social Work, 5,* 269–280.

Rosenberger, J. (1989). [Parents' self-education in coping with learning disabled children]. Unpublished raw data.

Small, S. (1986). Learning to get along: Learning disabled adolescents. In A. Gitterman & L. Shulman (Eds.), *Mutual aid groups and the life cycle* (pp. 161–176). Itasca, IL: F.E. Peacock.

Vigilante, F. W. (1983). Working with families of learning disabled children. *Child Welfare, 62,* 429–436.

Vigilante, F. W. (1985). Reassessing the developmental needs of children with learning disabilities: Programmatic implications. *Child and Adolescent Social Work Journal, 2,* 167–180.

Vigilante, F. W., & Dane, E. (1989). Multiple strategies in response to the identification of learning disabilities. *Churchill Forum, 11,* 5–6.

Weil, M. (1985). Professional and educational issues in case management practice. In M. Weil & J. M. Karls and Associates (Eds.), *Case management in human service practice* (pp. 357–390). San Francisco, CA: Jossey-Bass.

Ziegler, R., & Holden, L. (1988). Family therapy for learning disabilities and attention-deficit disordered children. *American Journal of Orthopsychiatry, 58,* 196–210.

Resources

This resource file is intended to assist social workers in their work with children with learning disabilities, with parents, and with other professionals. Most of these listings were provided by the National Center for Learning Disabilities.

Information Centers and Organizations

Association of Educational Therapists
P.O. Box 946, Woodland Hills, CA 91365
(818) 344-4712
A national directory of educational therapists is available.

Children with Attention Deficit Disorders (CHADD)
1859 N. Pine Island Rd., Suite 185, Plantation, FL 33322
(305) 384-6869

Council for Exceptional Children (CEC)
1920 Association Dr., Reston, VA 22091-1589
(703) 620-3660
CEC is a professional membership program serving persons who serve the educational needs of exceptional children. CEC works to expand the body of special education knowledge. CEC is organized in divisions that concentrate on a particular exceptionality or on an aspect of special education. The Division for Children with Learning Disabilities publishes two journals and three newsletters.

General Federation of Women's Clubs
1734 N St., NW, Washington, DC 20036
(202) 347-3168
More than 30 state chapters of Women's and Junior Women's Clubs have education projects on learning disabilities. The booklet *I Can Jump the Rainbow* can be ordered through your state or local chapter.

Learning Disabilities Association of America (LDAA)
4156 Library Rd., Pittsburgh, PA 15234
(412) 341-1515
Formerly the Association for Children and Adults with Learning Disabilities, LDAA is an organization of professionals, parents, and interested persons devoted

to advancing the education and well-being of children and adults with learning disabilities. A wide variety of materials on learning disabilities may be ordered. Local and state chapters also publish materials, sponsor events, and are an excellent resource. LDAA publishes *A Directory of Summer Camps for Children with Learning Disabilities.*

National Center for Learning Disabilities (NCLD)
99 Park Ave., New York, NY 10016
(212) 687-7211

NCLD (formerly the Foundation for Children with Learning Disabilities) promotes public awareness about learning disabilities, neurological disorders, and deficits that can be a barrier to literacy. NCLD provides grantmaking, legislative advocacy, publications, and training seminars for professionals and volunteers. An annual publication entitled *Their World* lists resources for parents. In 1990, a state-by-state listing of schools, colleges, and diagnostic centers and a multimedia training package will be available.

National Information Center for Handicapped Children and Youth (NICHCY)
7926 Jones Branch Dr., McLean, VA 22102
(703) 893-6061

NICHCY collects and shares information and ideas that are helpful to handicapped children and youths and the people who care for and about them. Staff members answer questions and link people with others who share common concerns. NICHCY also sponsors workshops and publishes newsletters.

Orton Dyslexia Society (ODS)
724 York Rd., Baltimore, MD 21204

ODS is a professional and parent membership organization offering language programs, research, and publications on dyslexia. ODS chapters are located in most states. All branches hold at least one public meeting or workshop per year.

Advocacy Groups

Advocates for Children of New York, Inc.
2416 Bridge Plaza S., Long Island City, NY 11101
(718) 729-8866

American Bar Association Child Advocacy & Protection Center
1800 M St., NW, Washington, DC 20036
(202) 331-2250

A manual for attorneys, *Representing Learning Disabled Children*, may be ordered.

American Coalition of Citizens with Disabilities
1200 15th St., NW, Suite 201, Washington, DC 20005
(202) 785-4265

Education Law Center
801 Arch St., 6th Fl., Philadelphia, PA 19107
(215) 732-6655

Mexican-American Legal Defense Fund
28 Geary St., San Francisco, CA 94108
(415) 543-5598

National Council of Juvenile and Family Court Judges (NCJFCJ)
P.O. Box 8978, Reno, NV 89507
(702) 784-6012
   NCJFCJ publishes a bench book on learning disabilities for juvenile and family court judges and *Juvenile and Family Court Journal: Learning Disabilities and the Juvenile Justice System.*

Parent Educational Advocacy Training Center
228 S. Pitt St., Suite 300, Alexandria, VA 22314
(703) 836-2953

Technical Assistance for Parent Programs Project (TAPP)
95 Berkeley St., Suite 104, Boston, MA 02116
(617) 482-2915
   TAPP is a federally funded program to assist both established and developing organizations of parents or special education students. TAPP uses experienced parent-operated organizations to offer technical assistance to groups, providing training about special education laws and procedures to parents of children with any handicap.

Educational Resource Organizations and Testing Services

American College Test (ACT) Administration
P.O. Box 168, Iowa City, IA 52243
(319) 337-1332
   Special ACT testing is available for students with documented learning disabilities. Untimed tests and tests on cassette tapes are offered. Reader services are available.

Educational Testing Service
Princeton University
Princeton, NJ 08541
(609) 734-5068
   ETS offers special administration of the Scholastic Aptitude Test (SAT), Graduate Record Examination (GRE), and the Graduate Management Admissions Test

201

(GMAT) for individuals with visual, physical, hearing, or learning disabilities. Tests are offered in regular type, large type, on cassette tape, and in Braille. Accommodations may include frequent rest periods and additional time. The services of a reader, amanuensis, and interpreter also are available.

ERIC Clearinghouse on Education for Training and Employment
1900 Kenny Rd., Columbus, OH 43210
800-848-4815

ERIC Clearinghouse on Handicapped and Gifted Children
see Council for Exceptional Children (p. 199)

National Clearinghouse on Postsecondary Education for Individuals with Handicaps
Health Resource Center, American Council on Education
One Dupont Circle, Suite 800, Washington, DC 20036
800-544-3284
The clearinghouse offers resources for adults with learning disabilities.

Project Literary U.S. (PLUS)
4802 Fifth Ave., Pittsburgh, PA 15213
(412) 622-1491
PLUS and NCLD cooperate to promote volunteer tutoring programs and training for volunteer trainers to assist children and adults with learning disabilities.

Educational and Career-Related Resources

Brown, D. (1983). *Post-secondary options for learning disabled students* (Monograph). Reston, VA: ERIC Clearinghouse for Handicapped and Gifted Children.

Dias, P. S. (1989). *Diamonds in the rough: Infancy to college reference guide on the learning disabled child.* East Aurora, NY: Slosson Educational Publications.

Fielding, P. M. (Ed.). (1985). *A national directory of four-year colleges', two-year colleges' and post-high schools' training programs for young people with learning disabilities* (5th ed.). Tulsa, OK: Partners in Publishing.

Mangrum, C. T., & Strickhart, S. F. (1989). *Peterson's guide to colleges with programs for learning disabled students.* Princeton, NJ: Peterson's Guides.

Moss, J. R., & Fox, D.L. (1980). *College-level programs for the learning-disabled.* Tulsa, OK: Partners in Publishing.

Partners in Publishing. (published monthly). *PIP college "helps" newsletter.* Tulsa, OK: Author.

Pernecke, R. B., & Schriener, S. M. (Eds.). (1983). *Schooling for the learning disabled.* Glenview, IL: SMA.

Porter Sargent Publishers. (1987). *Directory for exceptional children.* Boston, MA: Author.

Porter Sargent Publishers. (1989). *Handbook of private schools.* Boston, MA: Author.

Schieber, B., & Talpers, J. (1985). *Campus access for learning disabled students.* Washington, DC: Closer Look.

Schieber, B., & Talpers, J. (1987). *Unlocking potential: College & other choices.* Bethesda, MD: Adler & Adler.

Skyer, R., & Skyer, G. (1986). *What do you do after high school?* (A nationwide guide to residential, vocational, social and collegiate programs serving adolescents, young adults, and adults with learning disabilities). Rockaway Park, NY: Skyer Consultation.

Zwerlein, R., Smith, M., & Diffley, J. (1984). *Vocational rehabilitation for learning disabled adults* (a handbook for rehabilitation professionals). (Available from the National Center on Employment of the Handicapped at The Human Resources & Abilities Center, 201 I. U. Willits Rd., Albertson, NY 11507)

Periodicals and Newsletters

Challenge (a newsletter on attention deficit disorder)
Challenge, Inc.
42 Way of the River, West Newbury, MA 01985

Churchill Forum
Churchill Center for Learning Disabilities, Inc.
22 E. 95th St., New York City, NY 10128

Exceptional Parent
296 Boylston St., Boston, MA 02116
This magazine offers a pen pal program for children with learning disabilities.

The Exchange
Learning Disabilities Network
30 Pond Park Rd., Hingham, MA 02043

Journal of Learning Disabilities
Professional Press, Inc.
11 E. Adams St., Chicago, IL 60603

LDAA Newsbriefs
see Learning Disabilities Association of America (p. 199)

Reaching Children
New York Institute for Child Development
205 Lexington Ave., New York City, NY 10016

School of Social Work Information Bulletin
National Association of Social Workers
7981 Eastern Ave., Silver Spring, MD 20910

Spectrum
Hill Top Preparatory School
Rosemont, PA 19010

Update
National Institute of Dyslexia
3200 Woodbine Ave., Chevy Chase, MD 20815

Books on Tape

Services for the Blind and Physically Handicapped
National Library of Congress
First Street & Independence Ave., SE, Washington, DC
(800) 424-8567
  Resources are available for learning-disabled persons. Inquire at public libraries.

Recordings for the Blind
Anne T. MacDonald Center
20 Roszel Road, Princeton, NJ 08540
(609) 452-0606
  Textbooks on tape are available.

Youth Groups

  Major agencies serving youths, such as the Boy and Girl Scouts, Boys' and Girls' Clubs, and YMCAs and YWCAs are committed to mainstreaming youths with learning disabilities into their programs. Contact local or national offices to inquire about groups in your community with leaders trained in meeting needs of learning-disabled children. Contact local United Way offices for referrals to these agencies. For copies of *Scouting and the Learning Disabled: A Manual for Scouting Leaders*, contact the Direct Mail Supply Division, Boy Scouts of America, Irving, Texas. YMCA Project MAY (mainstreaming youths in recreation) manuals, including excellent information on fitness and aquatics, are available from the Director, Special Populations, YMCA of USA, Box 1781, Longview, WA 98632.

Recommended Reading for Parents

  Cordoni, B. (1987). *Living with a learning disability*. Carbondale, IL: Southern Illinois University Press.

  Cruickshank, W. M., Morris, W., & Johns, J. (1980). *Learning disabilities: The struggle from adolescence toward adulthood*. Syracuse, NY: Syracuse University Press.

  Gottesman, D. M. (1982). *The powerful parent: A child advocacy handbook*. Norwalk, CT: Appleton-Century-Crofts.

  Lavoie, R. D. (1988). *The learning disabled child: Round holes, square pegs; a guide for parents*. Greenwich, CT: Eagle Hill Outreach Project.

  McGuinness, P. (1985). *When children don't learn: Understanding the biology and psychology of learning disabilities*. New York: Basic Books.

New York Association for Learning Disabilities. (1973). *On being the parent of a handicapped youth.* Albany, NY: Author.

Nichamin, S. J., & Windell, J. (1985). *Coping with your inattentive child: A practical guide for management.* Waterford, MI: Minerva.

Nuzum, M. (1985). *What do teens with learning disabilities want to know?* (Available from 92nd Street YWCA, 1395 Lexington Ave., New York City, NY 10128)

Orton Dyslexia Society. (1985). *Readings for parents.* Baltimore, MD: Author.

Orton Dyslexia Society. (1990). *Guidelines for seeking help.* Baltimore, MD: Author.

Osman, B. B. (1979). *Learning disabilities: A family affair.* New York: Random House.

Osman, B. B., & Blinder, H. (1982). *No one to play with: The social side of learning disabilities.* New York: Random House. (Spanish edition available.)

Painting, D. H. (1983). *Helping children with specific learning disabilities.* Englewood Cliffs, NJ: Prentice-Hall.

Rowan, R. D. (1977). *Helping children with learning disabilities in the home, church and community.* Nashville, TN: Abingdon.

Silver, L. B. (1980). *Attention deficit disorders.* Summit, NJ: CIBA.

Silver, L. B. (1984). *The learning disabled child: A guide for parents of learning disabled children.* New York: McGraw-Hill.

Smith, S. (1979). *No easy answers.* Cambridge, MA: Winthrop.

Stevens, S. H. (1980). *The learning disabled child: Ways that parents can help.* Winston-Salem, NC: John F. Blair.

Stevens, S. H. (1984). *Classroom success for the learning disabled.* Winston-Salem, NC: John F. Blair.

Ungerleider, D. (1985). *Reading, writing and rage.* Rolling Hills Estates, CA: Jalmar Press.

Weiss, H., & Weiss, M. (1976). *A survival manual: Case studies and suggestions for the learning-disabled teenager.* Great Barrington, MA: Treehouse Associates.

Weiss, H., & Weiss, M. (1981). *Parent's and teacher's guide to activities which interest and instruct youngsters.* Great Barrington, MA: Treehouse Associates.

Activities Resources

Golick, M. (1986). *Reading, writing and rummy: Card games to develop language and social skills.* Ontario, Canada: Pembroke.

Golick, M. (1987). *Playing with words.* Ontario, Canada: Pembroke.

Lengel, J. K. (1982). *I can play the piano.* Boston, MA: Boston Music.

Lurio, D. (1982). *Special recipes for special people.* Philadelphia: Skylight Press.

Lurio, D. (1984). *More special recipes.* Philadelphia: Skylight Press.

Riccardi, J., & Vella, A. (1981). *Elementary piano with one hand.* Boston, MA: Boston Music.

Fiction about Learning Disabilities for Children and Adolescents

Albert, L. (1976). *But I'm ready to go*. Scarsdale, NY: Bradbury.

Behrmann, P. *Why is it always me?* (Available from P. Behrmann, 115 Lake Rd., Framingham, MA 01701)

Byars, B. (1979). *The summer of the swans*. New York: Viking.

Cassedy, S. (1987). *M. E. and Morton*. New York: Thomas Y. Crowell.

Corcoran, B. (1975). *Axe-time, sword-time*. New York: Atheneum.

Gilsan, J. (1980). *Do bananas chew gum?* New York: Lothrop, Lee & Shepard Books.

Glazzard, M. H. (1978). *Meet Scott: He's a special person*. Lawrence, KS: H & H Enterprises.

Greenwald, S. (1983). *Will the real Gertrude Hollings please stand up?* Boston, MA: Little.

Janover, C. (1988). *Josh: A boy with dyslexia*. Maplewood, NJ: Waterfront Books.

Krauss, R. (1971). *Leo, the late bloomer*. New York: Windmill.

Lasker, J. (1974). *He's my brother*. Chicago, IL: Albert Whitmay.

Levine, M. D. (1989). *Keeping a head in school*. Cambridge, MA: Educators Publishing Service.

Levinson, D. (1984). *Kevin's story*. Toronto, Ontario, Canada: IPI.

Pevsner, S. (1977). *Keep stompin' till the music stops*. New York: Seabury.

Raccioppi, C. A. *Dyslexia* (A photo essay by a teenager with learning disabilities). (Available from RMR Educational Consultation, 124 Washington St., Tappan, NY 10983)

Smith, D. B. (1975). *Kelly's creek*. New York: Harper & Row.

Index

About the Author

ELIZABETH DANE, DSW, ACSW, is Associate Professor at the Hunter College School of Social Work, in New York City. She also serves as a consultant to child welfare agencies and educational institutions in the areas of staffing, interdisciplinary communication systems, and social work roles with children with learning disabilities and their families.

Dr. Dane's research focuses on the educational and training needs of social workers in child welfare and family service agencies. Currently she is involved in a research project to analyze family system concepts and classroom organization to develop professional understanding about the impact of transitions from home to school for children in special education.

Dr. Dane has written on professional and parent collaboration in working with learning-disabled children, organizational issues in planning services for these children, and the use of social workers in serving this population. She has been published in *Social Work*, the *Journal of Continuing Social Work Education*, and *Administration in Social Work*.

She was recently elected to the Professional Advisory Board of the Learning Disabilities Association of America.